To Dickie Breathing
love and kisses

M W
& R

SELF
SERVE

Also by Peter Foster

The Blue-Eyed Sheiks (1979)

The Sorcerer's Apprentices (1982)

Other People's Money (1983)

The Master Builders (1986)

Family Spirits (1990)

How Petro-Canada Pumped Canadians Dry

SELF SERVE

PETER FOSTER

Macfarlane Walter & Ross
Toronto

Macfarlane Walter & Ross
37A Hazelton Avenue
Toronto, Canada M5R 2E3

Canadian Cataloguing in Publication Data

Foster, Peter, 1947–
    Self-serve : how Petro-Canada pumped
Canadians dry

Includes index.
ISBN O-921912-38-2

1. Petro-Canada.   2. Petroleum industry and trade
– Government ownership – Canada.   I. Title.

HD9574.C24P47 1992   338.7'6223382'0971
C92-095031-0

The publisher gratefully acknowledges the
assistance of the Ontario Arts Council

Printed in Canada

To the memory of my father

Contents

Acknowledgments

In some ways, this book has been fifteen years in the writing, since it brings together strands of five other books I have written. This means that many of those to whom I owe thanks did not realize where their contributions would end up. Neither did I. For that reason, I felt it inappropriate to repeat their names here. In addition, most of those who assisted me directly did so on the basis of anonymity. I also feel that others who remain in the oil patch might not want to be named. Nevertheless, I thank them all.

At Macfarlane Walter & Ross, Jan Walter proved once again a model of skill and kindness. Gary Ross gave me more help than might be expected of a man up to his neck in elephants. Barbara Czarnecki was both painstaking and inspired in her editing. Selena Forsyth did a fine job in digging up the photographs.

Last but foremost, I have to thank Indira Somwaru for putting up with me.

ONE

Sharing the Blame

BILL HOPPER struts into an antechamber of one of the big meeting rooms of the Four Seasons Hotel on Toronto's Yorkville Avenue. A short, stocky man with a large head and no discernible neck, he resembles a cross between a midget sumo wrestler and a corporate Truman Capote. His face beams beneath his grey-blond wavy hair as he chats to a colleague. His air of self-confidence, even self-satisfaction, seems, given the circumstances, somewhat strange.

Hopper is about to deliver a speech about the privatization of Canada's state oil company, Petro-Canada, which he has headed virtually since its creation. The privatization took place in July 1991 with a $523-million public share issue. The shares have slumped from $13 to $11 in only three months and are moving lower, leaving disgruntled shareholders who were told that Petrocan was cheap: a good bet for a quick flip. The Tories and investment dealers have cause for embarrassment, but nothing sticks to Bill Hopper. He has, as usual, extricated himself from the blame zone with the facility of a business Houdini. Still, there seems little for Hopper to be happy about. He runs a company that is struggling financially, squeezed between slumping oil and gas prices and huge capital commitments. Perhaps what buoys him is that, since the privatization, although the government still owns 80 per cent of Petrocan, it is no longer a Crown corporation or "public instrument." Bill Hopper is his own man at last.

Hopper's has been a long and very expensive journey. From 1976 until 1984, $4.2 billion was invested in Petrocan by the Canadian government. Assuming that the money was borrowed and that the government had to pay interest of 10 per cent per annum, the national debt associated with Petro-Canada by October 1991, the time of Hopper's speech, is around $11 billion. If the exploration grants Petrocan received under the Trudeau Liberals' 1980 National Energy Program are included, the present value of the debt associated with Petrocan climbs to more than $14 billion. Petrocan's market value, following privatization, is little more than $2 billion. What could justify these horrendous costs? Bill Hopper must have the answers. But only one message emerges from his speech: whatever happened, it wasn't his fault.

Following the rubber chicken and the stock introduction, Hopper moves to the podium and begins his version of laying it on the line. "I've always been very frank with people," he declares, "and I'm sick of talking about privatization."

Damned privatization.

"I'd much rather talk about Petro-Canada and where we're going, but I've got lawyers in Toronto and New York and Calgary all breathing down my throat because we're under registration [to issue new debt]."

Damned lawyers.

The privatization process is "not one I'd like to repeat, unless you want to talk to bureaucrats over and over and over again."

Damned bureaucrats.

Profitability? Profitability was never an initial priority for Petrocan, stresses Hopper. Even the supposedly bottom-line mandate imposed by the Tories in 1984 hadn't meant they'd keep their hands off. "When politicians have the ability to influence a major sector like oil, it is almost too tantalizing not to. I get calls from members of Parliament when service stations are shut down. I have a huge staff of people just writing letters."

Damned politicians.

Then of course the Tories had "urged" Petrocan to take over Gulf Canada's refining and marketing assets in 1985 so the rest of Gulf could be acquired by Toronto's Reichmann family. "Paul Reichmann basically wanted to buy the upstream on the basis that prices were going to go up, so Paul isn't always right. He didn't like the downstream. He was right there."

Damned Reichmanns.

Hopper portrays himself as the guardian of the widows and orphans who might have been, or indeed have been, sucked into buying shares by Tory enthusiasm. "Several Cabinet ministers wanted every man jack to have these shares, so they could become very popular and buy a bunch of votes."

Damned Cabinet ministers.

Hopper complains that analysts always claim that Petrocan is bureaucratic, has too many employees, and spends too much money.

Damned analysts.

He outlines the difficulties the industry has faced because of the decline in prices following Saddam Hussein's invasion of Kuwait and the Gulf War. He bemoans public ignorance of refining and marketing. He notes the burden of Petrocan's heavy financial commitments, particularly the Hibernia development off the coast of Newfoundland.

Damned Saddam Hussein. Damned public. Damned expensive great chunks of concrete built so Newfies can have jobs. Hopper's speech is typical: a profession of frankness and honesty from one of Ottawa's most skilled operators, mixed with sideswipes at virtually everybody, all coated in the style of a stand-up comedian. A psychologist might say Hopper is a man with a chip, an almost Oedipal need to dump on his creators: the politicians and the bureaucrats. It is not insignificant that Hopper owes his position to the fact that he was once one of those bureaucrats.

Hopper has proved a master of survival. Depending on which way you look at it, either he has cleverly moved with political currents through the corporate food chain, or he has manfully struggled with a financially reckless exploration mandate imposed on him by his political masters. In fact, these views are not mutually exclusive. Hopper has always preached size as a *sine qua non* of achieving his policy objectives. He certainly attained a huge corporate empire, but somehow the public purpose was never achieved.

Hopper is a paradox: a self-professed "free-enterpriser" who fought to head an organization based on the premise that the market didn't work and/or was injurious to Canada; a bureaucrat who won friends and influenced people in red-blooded, capitalist Calgary even as he headed the city's most reviled interventionist instrument; a man who consciously projects an outspoken, no-bullshit image while quietly manipulating his Ottawa network.

A complex, profane, and charming character, Hopper once described himself as a "bureaucrat for all seasons," and in one sense he has served his shareholders — that is, until 1991, federal governments — well, given that Ottawa's shifting objectives over the years have been geologically ill-informed, philosophically and financially muddled, and politically expedient. He has always claimed that he just "did what he was told." But Hopper has also pursued his own mandate, comprehensively outflanking political masters concerned that they were creating a monster.

Hopper's skills have been used in building a wealth-destroying and ultimately pointless entity. To review the three goals of Petrocan's original mandate: "Canadianization" has been achieved by overspending taxpayers' money; the Crown corporation's "window on the industry" has revealed primarily that the company itself wasn't necessary; and the pursuit of "security of supply" has been a failure. So what *has* Hopper managed to achieve?

Hopper likes to downplay his own significance in Petrocan's sorry history, but one particular aspect should not be overlooked. Privatization, he says, "meant, incidentally, that I got a raise. The government hadn't let me have a raise for eight years. They gave me another thirty-seven fifty a week." The joke fell flat.

Bill Hopper had complained a great deal both privately and publicly about the income limits on heads of Crown corporations: $475,000 by 1991. But Bill Hopper's salary of $414,000 back in

1984 was still more than ten times greater than it had been a decade before, when he was a far-from-humble assistant deputy minister in Ottawa's Department of Energy, Mines and Resources. And by 1984, Bill Hopper had been earning several times as much as the prime minister. He also had a much bigger and more opulent office, a well-equipped corporate jet — which he frequently took on long trips to Europe, South America, and the Far East — his own dining rooms both in Calgary and Ottawa, limousines, and uniformed servants. So life still wasn't bad enough that Hopper might decide to quit and teach the government a lesson. Moreover, despite that eight-year freeze, Bill Hopper's relative remuneration, as far as we know, had never fallen far enough to make him a bargain in the corporate marketplace. One could be excused for concluding that Bill Hopper had done very well out of Petrocan. Also, Hopper's salary increase after privatization was not $37.50 a week. It was closer to $4,000 a week, bringing him to between $600,000 and $700,000, not including a six-figure salary he received as chairman of a Petrocan subsidiary, Westcoast Energy (formerly Westcoast Transmission).

The issue of salary is not a minor point. Those who subscribe to the delusions of the "public interest" school of policy-making — that Crown corporations and other "policy instruments" are manned by selfless automatons who doggedly pursue their public mandate without concern for their personal welfare — might think that Bill Hopper's salary is a relatively small cost in the great scheme of things. But it highlights one of the less publicized but no less important concomitants of Petrocan's creation and growth: the benefits to those who created and grew it. That self-interest flourished in a political environment in which the value of government intervention was greatly overestimated, and it proved very hard to dislodge.

When Finance Minister Michael Wilson finally announced in his budget of February 20, 1990, that the Tories would be privatizing Petro-Canada, his party's fifteen-year struggle with the Crown corporation had taken on aspects of a peculiarly Canadian version of Moby Dick, a psychological drama with the Tories as

Captain Ahab and Petrocan — personified in the appropriately beluga-ish form of Bill Hopper — as the White Whale. The Canadian twist? Captain Ahab abandons his fixation for destroying his foe, joins Greenpeace, and gives Moby a pat on the head and a Godspeed as the reputedly streamlined beast moves off into the invigorating seas of the private sector. Only on the Canadian *Pequod*-of-state could a Captain Ahab, with one eye on the opinion polls, learn to be "pragmatic."

The unlikely role of the kinder, gentler Tory Ahab in this Maple Leaf tragicomedy fell to the minister for privatization, John McDermid, a former television newsman reputedly to the right of the party, but who in fact appeared to have a slim grasp on the conservative principles under which he claimed to be acting. He sat uncomfortably during an interview early in 1991 and said: "It's a funny phenomenon when you talk to people about these things, and you say: 'Well, don't you think it's just another oil company?' 'Yes,' they say, 'but it's ours.' You ask: 'You don't care if it loses money?' They say: 'Does it lose money? It can't lose money. It's an oil company. Oil companies don't lose money. They make billions.' That's the problem. Jesus, do you think taxpayers sit there and look at Petrocan's losses? To them, it's a national symbol: they're the ones who did the Olympic flame thing."

Obviously, what people thought, rather than the real world, dictated McDermid's actions, as it had come to dominate the actions of his party and Canadian politics more generally. And the "Olympic flame thing" had certainly had an impact.

Petrocan's Olympic Torch Relay before the 1988 Calgary Olympics was a stroke of marketing genius, but it also further confused Canadians' already muddled feelings about Petrocan. The Olympic organizing committee, headed by Calgary oilman Frank King, had been far from happy about the prospect of Petrocan taking such a key sponsorship, but the state oil company put up the money and the people, and wound up doing a thoroughly professional job. When application forms were sent out to Canadian households, a stunning 6.7 million responses were received. A lottery was used to select the 7,000 people who participated. An 11,000-kilometre route was mapped to pass within a two-hour drive of 90 per cent of Canadian homes. Hundreds of Petrocan employees worked not just on company time but on their own to make the relay a success. Some who travelled with the flame worked fifteen-hour days virtually throughout the three-month odyssey, staying in dingy motel rooms but convinced they were doing something worthwhile. Seven hundred employee volunteers spent week-long shifts working on the caravan. They drove the vehicles, ran as escorts, and coordinated the complex logistics.

From the time the first two runners wound their way down Signal Hill in St. John's, Newfoundland, coverage snowballed into a media phenomenon. Everywhere the torch relay went, it made the front page and the evening news. At each town the torch passed through, the flame was "shared" with locals carrying candles. "O Canada" was sung, and a wellspring of emotion was tapped. There was never a dry eye in the house. Even the most cynical were won over by the spontaneous response of the Canadians who participated. Politicians started gathering like moths round the flame, but there were no speeches. The flame was carried by the young and old, fit and handicapped, native and immigrant. It travelled by snowmobile and hot-air balloon and dogsled. When it finally arrived in Calgary after eighty-eight days on the road, 250,000 people were waiting to greet it.

As Petrocan's 1987 annual report noted: "During the 88 days that the flame passed across the country, the response of Canadians was impressive and moving. For the Corporation, the endeavor was so successful that benefits go far beyond any incremental retail sales. For the nation, new meaning has been injected into the concept of Olympic spirit. Canadians have set a new standard by which all future Olympics will be judged."

The problem was that the torch relay, insofar as it was promoting Petrocan, was promoting an impossible dream, and one that could only end in disillusion. The Olympic Torch Relay was used to glorify an organization that had lost billions of dollars in public money and would lose billions more.

Again, at the end of his 1988 annual review, Hopper noted: "We continue to be gratified by the enduring success of the Olympic Torch Relay... The event raised Petro-Canada's profile and confirmed for many the Corporation's ability to take on a major challenge and carry it through with distinction." This was hardly the challenge that those who created the corporation had had in mind.

TWO

Spiritual Father

PRIVATIZATION WAS a tough sell in Canada because Canadians had been told that Crown corporations were an essential and useful part of nation-building. This view was so deep-rooted and impervious to examination that even the Tories themselves peddled it.

In a speech about privatization in 1989, John McDermid declared that many Crown corporations "were created at a time when the private sector was incapable or unwilling to provide services that were essential to Canadians." He continued: "The CBC is one well-known example; it was set up in 1932 to ensure a national broadcasting service. Air Canada is another; it was established in 1937 to develop coast-to-coast air service. I could name a great many other companies I know you are all familiar with: the CNR, which was established in 1919; the Cape Breton Development Corporation in 1967; de Havilland, in 1974; and Canadair in 1976. The list goes on."

McDermid was regurgitating the conventional wisdom about Canadian economic history. But it was at best simplistic, at worst untrue. The CBC's creation had certainly not come from any groundswell of popular sentiment. Rather it was an élitist vehicle to "counter" the American programming that most people wanted to listen to in the 1930s. The CBC originally both competed with and regulated the private sector, whose growth it deliberately inhibited. In the end, the CBC found that it, too, had to carry American programming to attract listeners. One of its main functions, as historian Michael Bliss points out in his classic study *Northern Enterprise,* was to provide a "safety valve for nationalism in broadcasting. Its presence lessened pressure on the private stations to give Canadians programming that was good for them instead of the programs they wanted." Although it produced some quality programming, and a radio network superior to anything south of the border, it evolved into a horrendously costly organization — requiring subsidies of around $1 billion a year by the late 1980s. And most people still watched American TV.

In the case of Air Canada, government deliberately kept out the private sector by granting itself a monopoly. The Liberal wartime "minister of everything," C.D. Howe, created Trans-Canada Airways, the predecessor of Air Canada. Howe, fascinated with both aviation and power, ignored Canadian expertise and experience. When Canadian Pacific Air Lines emerged during the Second World War as a private-sector rival, the government kept it out of Trans-Canada's choice routes. According to Bliss: "The government-owned firm flew on through Canadian skies kept empty of competition by public policy."

Canadian National Railways, created to bail out an at least partially government-promoted mess of overambitious transcontinental railroads unable to recover their costs because of political pressures, was called by Bliss "the largest and most ill-conceived company in Canada." It cost hundreds of millions, then billions, to keep going. By the time McDermid spoke, CNR had, even by its own admission, become bloated and inefficient. It had also grown out of government control. An internal study in 1991 revealed that CNR ran "one of the least competitive railways in North America."

Citing de Havilland and Canadair as pieces of Canadian state-sponsored economic achievement amounted almost to satire. From 1974 until 1986, de Havilland was a disaster under Canadian federal ownership, swallowing the best part of $1 billion. In 1986, the company was sold to U.S. aerospace giant

Boeing, who sank more than $400 million trying to turn it around. Even as McDermid spoke, Boeing had realized it had made a massive mistake, and wanted out. Eventually, further huge public subsidies had to be offered to Bombardier, the Montreal-based conglomerate, to persuade it to take de Havilland over. Bombardier already controlled Canadair, which, under government ownership, had reported an all-time Canadian record corporate loss of $1.4 billion in June 1983. Bombardier had agreed to take over Canadair only after the taxpayers had swallowed its more than $1 billion of debts. Neither de Havilland nor Canadair would ever provide net benefits to the Canadian economy, because they could never possibly recover the public money that had been sunk into them. But instead of holding them up as horror stories, McDermid used them as examples of Crown corporations that had played a role "in the building of our country."

It wasn't clear whether McDermid and his speechwriters simply didn't know their history or were merely afraid of waking the electorate from its dreams. The minister noted that many Crowns had become national symbols, but what they had become national symbols of was the destruction of taxpayers' hard-earned money.

With the collapse of communism and the move towards market-based economies in the late 1980s, privatization of state-owned organizations had become a global phenomenon. The grounds for privatization were simple: state-owned companies, in both East and West, were manifestly inefficient and wasteful. High-minded social purposes had become bogged down in political expediency and vote-buying. Crown corporations inevitably wound up serving their own interests rather than the "public purpose." But there were still many Canadians who either didn't understand the costs of public ownership or clung to their belief in the power of good intentions, ignoring damning evidence. Many believed that public corporate ownership was still viable; it was just a matter of fine-tuning the monitoring process.

Why did Canadians have such faith in government intervention, particularly when it turned out to be so destructive? Partly it was a matter of historical misrepresentation by those with a vested interest in promoting the power of the state; partly it was an almost universal desire to believe that governments really could do what they claimed; partly it was a very deliberately promoted distrust of private enterprise; partly it was concern about American "domination." In the early 1970s, this jumble of concerns melded around the issue of oil. The champion of action was a complex public figure, Walter Gordon.

. . .

Walter Gordon was in many ways the spiritual father of Petrocan. It has been suggested that the psychic origins of Gordon's economic nationalism might have been acquired at the bottom of a pile of derisive English schoolboys when Gordon was briefly enrolled at a British preparatory school during the First World War. It certainly wasn't based either in reason or in the more normal attitudes of those of his station.

Gordon was a child of the Canadian Establishment. Rosedale-bred and Upper Canada College–educated, he went from the Royal Military College at Kingston to his father's accounting firm, Clarkson, Gordon & Dilworth. In the 1930s, like so many of his class, he became infected with radical notions, but he joined the mainstream politics of the Liberal Party while developing comprehensive knowledge — if skewed understanding — of Canadian business and industry through his consultancy work. He became rich, reportedly in his own right, travelled extensively, and owned a house in Rosedale and a farm northwest of Toronto. "But," as Christina McCall-Newman pointed out in *Grits*, "behind his armour of social and professional success, impeccable moustache, and unassailable self-regard, Gordon harboured an eccentricity. He was a passionate nationalist."

According to a *Maclean's* column by Peter C. Newman — co-founder with Gordon of the Committee for an Independent Canada, and hence hardly a harsh critic — Walter Gordon was "one of those rare figures in Canadian public life who has deliberately cast off what Don Quixote disdainfully called 'the melancholy burden of sanity' to wage a lifetime crusade against foreign investment." Foreign investment to Walter Gordon was what germs were to Howard Hughes. He was a strange contradiction, an Establishment renegade, a businessman capable of ignoring the fundamentals of a market economy. But he was more than simply a theorist.

In the 1930s, Gordon had formed a holding company, Canadian Corporate Management, or Cancorp, whose purpose, according to Gordon, was to buy Canadian companies in danger of being "sold out" to Americans. But there was only so much one man could do. By 1955, according to McCall-Newman, Walter Gordon's "old concerns had turned into a suppressed anger at the federal government's complacent attitude towards the accelerating sell-out to foreign business interests of Canadian resources and industries."

Gordon brought this anger with him when he chaired the Royal Commission on Canada's Economic Prospects, which further increased his knowledge of the shape of the Canadian economy but changed not a whit his xenophobic economic convictions. Postwar attempts by radical organizations to sow concern about American "economic imperialism" had been largely ignored. But the climate changed with the furor over the TransCanada PipeLine, when C.D. Howe bulldozed through legislation to have the federal government underwrite the uneconomic northern Ontario portions of the proposed transcontinental natural gas transportation system. The Liberal government subsequently fell over the issue.

The time was ripe for Gordon to broadcast his fears about foreign investment. "There is concern that as the position of American capital in the dynamic resource and manufacturing sectors becomes ever more dominant, our economy will inevitably become more and more integrated with that of the United States," declared the report of the Royal Commission in 1957. "Behind this is the fear that continuing integration might lead to economic domination by the United States and eventually to the loss of our political independence."

This sounded plausible. But what did economic "domination" mean? And what did Gordon and his cohorts have in mind when they talked of loss of "political independence"? Political independence to do what? There were sinister undertones. Some of those who wailed about political independence had economic plans that would not work without a little state-sponsored arm-twisting. It was harder for the government to twist arms when the company's head office was not in its jurisdiction.

There was no clear remedy for Gordon's debatable problem. Buying out U.S. interests would be expensive and would deprive the country of U.S. expertise. Blocking further investment would retard Canada's growth. Preventing sales of Canadian companies to U.S. interests would certainly infuriate Canadian sellers.

Gordon pursued his personal mandate when he was appointed finance minister by Prime Minister Lester Pearson. In 1963, he brought down a first budget, whose principal *bêtise* was an attempt to slap a 30-per-cent tax on foreign purchases of Canadian shares. The proposal was treated with outrage. The tax told Canadians that they were not free to dispose of what they had created as they wished. They would be penalized if they sold to foreigners.

The tax proposal was withdrawn, but Gordon persuaded his colleagues to set up a state-funded version of Cancorp to buy out foreign companies. The majority of shares in this organization, the Canada Development Corporation, would then be sold to the Canadian public. The proposal would lie dormant for six years, and the CDC would ultimately become a key battleground for those who supported and opposed Gordon's views.

Following the budget débâcle, Gordon was seen as a liability and he left politics. Tory Prime Minister John Diefenbaker described him as "the flossy Toronto taxidermist who stuffs the Grits with zany ideas." Nevertheless, Walter Gordon's wealth and influence remained, enabling him to pursue his crusade. His message became more strident with time: American corporations operating in the Canadian economy were a pernicious force; they caused us to import too much and export too little; they held back our research and development; they operated like puppets, with their strings pulled from New York or Chicago or Los Angeles.

Gordon's solutions too became more extreme as the years passed. Americans had to be forced to sell back majority control. And if they didn't? Well, just nationalize them. Canada should join a long line of political expropriators — from Bolshevik commissars through Latin American dictators to Muslim rabble-rousers — who had gained political capital by decrying the American devil and taking over his corporate works. These same heroes of the people had also watched with more or less equanimity as the things they had seized subsequently broke down, and their countries descended into poverty and repression. But Canadians didn't know much of history or its processes. They had a much greater than average belief in the power of government's healing hand. After all, they had been told throughout their schooling, government intervention had been necessary to create this geographical and economic anomaly of a country.

Gordon was regarded by some as a hypocrite. Over the years, Cancorp sold a number of companies to Americans. When asked about two of these sales, Gordon replied: "We were forced to sell those companies against our will. In both cases they were sold to Americans because we had a gun to our head — and when there's a gun at your head, you have to decide whether the fellow who's holding it is going to pull the trigger."

Of course, the thing to do when somebody puts a gun to your head is to call a policeman. But the "gun to the head" was one of the many rhetorical devices used by those who espoused intervention to cast the workings of a free economy as an exercise in coercion. His critics said it was Gordon who was really in favour of using the "gun to the head" of political violence through discriminatory taxation or expropriation.

Nevertheless, for his supporters, Gordon was a Great Patriot. And although he infuriated some in the business community, even there he wasn't condemned too harshly. Canadians are, after all, a tolerant people. Many of Gordon's business associates simply didn't take his rantings seriously. Donald G. (Bud) Willmot, then chairman of the board of the Molson Companies, a certified member of the Canadian Establishment, and one of Canada's most respected executives, used to socialize with Walter and his wife, exchanging dinner invitations every couple of months and playing bridge. Gordon would expound his theories and Willmot would leave him in no doubt about what he thought of them. But it always remained friendly. In fact, Willmot thought Gordon was just being provocative.

Ironically, Bud Willmot would later agree to be one of the founding directors of Petro-Canada. He saw it in no way — nor was it sold to him — as partial fulfillment of Walter Gordon's nationalist dreams. But like most practical businessmen, Willmot may have missed the more irrational aspects of the drift of government policy, believing that a level-headed man like himself might be able to "talk some sense" into those who thought like Gordon, even though he was never able to do so with Gordon himself.

From the point of view of the business establishment, Gordon was considered economically *non compos mentis,* as mad as a March Hare, a figure with a sandwich board bearing a hand-scrawled message of doom, as embarrassing as a wild-eyed drunk who grabs your arm in a bar and tells you he has The Answer. But Gordon's views found increasing favour in Ottawa.

A series of laws discriminating against non-Canadian corporations culminated in 1973 with the creation of the Foreign Investment Review Agency. FIRA was formed to bar foreign investments that would not bring "significant benefit" to the Canadian economy. How the benefits of any investment could be judged before it had been made was not explained. The legislation assumed that foreign investment was guilty until proven innocent, and it suggested that, in any case, Canada was so inundated with investment that the nation could afford to pick and choose.

Gordon's policies were being implemented because they had political appeal and brought undoubted material advantages to those who could most becomingly cloak themselves in the

Canadian flag. The creation of public "instruments" was supported by some with both political experience and corporate connections because they realized there might be some interesting opportunities in "bridging the gap." There was plenty of personal growth potential in "taking back control" of the Canadian economy. If the Canadian private sector was "too weak" to take on the task, then the only alternative was for government to do the job. And if government was to take a greater role in running the economy, then there were some very powerful, and possibly even very well-paid, jobs to be had.

In the 1960s and 1970s, anti-capitalism was the required stance of those with a good liberal education. The dismal science taught university students that markets were prone to failure and inefficiency. The most dangerous form of failure and inefficiency was monopoly, against which a wise government had to be constantly on guard. Which is where we come to the oil business, John D. Rockefeller, the greatest monopolist of them all, and his empire's Canadian subsidiary, an organization whose very name was enough to raise Walter Gordon's blood pressure.

THREE

The Imperial Legacy

WHEN CANADIANS thought of oil companies in the 1950s and 1960s, one name came to mind: Imperial Oil. Like the mythical blind men encountering the elephant, what you thought of Imperial Oil depended upon where you stood in relationship to it, which part of it you touched, or which part of it touched you.

For motorists, Imperial was the most prominent of the four major international oil companies — Imperial, Gulf, Shell, and Texaco — whose gasoline stations dotted the highways from coast to coast and fuelled the tail-finned booms of the postwar years. Imperial meant "happy motoring." Its gasoline put a user-friendly "tiger in your tank." It promoted the national institution of *Hockey Night in Canada.* For shareholders, it was the classic widows-and-orphans investment. Its annual meeting was a congregation of the faithful who believed Imperial stood for the old-fashioned values. For employees, Imperial was a company that had pioneered the eight-hour workday in Canada, that looked after their careers, that encouraged them to contribute to the community as a matter of conviction, not as a marketing gimmick.

Imperial had established itself as the major corporate force both in the "upstream" — the exploration and production arm of the industry — and the "downstream" — the refineries where petroleum was converted into gasoline and other products, and the gas stations where the gasoline was sold. It also took the lead in petrochemicals, where petroleum's versatile molecules were moulded into an enormous range of synthetic products.

Imperial's roadside logo went back to the very beginning of Canadian motoring, when it opened the first drive-in gasoline station in Vancouver in 1908. Imperial had also heralded the modern age of Canadian petroleum with its seminal find near the village of Leduc, southwest of Edmonton, in 1947.

Alberta's involvement with petroleum went back to before the turn of the century, when engineers working for the Canadian Pacific Railroad had struck natural gas at Langevin while drilling for water. The discovery was not considered a cause for joy. Natural gas is one of the many forms of petroleum; often, both oil and natural gas emerge from a well. But natural gas was treated for decades as at best a nuisance, at worst a danger. Although it was sometimes used for local heating and lighting, it was usually ignited and "flared off." Only with the advance of compression and pipeline technology after the Second World War did the natural gas business really take off. The key Canadian development was the construction of the TransCanada PipeLine, which brought natural gas from Alberta to Ontario.

Alberta's first major oil find had been in the Turner Valley, southwest of Calgary, in 1914. The Turner Valley would remain the focus of exploration for more than thirty years, as well as the nursery of some of Canada's greatest and most colourful oilmen, like Bobby Brown of Home Oil and Frank McMahon of Pacific Petroleums. For many of those years, the flames from the Turner Valley's natural gas flares lit the Calgary night sky.

Until 1947, petroleum was largely an Alberta affair, and periodic bouts of Turner Valley–inspired oil fever were mostly restricted to the dusty streets of Calgary. Local production could not nearly keep pace with the growing demands of Canada's economic development, which were fed by imports. That changed with Imperial's find at Leduc.

Leduc was not merely important as a 200-million-barrel field; it provided the geological key to similar finds in structures known as Devonian reefs. In 1948, Imperial used the key in making a much larger find at Redwater, northeast of Edmonton, and from then until the mid-1950s, a Devonian find at least as large as Leduc was made every year. In 1953, Mobil Canada found the huge Pembina field in the Drayton Valley west of Edmonton.

These finds led to a surge in Canadian production. In 1947, Canadian oil had provided only 19,500 of the 211,000 barrels used daily by Canadian refineries. Ten years later, Canadian oil was providing 347,500 barrels a day towards total refinery demand of 654,000 barrels.

Imperial not only found and developed a lot of oil — not just Leduc and Redwater, but other large fields like Judy Creek and Golden Spike — it built the pipelines to move the oil both east and west from Edmonton. In 1950, it masterminded the Interprovincial line to Lake Superior, extending the line two years later to Sarnia. It also put together the consortium to build the Trans Mountain Pipe Line over the Yellowhead Pass and down the Fraser Valley into Vancouver.

In 1957, Imperial moved its headquarters from a bevy of buildings in downtown Toronto to a huge new office block at 111 St. Clair Avenue West, midway between the mansions of its largest shareholders in Rosedale and Forest Hill. The modern yet suitably sedate nineteen-storey building of granite, limestone, and tinted green glass provided the highest observation point in the city. The spreading developments that could be seen from the building's upper stories — Scarborough to the east, Port Credit to the west, Richmond Hill and Thornhill to the north — indicated the suburban conquests of the gasoline-fuelled automobile. The far-off haze above Niagara Falls was another symbol of gasoline-driven tourism. From its St. Clair Avenue headquarters, Imperial was the lord of all it surveyed. But Imperial had always had a problem: its parent.

• • •

For economic nationalists and those concerned about the supposed evils of "corporate power," Imperial's single most important feature was that 70 per cent of its equity was owned by Standard Oil of New Jersey, which was the largest of the companies that had emerged from the dissolution of John D. Rockefeller's Standard Oil Trust in 1911. Rockefeller was one of the most admired and reviled men of his dynamic generation. It was the Rockefeller connection that made Imperial a lightning rod for the paranoia of economic nationalists and socialists, who had been educated to fear and despise the largely fictitious terrors of the objective for which Rockefeller reputedly strived: monopoly. It was in pursuit of this elusive goal that Imperial had been purchased.

Rockefeller was born in 1839 in rural New York state. His father, who sold herbal remedies and patent medicines, moved the family to Ohio and inculcated the young John D. with commercial skills. By the age of twenty, Rockefeller had moved to Cleveland and formed a trading partnership that dealt in farm and other produce, then oil, which had recently almost literally started to flood markets.

The U.S. oil industry had its origins around the time of the Civil War, when entrepreneurs were looking for alternatives to whale oil and other animal fats for lighting and lubricating. Oozing seeps of tarry bitumen, or asphalt, had been known for thousands of years, and had been used for waterproofing vessels, covering roads, and healing wounds. Moses' Burning Bush and the "eternal flame" of the Delphic Oracle were both probably flares of gas that had somehow been ignited. Similar mysterious flames were at the root of Middle Eastern fire-worship. But it was a combination of technology and entrepreneurial vision that heralded the modern oil age.

Dr. Abraham Gesner, a twice-shipwrecked former horse trader, medical doctor, and ultimately geologist for the province of New Brunswick, developed a process for extracting and refining illuminating oil from asphalt and other "heavy" oils. He called his refined product "kerosene," from the Greek words for wax and oil.

Kerosene could also be produced from lighter "rock oil," or petroleum, but supplies seemed limited to what bubbled up through marshy seeps.

In the 1850s, a group of New Yorkers led by a lawyer, James Bissell, decided to invest in the development of rock oil in western Pennsylvania. Bissell and his fellow investors believed there were large underground "pools" that could be tapped by salt drilling techniques. In fact, oil did not lie in subterranean caverns, as some suspected; it sat under enormous pressure in porous rocks where its upward migration had been stopped by an impermeable rock "cap." When this cap was penetrated by a bore hole, the oil and natural gas rushed to the surface, providing the classic "gusher," which became the symbol of oil wealth.

The first well for Bissell's Pennsylvania Rock Oil Company was drilled in Titusville by "Colonel" Edwin L. Drake. In August 1859, at sixty-nine feet, Drake struck a modest flow of oil and sparked a drilling boom, leading to a proliferation of wells, a flood of oil, and a collapse of prices.

Oil played havoc with markets because it wasn't like other minerals. You didn't have to extract it from reluctant rock. Once you hit the spot, oil came to you, often in super-abundance. Oilmen soon came to respect their petroleum prey as a beast that needed a strong master. Many tried to tame it. The one who came closest was Rockefeller.

With oil gushing and prices falling between the end of the Civil War and 1870, Rockefeller decided to try to consolidate the refining industry. In 1870, he and four partners established the Standard Oil Company, so named to indicate a reliable consistency of product. He pioneered modern business methods, expanding to take advantage of economies of scale, and vertically integrating to bring both production and distribution under his control. Economies of scale and vertical integration helped lower costs and make planning possible. The railroads who carried his products offered him secret rebates, thus further increasing his price advantage. By 1872, he was master of the largest refinery group in the world.

Standard's size and market control enabled it to lower prices, thus forcing rivals into the fold or out of the business. But Rockefeller's business practices were not unusually predatory for the times. Of his "secretive" approach, Rockefeller once said: "It is all too true! But I wonder what General of the Allies ever sends out a brass band in advance with orders to notify the enemy that on a certain day he will begin an attack?" The important point — and one that has since been deliberately obscured — was that Rockefeller's attack was not on the consumer; it was on his business rivals.

By 1879, Standard controlled 90 per cent of America's refining capacity. When the development of pipelines threatened to circumvent Rockefeller's control, Standard acquired those too. Standard grew as a conglomeration of individual companies coordinated through a trust, which controlled the companies on behalf of Rockefeller and his fellow shareholders. Said financier William Vanderbilt: "I never came into contact with any class of men so smart and able as they are in their business."

These smart men inevitably turned their eyes to capturing foreign markets. One of the most promising was neighbouring Canada, which was hardly considered a "foreign" market at all.

Canada's most prominent oil company was Imperial. Imperial's origins went back to those of the Canadian oil business in southwestern Ontario, where oil was found at around the same time as in the U.S. The company was organized in 1880 by the leading petroleum refiners in the Ontario towns of Petrolia and London, Frederick Fitzgerald and Jacob Englehart, to bring order to a chaotic industry. Fitzgerald and Englehart bought eleven local refineries, closed nine, and made Imperial the dominant Canadian oil company. By 1891, Imperial produced 45 per cent of Canadian-refined oil, but its market was being invaded by a superior and lower-priced product from south of the border. On July 1, 1898, the manufacturer of the cheaper, higher-quality product, Standard Oil, acquired 75 per cent of Imperial's stock, giving it control of the largest Canadian refiner.

The consumer was well served by the Rockefeller empire.

Kerosene prices came down sharply. But outraged and outsmarted business opponents in the U.S. denounced "the overweening control of the oil business by the Standard Oil Company." Unable to beat Rockefeller in the market, they turned to politics, the populist media, and the courts, accusing Rockefeller of trying to build a "monopoly," a word that deeply offended the egalitarian, Republican spirit.

Monopolists were the bogeymen who wanted to seize control of markets at all costs so they could extort higher than "normal" prices from a helpless consumer. In fact, the reality was something else. The latter half of the nineteenth century saw the rapid development of larger and larger industrial facilities whose economies of scale and scope produced higher-quality products at lower prices, thus driving smaller and less efficient operations out of business. Competition was fierce, and industrialists desired control of markets not primarily to make extortionate profits but to avoid losses from "ruinous competition," a particular problem in the volatile oil business. For someone to approach as close as Rockefeller to dominating a market required both a limited market and extraordinary skills, organization, and excellence. What Rockefeller tried to do was to introduce order to the most chaotic commodity ever known to man. His attempt failed.

Despite the brilliance of his organization, and the occasional ruthlessness of his methods, he was under constant attack from new supplies and new competitors. Standard's control of overseas markets was tenuous from the beginning. The Russian oilfields around Baku on the Caspian Sea, which were developed by the Nobels and the Rothschilds, became the principal alternative source of supply. By 1888, Russian production was almost as great as that of the U.S. The Rothschilds linked up with a London-based merchant, Marcus Samuel, who would go on to found Shell. Samuel outflanked Standard by developing bulk oil tankers and dispatching them through the Suez Canal to put Russian oil into the Far East.

During the "Oil Wars" of the 1890s, Standard, the Nobels, the Rothschilds, and the other Russian producers not only fought for markets but courted one another with a view to merging or apportioning markets in order to avoid "ruinous competition." The cast of characters expanded with the entry of the Royal Dutch company.

The new century brought both massive new finds and the automobile. The incandescent light bulb sounded the death knell for kerosene, just as the internal combustion engine heralded the boom in another refined product, gasoline. Refining technology was adapted accordingly. The gusher at a little hill called Spindletop started the great Texas oil boom, which in turn provided the foundations for two more of the industry's giants, Gulf and Texaco.

As new discoveries were made in other parts of the U.S. and the rest of the world, Standard, which incorporated its interests in New Jersey in 1899, could not hold its pre-eminent position. Nevertheless, Standard's size, secrecy, and "power" provided fertile ground for populist assault. In particular, Standard drew the unwelcome attention of the American Progressive movement and its "muckraking" journalistic wing, the best-known member of which was the journalist Ida Tarbell. Tarbell's *The History of the Standard Oil Company* was described by oil historian Daniel Yergin as "the single most influential book on business ever published in the United States." Tarbell was not a socialist, but her exposé inevitably implied that a countervailing force was necessary to corporate power. Only one countervailing force was possible: government. She thus set the stage for a struggle between governments and oil companies that would span the twentieth century. The story of this struggle is brilliantly told in Yergin's book *The Prize*.

President Theodore Roosevelt, who came to power in 1901, thought the muckrakers too negative, but he saw their populist appeal. He believed that corporate power had to be controlled in order to short-circuit radicalism. Nevertheless, he was not above taking pot-shots at the easy targets in the Standard boardroom. In 1906, his administration brought suit against Standard under the Sherman Anti-Trust Act of 1890, accusing the empire of conspiring to restrain trade. The case went to the Supreme Court, whose chief justice declared: "No disinterested mind can survey the period in question [since 1870] without being irresistibly drawn to the conclusion that the very genius for commercial development and organization...soon begat an intent and purpose to exclude others...from their right to trade and thus accomplish the mastery which was the end in view." Standard Oil was ordered dismembered. From the break-up came Standard Oil of New Jersey (today called Exxon), Standard Oil of New York (Mobil), and Standard Oil of California (Chevron) — companies that would tower over oil development in the twentieth century — as well as other great oil names like Amoco and Sohio.

The three Standard Oil companies would be joined by Gulf and Texaco, and two European companies — the amalgamation of Royal Dutch/Shell, and British Petroleum (originally Anglo-Persian, then Anglo-Iranian) — to form the "Seven Sisters." Their reign was one of technological excellence and commercial reason. But oil continued a most unruly commodity. And the politics of the countries in which the Sisters found their oil provided frequent challenges and frustrations.

Oil's importance grew strategically as well as commercially with its development as a transportation fuel. The British government became directly involved as a result of the Royal Navy's conversion from domestically abundant coal to oil — more efficient, but foreign — before the First World War. Winston Churchill was the formidable champion of government involvement. Like Teddy Roosevelt, Churchill felt no compunction about taking aim at Standard and Royal Dutch/Shell when he found it politically useful. When he sought parliamentary approval to buy 51 per cent of the exploration company Anglo-Persian, he shamelessly and cynically attacked the "monopolies and trusts."

The Great War inevitably drew politicians and bureaucrats into the business, waving the flags of both prosperity and power. The French government created Compagnie Française des Pétroles (CFP). The British government tried to gain control of Royal Dutch/Shell, but was rebuffed by its brilliant Dutch head, Henri Deterding. The Americans didn't like the idea of state-owned companies, although political considerations would lead Big Oil into many uneasy alliances with Washington.

The issue of national "control," which would become so prominent in Canada in the 1970s and early 1980s, was already a feature of global oil by the 1920s but was treated dismissively as an irrelevance by some of the more outspoken members of the oil sorority. Robert Waley Cohen of Shell declared in 1923: "The whole question of control is very largely nonsense. It is a matter of sentiment, but if by transferring control to the Hottentots we could increase our security and our dividends, I don't believe any of us would hesitate for long."

Others took a more understanding line towards national aspirations, or at least understood their potential power. Deterding said of Shell's operations in the U.S., "It is contrary to human nature, however well a concern like that may be directed, or however much it may have the interest of the people at heart, not to anticipate there will be a kind of jealous feeling against such a company."

Oil became a symbol of sovereignty. That inevitably meant a collision between the objectives of oil companies and the interests of nation-states. Ultimately, governments had the "legitimacy" to do whatever they could get away with. Their only real constraints were fear of reprisal by the international oil companies' home governments, or the realization that they needed a company's exploration and production expertise and marketing networks. But oil's often super-abundant nature also meant that the industry sometimes sought government involvement.

In the 1930s, with a new flood of supplies from the giant East Texas field and rock-bottom prices, the U.S. industry begged for government intervention. A system of production controls was introduced under the aegis of the Texas Railroad Commission, which provided both precedent and model for the Organization of Petroleum Exporting Countries and the Alberta Energy Resources Conservation Board. Output controls stabilized prices, but stability had been bought at the expense of further government intervention.

At a global level, there had been an attempt among the companies — prodded by the British government — to bring order to the chaotic market at a famous, although at the time supposedly secret, meeting at Achnacarry Castle in Scotland. The result was the "As-Is" agreement, under which world markets were meant to be divided according to corporate shares in 1928. The "As-Is" agreement was subsequently portrayed as a dastardly plot, but was more accurately a defensive response to increased assaults from governments. In any case, it didn't work. The Soviet Union was not a signatory, and there were always "fringe" players who would overturn such supposedly tidy arrangements. The "market" — in the shape of new finds and new competitors — invariably overwhelmed attempts at control, by either companies or governments.

Governments had blunter instruments at their disposal. The greatest challenge of the 1930s came in Mexico, where British and American interests had made large finds. "Yanqui" domination was an obsession, even though the majority of the industry was British-controlled. Following an oil workers' strike in May 1937, President Lázaro Cárdenas set up a commission, which accused the oil companies of "raping" the Mexican economy and adding nothing to economic welfare. It demanded huge wage and benefit increases. The oil companies — with conspicuously little support from the government of Franklin Delano Roosevelt — buckled on most demands, but the die was cast. On March 18, 1938, foreign oil was expropriated. A state oil company, Petroleos Mexicanos, was set up with great fanfare. The immediate consequence of the great 1938 battle over higher wages was that Pemex was forced to impose a wage cut. Pemex would become a model, primarily of corruption and waste.

Although hostility to foreign oil was not as vehement in Canada as in Mexico, it nevertheless existed as a powerful echo of the muckrakers' propaganda. Imperial executives were uniquely sensitive to their parentage. For years they resisted the suggestions of Standard that they change the name of their gasoline from Imperial to Esso, because Esso stood for S.O., and S.O. stood for Standard Oil, and Standard Oil stood for Rockefeller.

Meanwhile, some provincial Canadian governments could match any *caudillo* for windy rhetoric. In the 1930s, Frank McMahon's efforts to drill in the Peace River area of northeastern British Columbia were held up by the Liberal provincial government of Duff Pattullo, a Big Oil–hater and interventionist who wanted to preserve the undiscovered riches of the Peace River area "for the government and the people."

Pattullo did not understand the oil business, or indeed any business. A diminutive, dapper former newspaperman with a taste for pomposity, he was dead set against private exploitation of "the heritage of the people." His government hounded gasoline retailers and accused them of gouging, leading the companies to refuse to supply gasoline to Vancouver. In retaliation, his government introduced the Petroleum Powers Act, which gave the government the authority to take over part or all of the petroleum industry in Vancouver. Pattullo told the legislature, "Gasoline is so vital in the life of our people, it seems unreasonable that its sale and distribution should be at the sole dictation and control of the companies who sell it."

Duff Pattullo would become the model for later oil interventionists. He wanted more oil but refused to allow the prices that would stimulate investment. He declared that since the oil companies weren't drilling, then the government had to. But Duff Pattullo never found any oil.

• • •

Following the Second World War, the giant Middle East "concessions" were signed. Companies agreed to explore for and produce crude oil, which would belong to the company or consortium for the duration of the concession. The company or consortium would set prices and find markets and, in return, pay local governments royalties and taxes on production. The petroleum world's centre of gravity shifted decisively to the Middle East, with profound geopolitical consequences.

Despite the concession system, the struggle between governments and companies over the division of spoils, or "economic rents," continued. The concept of economic rent was developed by nineteenth-century stockbroker-turned-economist David Ricardo. Ricardo applied his analysis first to grain-growing land. Rents represented the "excess" profit that accrued from having highly productive, as opposed to marginally economic, acreage. The same theory was applied to oil, which was similarly regarded as a "bounty of nature." The marginal well, which returned just enough to pay its costs and keep its producer in business, was contrasted to the gusher, whose production costs were mere cents per barrel. All income above the "normal" return was regarded as a "rent." This sum was particularly large on Middle East oil.

How the rent was to be divided could be settled only by a power struggle. For the oil-producing countries, the struggle was interwoven with nationalist aspirations. Nationalists often found it convenient, as in Mexico, to cast the foreigners as exploiters who had held back development rather than promoting it; they claimed Big Oil had "corrupted" the political leaders whom the revolutionaries sought to unseat. There was much talk of oil as a "birthright" and "national heritage" from people who, without the oil companies, would never have known the petroleum was there.

The oil companies wrote off much of this behaviour as posturing, and regarded talk of exploitation as nonsense. After all, they were the ones who had put up the money, taken the risks, created the values, and suffered the costs of the dry holes. The men who ran the multinationals were practical people, engineers and geologists who wanted to drill the prospects, put in the production systems, build the terminals, and move on to the next job. They wanted to leave local politics alone. But inevitably, when they found oil under a dictatorial regime, they were cast as supporters of the regime — and cast out alongside it, come the revolution.

The arena for the first epic postwar contest for control of oil was Venezuela, the major source of low-cost oil for Standard Oil of New Jersey's subsidiary, Creole. Venezuela's minister of development, Juan Pablo Pérez Alfonzo, later one of the founders of OPEC, introduced a revolutionary "fifty-fifty" arrangement, under which the government and the companies shared the "rent" equally. By 1948, Venezuela's oil income was six times the level of 1942.

The Venezuelans' concessions set a model that others inevitably wanted to follow. Fifty-fifty deals were soon signed with Saudi Arabia, Kuwait, and Iraq. But despite the fair-sounding nature of fifty-fifty, the split would always be subject to pressure from countries who thought they could gain more, or companies who were prepared to offer more. Nationalist aspirations added an extra element of instability to the equation. That soon became apparent in Iran.

Shah Mohammed Reza Pahlavi's father, Reza Pahlavi, had seized power in what was then Persia in the 1920s. He was deposed during the Second World War by the Allies because of his friendliness to the Nazis. His son, enthroned in his place, would always be haunted by his own puppet image. Riven by every kind of political division, Iran needed a very strong man indeed. Its politics were full of wild exaggeration and violent emotion. Its business was rife with graft and corruption. The single unifying force was hatred of the British. Every political opponent was assumed to be a British agent. Every misfortune, from crop failure to earthquakes, was the work of the British infidel. The source of, and focus for, the hatred was the Anglo-Iranian Oil Company.

The British government had little control over Anglo-Iranian, despite its 51-per-cent shareholding. That had been Churchill's intention. The company was Iran's largest industrial employer and its major source of foreign earnings. But these were mere economic details. What counted were emotions and symbols. Anglo-Iranian was a very useful scapegoat.

Mohammed Mossadegh was a cosmopolitan, European-educated lawyer who was fiercely nationalistic and apparently obsessed by his opposition to the British. He was also full of humbug. He sent his son to a British school — "Where else?" he asked — and would feign fainting fits for effect at the climax of speeches. Given to greeting visitors from his bed, clad in pajamas, he was a veritable showman of the side-step, arguably devoid of conviction. Mossadegh, said to show "little gift for governing" according to

Yergin, was made prime minister in 1952, "with the specific and wildly popular mandate to execute the nationalization law."

"The source of all the misfortunes of this tortured nation," he declared, "is only the oil company." Mossadegh dispatched the governor of Khuzistan province to sacrifice a sheep in front of Anglo-Iranian's headquarters at Khorramshahr, then announced to a delirious crowd that the concession was voided. In fact, the deed was not so easily done. The Americans were terrified that if Mossadegh fell, a communist government would follow. They joined the British in organizing a counter-coup in favour of the Shah, arousing a storm of controversy. A multinational consortium was subsequently formed to work in Iran, consisting of all the great concessionaires: the Seven Sisters plus the French CFP.

The fact that Western governments were prepared to interfere in foreign politics — even overthrow national governments — in pursuit of a secure oil supply did not mean that the oil companies had their home governments in their pockets. U.S. policy was marked by dramatic swings. At times, Washington would champion the companies in order to promote America's political and economic objectives. At other times, the same companies were subjected to assaults by branches of government that seemed to have no knowledge of the realities of either business or international oil diplomacy.

Anti-trust lawyers in the Justice Department still saw the ghost of John D. Rockefeller stalking the corridors of oil power. In 1949, the Federal Trade Commission used subpoenaed documents to write a huge study — *The International Petroleum Cartel* — that became a key reference work for industry knockers. According to Yergin: "It generally interpreted complex events in such a way as to support its overriding thesis that international oil was indeed a cartel. In particular, it showed a fundamental blind spot; in the world of *The International Petroleum Cartel,* oil companies did not have to adapt and bend to the will and requirements of governments — the cartel-minded governments of the 1930s, dictatorships around the world, the British and French governments throughout the years, and the governments of oil-producing countries, which wanted higher revenues and could always cancel a concession." In the FTC's mind, it was all a great conspiracy.

The State and Defense departments, as well as the CIA, were appalled by the report. The White House's Intelligence Committee said it would "greatly assist Soviet propaganda" and "would further the achievement of Soviet objectives throughout the world." British Prime Minister Sir Anthony Eden described the FTC report as the work of "witch-hunters." Still, the mud stuck.

· · ·

The global system so carefully erected by the oil majors was not merely vulnerable to political attack both at home and abroad. Despite all its supposed monopolistic or oligopolistic powers, it remained vulnerable to competition from the strong-willed independent oilmen who were prepared to pay a price to break into the charmed circle — men such as Americans John Paul Getty and Armand Hammer, and the great Italian state entrepreneur Enrico Mattei. The premiums paid by these men threatened the major oil companies' united front and shifted the balance of power towards the producing nations.

A price reduction by Standard Oil of New Jersey in July 1960, led to the creation of the Organization of Petroleum Exporting Countries, to defend the price of oil and regulate production. The event was hardly noted, particularly in Canada, for whom the geopolitics of oil had always been a distant concern.

Until Imperial's find at Leduc, the Canadian oil business had concentrated on refining and marketing oil imported by the subsidiaries of the major oil companies, most of whom had entered Canada by buying Canadian operations. But once Leduc had unlocked Alberta's considerable petroleum treasures, domestic oilmen were quick to get into the act, although they had to operate in the shadows of the better-funded and more technically skilled majors. Where they scored was in their ability to move much more rapidly than the multinationals.

The Canadian independents made significant finds of their

own, but Canada never produced independents of the calibre of Getty or Hammer, players on the global oil stage. Home Oil's Bobby Brown and Pacific's Frank McMahon had world-class dreams but found their fortunes in Alberta. Because the Canadian oil business got a late start, the first really major Canadian oil fortune did not emerge until the mid-1950s, when lawyer Eric Harvie sold most of his Alberta holdings to a Belgian company, Petrofina.

Since the Canadian independents' fortunes depended on production and sale of Alberta oil, they had a natural conflict with the majors, most of whose supplies came from the gushing fields of the Middle East. Although more Canadian oil was sold into the Canadian market once Imperial built its pipelines in the 1950s, Canadian producers had continued to find more than they could sell. Moreover, Imperial and the other major companies didn't want to transport Canadian oil farther east. It made more financial sense to ship oil into Montreal from South America and Saudi Arabia than to pipe it from Alberta.

The Canadian independents campaigned throughout the 1950s for import controls or tariffs but got little support from eastern Canadian consumers. Nevertheless, as a concession to Alberta's producers, following a 1960 Royal Commission on Energy, the National Oil Policy reserved the area west of the Ottawa Valley for sales of more expensive Canadian oil. Alberta producers, still facing a surplus, kept lobbying for an even greater share of the domestic market on security grounds.

In 1969 and 1970, representatives of the independent producers came to Ottawa, trying to peddle the concept of extending the Interprovincial oil pipeline into Montreal. Pierre Trudeau was advised to tell the Western oilmen to look harder for markets in the U.S. That's what Imperial would have recommended. Indeed, many believed that's what Imperial *had* recommended, and that Canadian oil policy essentially came out of the executive offices on St. Clair Avenue. In fact, it was a little more complicated than that.

Joe Greene, Trudeau's energy minister, had set up the National Advisory Committee on Petroleum to receive advice from senior oil and pipeline executives on government policy. NACOP's strongest voice belonged to Bill Twaits, Imperial's outspoken chief executive, a man who displayed scarcely concealed frustration with anyone who refused to see that what was good for Imperial was good for Canada. But events in global oil, and in Canadian politics, were about to raise doubts about that maxim.

Economic nationalists found rich grounds for their paranoia in the reach of Imperial's history and the scope of its operations. For Walter Gordon, still denouncing foreign domination from the pages of the *Toronto Star,* the very idea that Imperial might have something to say about oil policy was offensive. What, Gordon would ask indignantly, did Imperial do that Canadians couldn't? Was it good for Canada that they had to run down to New York for orders from Exxon (as Jersey renamed itself in 1972)? And what was Exxon in business for, Gordon would ask darkly. They just wanted to maximize profits!

There was an amazing similarity between the views peddled by Walter Gordon and those expressed in the government offices and political cabals of Latin America and the Middle East. Like Iran's Mohammed Mossadegh, Gordon wanted to get up to 111 St. Clair West, sacrifice a sheep out front, and claim Imperial for the nation. And although he might have been paranoid, Gordon was acquiring some very powerful supporters.

In the early 1970s, the increasingly prevalent belief that Imperial Oil and its multinational sisters were lying about petroleum reserves and ripping off the Canadian people at the gas pump was a powerful element in popular support for the creation of a state oil company. The source of this belief lay in understandable incomprehension about what was happening in the oil world.

For its first decade, OPEC was not much feared and did very little. The global surplus had held it in check. Between 1960 and 1969, the market price of oil fell by 22 per cent in money terms and 40 per cent in real terms. These price cuts provided an enormous boost to Western industrial growth. They also led oil's bounty to be taken for granted, and made the shock of what happened in 1973 all the greater.

During these years of new finds and growing production, the majors had the delicate task of allocating output to various producers who were often rivals, in particular Iran and Saudi Arabia. Their task was made no easier by the increasing penetration of the independents into world markets. In the U.S., they continued to face import controls imposed by President Dwight Eisenhower in 1959, and in Canada their imports were barred from Western markets by the Ottawa Valley line of the 1960 National Oil Policy.

The U.S. quotas lasted for fourteen years and turned into an administrative nightmare. Nevertheless, they tilted investment to the U.S. and to Canada, because of its preferential access to the U.S. market. Canadian nationalists sometimes complained that Americans had an advantage in Canada because of U.S. tax laws that gave them generous write-offs for foreign exploration; in effect, U.S. taxpayers were subsidizing Canadian oil exploration instead of Canadian taxpayers. Moreover, in contrast to the concession system, where producers took ownership of the oil they found, all oil and gas in Canada belonged to the federal or provincial governments and was only produced under licence by oil companies, who paid both royalties and taxes. With these financial levers, government ultimately controlled both pricing and production.

While OPEC struggled to get its act together, and the independents fought their battles with the majors, it was the ineluctable power of supply and demand that would force the huge price increases of the early 1970s. These price increases would be misinterpreted, not entirely innocently, as the result of the exercise of political power by OPEC, and certainly politics was very much in evidence. But the major factor in what happened was the world's insatiable thirst for oil. Contrary to the fears of many, the world wasn't about to run out of oil, but it was about to run out of *cheap* oil.

The huge Middle East finds of the 1950s and 1960s had run ahead of demand, but that lead was rapidly running out by the early 1970s. Oil products were aggressively marketed by the majors, who were in turn pushed to sell more by the producing countries. World oil production and use had roughly doubled every decade since 1880. In 1960, 1 billion tonnes of crude oil was produced. By 1970, the figure was 2.3 billion tonnes. At some stage, something had to give. Perhaps even more astonishing than the trends in demand growth were the trends in prices. The international price of a barrel of crude in 1970, at US$1.80, was about the same as it had been in the 1920s, and much less than at times in the 1860s, when Pennsylvania crude had sold for almost US$10.

Another key factor in the 1970 crisis was a dramatic change in the pattern of supply and demand. From 1860 until 1950, the U.S. had dominated world production. In 1950, the U.S. still produced half the world's oil. U.S. production would continue to grow for the next twenty years, but the relative importance of American oil declined with huge finds abroad. By 1965, the Middle East had overtaken the U.S. in total production. In 1970, U.S. production peaked, but demand there did not. The country developed a massive thirst for imported oil. That demand increasingly had to be fed from the Middle East, which was becoming more and more politically unstable.

The Arabs attempted to use the "oil weapon" during the Six-Day War with Israel in 1967, but failed. Then, in 1969, Muammar al-Qadaffi seized power in Libya. President Gamal Abdel Nasser of Egypt, who had first recommended the use of oil as a political weapon, was his hero. Abdullah Tariki, the "Red Sheik" of Saudi Arabia became his advisor on oil. The company he chose to squeeze was Armand Hammer's Occidental, which had all its eggs in the Libyan basket. The squeeze — made more effective by a tightening market — resulted in a 30-cent-per-barrel price increase and a hoist in Libya's profit share from 50 to 55 per cent. The Libyan agreements decisively changed the balance of power. The Shah of Iran, not wanting to be outdone, reopened agreements and got 55 per cent too. Then the Gulf states got 55 per cent, and with that, a game of leapfrog began. Venezuela introduced legislation to raise its share to 60 per cent. OPEC declared 55-per-cent a minimum. Then Libya jumped over Iran and made new demands. In February 1971 in Tehran, fifty-fifty was formally buried by OPEC in favour of the 55-per-cent minimum government take. A 35-cent-per-barrel price increase was also agreed, with other annual increases to follow. It was the watershed. The buyers' market was over. In April 1971, there was another agreement in Tripoli. Now the OPEC posted price was raised by 90 cents. The rout was gathering momentum.

The fires of nationalism were fed by the commercial "victory." In earlier years the Bolsheviks, the Mexicans, and the Iranians had nationalized or tried to nationalize outright, but now some thought "participation" was preferable since it would keep the majors — who were essential to selling the oil — in the game. Algeria took 51 per cent of the French companies operating there. Venezuela passed legislation under which all concessions would revert to state ownership upon their expiry in the early 1980s. Libya nationalized BP's holdings. Iraq, which had cancelled all the unexplored concessions of the Iraq Petroleum Company in the early 1960s, nationalized the remainder of IPC. There were participation deals with Saudi Arabia and Kuwait. Then Libya took over 50 per cent of the Italian state oil company's operations there, completely expropriated another of the flamboyant independents, Bunker Hunt, and nationalized 51 per cent of all the others. The Shah already owned Iran's oil, but the National Iranian Oil Company was now made operator as well.

This seizure of political initiative based on underlying market changes indicated that the oil weapon might be used more effectively next time. By the time it was, Canadian energy policy was being run by those whose thinking had much more in common with Venezuela and Libya than with the U.S. They believed that government control was essential.

FOUR

The Policy Entrepreneurs

N OCTOBER 1990, Bill Hopper was being questioned in the usual desultory manner at the Senate Standing Committee on Energy and Natural Resources, one of Ottawa's myriad gatherings designed to create the impression of public surveillance of the workings of government. It came to the turn of Liberal Senator Jack Austin. Austin wanted details of Petrocan's plans to raise equity under Bill C-84, the proposal to privatize the Crown corporation. Hopper said that, before he answered, he wanted to say something: "Senator Jack Austin, if anyone, serves as father to this corporation."

Austin's round, rosy face beamed. "Thank you very much," he replied. "I think that is a compliment." But while the broad smile still played on Austin's face, Hopper said something else: "If you like it, you can thank him. If you do not like it, you can blame him." The moment of élite intimacy was given a sharp edge. The exchange perfectly indicated Bill Hopper's strange relationship with Ottawa, and his unique ability to shift blame and deliver sugar-coated barbs. His words also contained a subtle subtext, a compensatory pat for coming second, for both men knew that Bill Hopper had the job that Jack Austin had once coveted.

Smiling while acknowledging fatherhood of one of the great money-eating entities of modern Canadian times seems strange, but then bottom lines have never been treated very seriously in Ottawa. Bottom-line perspectives, particularly during the Trudeau era, were considered far too narrow, indeed almost crass when broader but more vague goals like the public interest had to be served.

By 1990, Jack Austin's star had long passed its zenith. But he had once been a real shooter, on the leading edge of a group of people who were prepared to take big risks with public money on the basis that all the things wise men knew about human nature and politics weren't true. This group of people was known as the "policy entrepreneurs."

When Pierre Trudeau came to power in 1968, he came as a still self-confident young nation's dream. He was academically brilliant and charismatic, promising the rule of "reason above passion." To bring about this rational revolution, he recruited a team of analysts and expediters. Of course, bureaucrats had always held much more power to influence policy than was publicly acknowledged. Moreover, Trudeau was well aware of bureaucracy's tendency to pursue its own interests and oppose government policies it found inconvenient. So he planned to seize control of the Ottawa machine through the creation of his own super-bureaucracy. These new men considered themselves the agents of reason, but they were also committed reformers, full of faith in the ability of their well-honed minds to solve social and economic problems. Trudeau's new élite were *engagés*. They were innovative. They took risks. They bent the rules.

The new men had a new style and a new approach. Their academic and professional backgrounds tended to be in economics and law. Many held doctorates. If they had ever worked, they were likely to have been lawyers or academics. In line with the shifting demands of politics, this élite tended to move between policy areas rather than sticking to any one department. They looked upon government not as a career or a vocation, but as a stepping-stone from which they could move on to bigger and better things.

There was an enormous competitive spirit among them. The game was to get to the key policy areas and come up with bright ideas. Ministers were treated as equals, although usually regarded as intellectual inferiors. The new men regarded themselves not as subordinates but as colleagues of the politicians; they were there not to serve their masters, but to help them come to the right decisions.

· · ·

The new men were moulded by the political and intellectual trends that had taken over postwar ivory towers. Broadly, academics of the 1950s and 1960s believed that the free market "worked" only in crude terms, and that the healing hand of government was necessary to correct its shortcomings. Among their leading gurus were economist John Maynard Keynes, who preached that central governments could pursue counter-cyclical spending policies in pursuit of full employment, growth, and stable money, and social critic John Kenneth Galbraith, who held the corporate world up both as an object of ridicule and as a potentially pernicious force, capable of perverting weak-minded consumers' priorities through advertising.

Keynes's recommendations may have had economic merit, but they were deeply flawed politically, for they could only be implemented by a benevolent despot. They assumed that democratically elected politicians would borrow to spend during recessions, but then run budget surpluses during booms. Inevitably, politicians got half the message. People who buy votes never run budget surpluses.

The Galbraithian critique suffered from the same fundamental fallacy of assuming benevolent rulers to whom more power should be given. "The need for remedial action to align the use of power with the public interest can no longer be escaped," wrote Galbraith in *Economics and the Public Purpose*. "And such remedial action ceases to be exceptional but becomes, instead, an intrinsic need." The crusade had to set sail at once. The destination could be worked out later.

In fact, Galbraith's analysis acknowledged its own central flaw but refused to accept its implications. He noted that organizations always served their own interests. "The problem of power derives not from private organization but from organization. All organization excludes interference from outside or above; its goals are those which serve the interests of its members." Where were we, then, to find the all-seeing agents of good will who would administer Galbraith's vague program, and how — since they had inevitably to work in an organization — could they possibly maintain their purity of purpose? And how could we be certain that these agents *were* pure of purpose ?

Those who found the Galbraithian view attractive never appeared to consider that bureaucratic self-interest might apply to them. When one suggested to the Trudeaucrats that they were in danger of acting beyond their powers of comprehension, or were straying into politically dangerous territory, they would look affronted. What, then, were they to do? Accept the imperfections of the economy and society? Do nothing? They claimed the force of reason would solve all problems. Their *Weltanschauung* was summed up by another guru, economist Robert Heilbroner, who wrote in his history of economic thought, *The Worldly Philosophers:* "To the extent that we no longer let the game of economics proceed unhindered to its natural outcome, we are going beyond the economic revolution. After two centuries of sailing almost as the winds directed us, the tiller of society is again in our grasp."

For those who espoused such views, it was more attractive to seize control of the wheelhouse than of the chartroom. That could be taken over later. Jack Austin, a great fan of both Galbraith and Heilbroner, saw himself as a steersman, but he also had a good idea of his course.

Austin's interventionist liberalism was compounded by his Canadian economic nationalism. His mentor in British Columbia had been Art Laing, a Liberal populist and a former feed and farm implements salesman whom Lester Pearson had chosen as his Pacific minister. Austin, who had law degrees from UBC and Harvard, ran Laing's election campaign in 1962, then followed him to Ottawa as executive assistant, in the process abandoning a doctoral thesis at Berkeley. Austin also became legal advisor to the Canadian team negotiating the Columbia River Treaty with Washington.

Austin was already a strong nationalist — he joined Gordon's minority group in Ottawa — but, in contrast to Gordon, believed that the resource industry was more important than manufacturing, and thus a stronger candidate to be "seized back." Gordon eventually came around to Austin's point of view. Two involvements during his first years in Ottawa galvanized Austin's nationalistic concerns and gave him opportunities to do something about them. He came away from the Columbia River Treaty negotiations with a feeling that Americans lacked appreciation for Canada. "The Americans saw us as a producer of resources for their cyclical requirements," he later said. "We were not seen as a steady source of supply to whom they needed to offer a certain degree of commitment."

Again, in 1965, Austin was a willing listener when conspiracy theories about the big oil companies' strategy for exploiting the oil and natural gas beneath the barren wastes and frozen waters of the Arctic Islands were related to him by a Calgarian visionary named Cam Sproule. Sproule painted a picture of major oil companies waiting in the wings for Canadians to make the finds, whereupon they would swoop in and take control. It was a wonderful theory if you wanted to persuade governments to invest in Arctic exploration. With Laing's backing, Austin worked on the creation of Panarctic Oils as a joint government-industry company to explore the High Arctic. It was an extraordinarily fruitless endeavour.

Austin ran unsuccessfully for Parliament in 1965, then returned to Vancouver to practise resource law and become involved in mining ventures. He maintained his political connections and his interest in power. He would find the bureaucratic route to achieving his personal visions both much more rapid and much more effective than the electoral alternative.

While in Ottawa, Austin had impressed a number of senior bureaucrats, including Gordon Robertson, then Clerk of the Privy Council and dean of the public service. It was Robertson who, in

1970, asked Austin to return to Ottawa for an interview with Pierre Trudeau for the job of deputy minister at the Department of Energy, Mines and Resources.

EMR had been formed in 1966 when responsibility for energy had been grafted onto the Department of Natural Resources, then concerned primarily with mining and water. The department was packed with boffins, beavering away on earth physics and mineral geology and cartography. It was not a policy powerhouse. Energy policy, such as it was, came from the National Energy Board, which had been set up a decade before. The main plank of oil policy was still the Ottawa Valley line, which provided protection for more expensive domestic oil.

The NEB put together reports on the basis of information from the oil companies. That made it an object of suspicion for the Trudeaucrats. The implication of manipulation was roundly rejected by the NEB's chairman, Dr. Robert Howland, who was also less than pleased at the prospect of an alternative source of policy advice within Ottawa.

Austin's job interview took place in Trudeau's limousine on the way to Ottawa airport and then aboard the prime minister's Jetstar as it flew to Toronto. Trudeau told Austin that the government wanted to understand the role of energy in Canadian society. How did the industry work? Was the public interest being served? What was the resource and price outlook? He wanted Austin to produce a White Paper.

When Trudeau asked Austin if he had any policy objectives, Austin replied: "A state presence in the oil industry." Trudeau, according to Austin, was non-committal. He declared he had an open mind on the issue. When Austin left Trudeau in Toronto, he was satisfied that he would be able to "build and take the big picture" within EMR. EMR was then, however, hardly equipped for such a role. Austin later recalled: "EMR existed only on paper. There were only three main energy policy officials — God, it was a different world then. Imperial Oil set the price of commodities according to its view of its own corporate interests. It had a research department that outmatched all the federal and provincial governments together."

These words betrayed a lot about Austin's thinking. The notion that Imperial set prices "according to its view of its own corporate interests" both stated the obvious in a darkly suggestive way and attributed more power to Imperial than it in fact possessed. Nevertheless, it was essential for the policy entrepreneurs to attribute strong powers to the corporate sector in order to justify extended powers for government. There was also a clear implication that Imperial's interests did not coincide with the "national" interest. Finally, Austin's statement indicated a conviction that research departments weren't there to give disinterested, objective analysis — or at least that of Imperial wasn't. The word "outmatched" implied that Austin needed some big analytical guns on his side. He already knew what the bottom line of their research should be.

Inevitably, Austin's arrival in Ottawa ruffled many feathers. Bob Howland and the NEB saw his appointment as an implicit criticism. Austin's elevation to instant deputy ministership stirred resentments in the rest of the bureaucracy. Within EMR, he was at first treated with a combination of suspicion and awe. His commitment to delve into the world of policy was seen by some in the department as a challenge, but many regarded it as a threat to their scientific purity. What, they asked themselves, was this part-academic, part-lawyer, part-businessman, part-Liberal policy guru doing in the role of senior bureaucrat, heading a department whose primary task was to be a knowledge base for pure and applied science? The answer was that he was there to create a national oil company.

The private sector, too, looked with suspicion on Austin. For Bill Twaits, head of Imperial, the appointment of Austin — who implied that he wanted to go through the books to get the *real* story, who suggested that he might have a higher purpose than Imperial — amounted almost to impudence. Moreover, Austin's dream of a state oil company was a solution to which there was, as yet, no problem.

· · ·

Two years before the Middle East heated to boiling point, Austin came within a whisker of achieving his state oil company without public debate, when one of Canada's most colourful oilmen, Bobby Brown, was forced to sell Home Oil. Brown, who caught the oil bug during the Turner Valley booms of the 1930s, had gained control of Home in 1950 and taken it on a switchback ride. His exploration successes were matched by equally ambitious and expensive failures, such as a huge gamble on the North Slope of Alaska in the wake of Atlantic Richfield–Humble's oil and gas find at Prudhoe Bay in 1968. When the bubble burst, in 1970, Home's shares plummeted from $81 to less than $10, forcing Brown, who was heavily in debt and whose health was wrecked by alcoholism, to sell.

Austin smelled opportunity. With Energy Minister Joe Greene's permission, he visited Brown and told him the government did not want Home to fall under foreign control. However, just before Christmas 1970, at a meeting in Ottawa, Brown told Austin and a group of senior bureaucrats that none of the Canadian companies with whom he had been negotiating had been able to come up with an acceptable offer. He wanted to sell to Ashland Oil of Kentucky. Brown left the meeting with the impression that the government had no more interest in acquiring Home. He was wrong.

Brown signed a deal with Ashland on January 18, 1971. The following morning, when he presented the agreement to Joe Greene in Ottawa, Greene told him that Ottawa had no intention of allowing the deal to go through. Although the government had no legislation to stop it, such legislation was pending.

Austin pressed behind the scenes for a government takeover, and he appeared to have won. On March 5, he called Brown in New York and told him to present himself with his advisors in Ottawa the following day: the government intended to purchase Home. The disgruntled Brown arrived in Ottawa for a weekend of discussions. The following Monday, March 8, he flew to Toronto to put the case to Greene once more for an Ashland takeover. He was unsuccessful. It appeared he would have to sell to Ottawa. But when faced with the moment of truth, pen in hand, Brown suddenly thrust the documents to one side, declaring: "I've come too damn far in life to sign everything away in half an hour. Tell them I won't sign today. I want the weekend to consider it."

After the next weekend, Brown issued a statement: "After careful and thoughtful consideration I have decided I would prefer to deal with the private sector...I now intend to try to put a consortium of Canadian and American companies together to see if I can accomplish my desires and still keep Home's control in Canada." A month later, Toronto-based Consumers Gas emerged as Home's Canadian "white knight."

Austin was undoubtedly disappointed. A buy-out of Home would have gone well beyond the government involvement in the TransCanada PipeLine or Panarctic Oils; financial support for those projects had been provided because they were considered nationally important but could not be wholly privately financed. Home would have been radically different: the purchase of a company with public funds to stop it from falling under American control.

Austin claimed he had rejected the "solution" of nationalizing the oil companies — urged upon the government by Gordon and the NDP — but his attitudes went beyond nationalism into a more fundamental belief in state control. He wasn't just talking about counterbalancing foreign power, he was talking about counterbalancing *private* power.

Austin had been frustrated, but he remained determined to create a national oil company. "So," he told an interviewer with a sigh, "I had to take the long route." Events in world oil would soon make his job much easier.

• • •

Canadians had never greatly concerned themselves with the sequence of revolutions, struggles, and expropriations that lay behind the evolution of the global oil business because the majors had largely succeeded in muffling these crises. There were always supply alternatives and prices hardly ever moved. Canadians may have noticed that they paid less for gasoline in Montreal than in Ontario because it was made from cheaper foreign oil, but otherwise the very stability of the oil business through the quarter-century after the end of the Second World War made the turmoil abroad almost invisible.

To say that Canadian oil development until the early 1970s had been "dominated" by the U.S. would be to fall into the semantic trap of implying that this U.S. involvement was in some way injurious. In fact, it was an almost wholly beneficial relationship. Certainly U.S. companies were the largest, they had been responsible for the majority of the most significant Canadian finds, and they had provided the conduit for cheap oil. The supply system they had erected with Shell, BP, and a number of other giants was an organizational wonder. But Jack Austin's deputy ministership at Energy, Mines and Resources between 1970 and 1974 coincided with a period of growing uncertainty, and then outright alarm, about oil.

A tightening in world markets enabled the oil weapon to be used successfully. This tightening also led to gradual, then very rapid, price rises, which were interpreted as a "power shift" from the consuming to the producing nations. In Canada, as elsewhere, these price increases were accompanied, in an atmosphere of ignorance, by widespread allegations of some ill-defined "conspiracy" on the part of Big Oil.

A more wide-ranging pessimism was abroad. The Club of Rome's gloomy report *The Limits to Growth,* published in 1972, painted a picture of resource depletion and environmental damage that pervaded subsequent policy formulation and bolstered the belief that capitalism didn't work, was too short-sighted, and was destroying the planet. (In fact, it would later be learned that far greater horrors were being perpetrated behind the Iron Curtain.) Environmentalists had already been flexing their muscles by delaying the development of the Alaskan oil find at Prudhoe Bay.

America was embroiled in Vietnam, and in Watergate, whose gradual unravelling coincided with the oil crisis. As Daniel Yergin wrote: "Things meshed in hazy, mysterious ways, and this impression left deep and abiding suspicions that fed conspiracy theories and obstructed more rational responses to the energy problems at hand." One lapel button summed it all up neatly: "Impeach Nixxon."

Canada, by contrast, felt a new sense of power. According to Michael Bliss, it was "becoming richer, more successful every year, a country whose infant cultural institutions and whose sense of distinctiveness were thriving as never before." The notion of being an economic colony of such a troubled power as the U.S. was distasteful to a young, self-confident nation. The desire for "authenticity," which Canadian economic nationalists shared with budding Third World leaders, was demanding its due. Authenticity was "doing your own thing" raised to a political level. But like the Flower Power that spawned that phrase, authenticity contained a hefty dose of irresponsibility, and a dangerous implication. America stood for free enterprise, so authenticity implied looking for some other way. That other way invariably meant more power for governments.

A 1964 Gallup poll revealed that 46 per cent of Canadians thought the country had enough U.S. capital; by 1972 the figure had risen to 67 per cent. The very fact that a poll should have been conducted on such a crucial economic issue said something about the times. The public had the barest understanding of economic issues, yet it was felt appropriate to consult them on this one. The assumption was similar to that which underlay FIRA: we could afford to pick and choose where our investments came from; people would always be clamouring to put their money into Canada. Moreover, a greater role for government seemed appropriate. We were used to more government; we needed more government to protect us from that huge, frightening, troubled entity to the south.

Energy uncertainties increased the attractiveness of an instrument that might give the public the "real goods" on the energy situation and might act in the "public interest" instead of just engaging in an unholy grab for profits. Moreover, such an agency might find oil to help domestic security, providing a blanket for a northerly nation easily spooked by phrases like "freezing in the dark."

Nevertheless, when Austin arrived in 1970, the coming oil crisis was a very distant rumble. There was little support for a state oil company, except from Walter Gordon and the NDP. Undaunted by his failure to orchestrate a state oil company through the purchase of Home — that is, in practice — Austin set about laying the basis for one in theory. He decided he needed a study. The man recommended to him for the job was a young Canadian consultant working in Boston named Bill Hopper.

· · ·

Wilbert Hill Hopper came within contractions of being born on the wrong side of the economic nationalists' great divide. His father, Wilbert, was doing his economics doctorate at Cornell in 1933. According to family legend, it was only Eva Hopper's decision to drive herself back across the border in the family's twelve-cylinder converted hearse that prevented Wilbert, Jr., from being born American.

The family moved to Ottawa when Wilbert, Sr., took a job with the federal Department of Agriculture. His next post was in Sydney, Australia, as agricultural counsellor in the Canadian Embassy. Young Wilbert attended Rockcliffe Park Public School in Ottawa and a private school in Sydney before going to American University in Washington for a degree in geology. He first worked for Imperial Oil as a junior geologist, but he wanted a faster track to the top. So he took an MBA at the University of Western Ontario, then returned to Calgary to work as a petroleum economist with Foster Associates. Hopper spent three years with the National Energy Board in Ottawa before moving back to the U.S. once more, this time to Cambridge, Massachusetts, as a senior petroleum consultant with Arthur D. Little, one of the world's leading consultancies. Hopper revelled in the globe-trotting, frayed-passport life of the international petroleum consultant, living out of a suitcase, dispensing advice to companies and governments in West and North Africa, Europe, and all over South America and Southeast Asia.

Hopper was well qualified to carry out the study for Austin because he had worked for a lot of national oil companies. In most cases, he had been less than impressed. Indeed, Hopper was reckoned to be downright skeptical about marrying public policy with commercial objectives under one corporate roof. Either national oil companies wound up trying to be mirror images of Big Oil, or they carried out often misguided government objectives with disastrous financial results. Nevertheless, Hopper had a hero who appeared to establish that "public entrepreneurship" in oil was possible: an Italian, Enrico Mattei.

Mattei came from a humble background, left school at fourteen, and by the age of thirty was running his own chemical plant in Milan. The Italian state oil company, Azienda Generale Italiana Petroli (AGIP), had been set up in the 1920s, following the example of France's CFP, to create a domestic refining company to compete with the majors. At the end of the war, Mattei was installed as its head, and determined to create a new major, cast in his own swashbuckling image. Hawk-featured and described as having "the look of a fervent but worldly Jesuit of the sixteenth century," Mattei was, according to Yergin, "willful, ingenious, manipulative, and suspicious. He had a talent for improvisation, and a propensity for gambling and taking risks, combined with a steely commitment to his basic objective, which was to obtain for Italy and AGIP, and Enrico Mattei, a place in the sun."

The discovery of major natural gas reserves in the Po Valley, in northern Italy, gave Mattei the cash for his ambitions. In 1953, AGIP and a number of other state-owned, petroleum-related companies were gathered together as ENI, Ente Nazionale Idrocarburi, with Mattei in charge. Mattei was a good businessman and a national hero, embodying the self-made man. He became the most powerful person in Italy, controlling both newspapers and politicians. Significantly, Mattei did not like politicians, but was prepared to use them. According to Paul Frankel's *Mattei: Oil and*

Power Politics, Mattei said: "To deal with a government is like sucking needles."

Mattei was rough-hewn but he instilled fierce loyalty in his employees. His overriding objective was to ensure that ENI — and Italy — had its own international petroleum supply, independent of the "Anglo-Saxon" companies. He loudly and continually attacked the "cartel," as he called the major companies, and was credited with coining the term "Sette Sorelle," Seven Sisters, in derisive reference to their close associations and multiple joint ventures. He conveniently excluded the French company, CFP, which was also a Middle East concessionaire, because it did not fit his dismissive Anglo-Saxon characterization.

Mattei's real complaint against the Big Oil club was that he was not a member. He was particularly angry at being excluded from the Iranian consortium after he had complied with the embargo on Iran following Mossadegh's attempted nationalization. And, according to Yergin, "in his own anticolonial rhetoric and his attacks on 'imperialism,' he was a fair match for the nationalistic fervor of the exporting countries."

Mattei thought dynastically, and even proposed marrying an Italian princess to the Shah of Iran in order to secure oil supplies. In the end, it was a less spectacular but more significant proposal that would horrify the major oil companies: a proposal under which Mattei would gain an Iranian concession on a twenty-five/seventy-five basis, thus destroying the fifty-fifty rule. No oil was found under the agreement, but the fifty-fifty principle had been breached. The majors regarded it as little more than treachery. In fact, it was just the market at work. Mattei also disrupted world markets by opening the spigots on Soviet oil in the 1950s.

Enrico Mattei died in an airplane crash in a thunderstorm in northern Italy in October 1962, as he was planning a deal to swap Russian oil for Italian pipe. His Soviet purchases had alarmed both the U.S. and NATO. Nevertheless, he was coming to some sort of rapprochement with the majors. With him on the plane when he died was the Rome bureau chief of *Time,* who was researching a cover story on the Italian magnate. Mattei had certainly achieved his ambition to carve out a niche in history. He had also shown the chinks in Big Oil's armour. Contrary to the popular image of tight control, the industry's structure was constantly changing. Newcomers continually broke in on the established order. But until Mattei they had been accommodated or absorbed into the establishment. Mattei's deal with Iran and his arrangements with the Soviets had changed that.

Mattei's vision and style were a model for the young Hopper, who had similar ambitions of painting his own picture on a global canvas. But Hopper was well aware of what had happened to ENI after Mattei's death. The government had forced it to locate new refining capacity in the depressed south as part of regional development policy, to the detriment of both the company's organization and its bottom line. Such was not the exception in the operation of state oil companies, it was the rule. But Mattei had shown while he was alive that a strong enough individual could control governments in his personal vision of the "national interest."

Hopper's report for Austin — which has since disappeared — was considered broadly negative. But Austin was not interested in a negative assessment; he wanted a state oil company. Moreover, he was sufficiently impressed with Hopper that he asked him to join EMR as a senior advisor to help work on Austin's broader mandate of an energy White Paper.

Austin found two other key members for his brain trust. Significantly, neither came from within EMR, whose slim policy-making team was considered too imbued with old ways of thinking. He recruited Ian Stewart, a brilliant academic economist and econometrician, from the Treasury Board. Stewart had studied at Queen's, Oxford, and Cornell, then taught at Queen's and Dartmouth. Econometrics was among the most arcane branches of economics. Its highest quest was for working mathematical "models" of the economy that would enable its guardians to unlock the mysteries of economic progress, allowing them both to see the future and to identify the levers that had to be pulled to achieve optimal results. Well liked by all for his Galbraithian sense of social concern, Stewart became genuinely anxious about macroeconomic issues like windfall profits or fiscal imbalance. Stewart's star would rise rapidly in Ottawa. He would introduce the works of Galbraith to Pierre Trudeau, who would later admit that Galbraithian thinking had "permeated" his thought.

The third member of the team was Joel Bell, an intellectually lean and policy-hungry Montrealer who had read law at McGill, then moved briefly into practice before taking a postgraduate degree in law and economics at Harvard. Before Bell had completed his Harvard course, he was commuting north to consult with an Ottawa task force working on labour legislation. He consulted for the Economic Council of Canada, advised the Department of Consumer and Corporate Affairs on proposed competition legislation, then joined Liberal MP and economic nationalist Herb Gray to prepare a report on foreign investment that would lead to the establishment of FIRA.

Bell had not been involved in energy before, but he was Austin's kind of man: somebody who could be intellectually flexible in dogged pursuit of underlying goals. Other EMR officials were involved, but the heart of analysis lay with Austin, Hopper, Stewart, and Bell, men with a whole phalanx of legal qualifications, economics degrees, and even, in the case of Hopper, knowledge about oil. They saw themselves as professional problem solvers who relished nothing so much as a big problem. Stewart knew the economics, Bell knew the law, and Hopper knew the industry and the jargon. As their minister, when Joe Greene left the post in 1972, they had Donald Macdonald, a powerful Cambridge-educated lawyer who never shrank from a challenge. Because of a certain bluntness and a tendency to pound tabletops, Macdonald was nicknamed "the Thumper."

The first sign in Canada of a changing world energy balance was an enormous increase in Canadian exports to the U.S., whose domestic production had peaked in 1970. In 1972, exports surged 22 per cent to 1 million barrels a day. This was not seen as a problem. Canada was said to have huge amounts of oil and natural gas. Indeed it did, but the important variable in whether all that energy was produced was economics.

Joe Greene had been keen to maximize oil exports to the U.S. He found his ammunition in a study carried out by the Canadian Petroleum Association, the representative organization of the big oil companies. The CPA study was later reckoned to have been crude rather than devious. It calculated Canada's ultimate reserves by estimating the country's total cubic mileage of sedimentary rock — which potentially bears petroleum — then estimating the presence of oil and natural gas within each sedimentary "basin" by analogy to similar basins in the U.S. The results of this study were given to Greene by the NEB's chairman, Bob Howland, who was eager to demonstrate that the NEB could give more pertinent advice than the newly beefed-up Department of Energy, Mines and Resources. Armed with the CPA figures (which some within the CPA thought were dangerous if misinterpreted), Joe Greene announced in a speech in June 1971 that "at 1970 rates of pro- duction, [Canada's] reserves represent 923 years' supply for oil and 392 years for gas." The statement would come back to haunt both the Liberals and the CPA. Joe Greene would later joke to Donald Macdonald: "What did you do with all that oil I left you?"

Then, in his statement in Imperial Oil's 1972 annual report, Imperial chairman and chief executive Bill Twaits made a state- ment that would become even more famous. Twaits was eager to meet booming demand from the U.S. This was not a matter of conspiracy with his U.S. parent; he was simply bolstering his own bottom line. Nevertheless, one sentence from that annual report was subsequently held up as a smoking gun by nationalists, giving Austin's project an unexpected boost. It read: "Canada is not in any way deficient in energy resources. Our present energy reserves, using present technology, are sufficient for our requirements for several hundred years."

There is no doubt that Twaits was biased towards promoting exports, but his remarks were taken out of context. Indeed, his very next sentence read: "But this fact alone cannot guarantee that Canada will not face interruptions in energy supply — or assure Canada the most economic development of supply." Twaits was primarily focusing on the Canadian frontiers in his reserve estimates. His bottom line was that the frontier exploration and development could not be justified on the basis of domestic demand alone. His reserve estimates were also predicated on rising prices. But he had no idea how far and fast prices were about to rise.

FIVE

Flawed Mandate

N OCTOBER 6, 1973, Yom Kippur, the holiest day in the Jewish calendar, Egyptian president Anwar Sadat launched a surprise attack on Israel. Ten days later, when the Israelis were counter-attacking, OPEC, in an increasingly tight market, raised the oil price by 70 per cent, to US$5.11. Arab members of OPEC, buoyed by the ease with which the increase had been imposed, announced production cuts and embargoes until Israel withdrew from what they considered Arab lands.

Panic gripped the consuming countries. Lines of overheating automobiles, stretching down the roads from U.S. gas stations, became the symbol of the problem. But the lines were created partly by a perverse government-imposed allocation system, and partly by consumers themselves, who headed for a gas station as soon as their fuel needle lost contact with the "F."

The oil majors tried to organize international supplies on a rational basis of "equal misery." Governments had other ideas. British Prime Minister Ted Heath, for example, who was having severe problems with the country's coal miners, summoned the chief executives of Shell and BP and demanded more oil. When they refused, British bureaucrats told them that if they didn't come up with supplies, they wouldn't get exploration licences in the North Sea. Blackmail did not seem a very rational basis for action.

The attitudes and actions of the major oil companies, as opposed to those of consuming governments, in the wake of the first OPEC crisis deserve some attention. One of the much-touted reasons for having governments override the "selfish" interests of the private sector is that governments are supposed to have a broader and longer-term view. In fact, in a crisis, they are often the first to panic, and they have no compunction about using their coercive powers to get what they want. The majors undoubtedly had a broader and more responsible attitude than many of the consuming governments. Among those governments, there was a sudden and desperate scramble to appear on top of events. In Canada, Jack Austin's team held the heavy responsibility for making the Liberals appear that they knew what they were doing.

Mounting global uncertainty and escalating federal-provincial political strife formed the background against which Austin's group made its deliberations throughout 1973. Austin, Hopper, Stewart, and Bell would stay late into the night at the department, letting down their intellectual hair, caught up in Ottawa's great policy-making power rush.

In June 1973, on the eve of the OPEC storm, Austin's team produced its White Paper, *An Energy Policy for Canada — Phase 1*. The report stepped on many bureaucratic toes. The National Energy Board was naturally miffed at the intrusion on its territory. The Department of Finance was appalled by the report's "gloomy" prediction that oil prices might rise to "double or triple present levels by the year 1990." In fact, they would rise fourfold in the following six months, a fact that in itself should have given Austin's forecasters pause about their understanding of the market, even if they were more accurate than anybody else.

The chapter on a national oil company, although broadly neutral in tone, did not fully reflect Hopper's skepticism. It was written by Austin. It laid out ten arguments in favour of a state oil company, eight against. A good deal of emphasis was given, reportedly at the insistence of doubters in Cabinet, to the high costs of entering the oil industry and to the inherent problems of reconciling policy goals with commercial norms.

Austin later confided to journalist Elaine Dewar: "The chapter had been carefully crafted, so as to give no offence to the powerful men in Cabinet who still had an ideological objection to the very idea of a government company… There is an enormous difference between what you *say* and what you want to *achieve*."

Austin seemed to be suggesting that the tone of the chapter was a smokescreen. Anyone who opposed his proposal could only be doing so on an "ideological" — which in Austin's view was synonymous with mistaken — basis.

For the Trudeau Liberals, the situation was all the more tenuous because of their minority status. The party had narrowly escaped defeat in the 1972 federal election and had been forced to forge an alliance with the NDP, whose leader, David Lewis, and energy spokesman, Tommy Douglas, were both advocates of government takeovers of foreign oil companies, particularly Imperial. The Walter Gordon wing of the Liberal Party heartily agreed.

It has frequently been claimed since that the NDP was the true seminal influence in the creation of Petro-Canada, but the real pressure was coming from the Liberals' advisors, who were more than happy to take advantage of NDP rabble-rousing. Moreover, when the Liberals regained a majority in 1974, they could have dropped their commitment to a state oil company. They did not.

Popular concern about the oil situation had been increasing in the months before the first OPEC crisis. The Canadian domestic oil price had risen 32 per cent in the nine months to August 1973. The NEB had revised dramatically downwards its estimates of the availability of oil to meet domestic and export commitments. Ignorance, once again, proved fertile ground for nationalist paranoia. How could Big Oil be trusted? Wouldn't the Seven Sisters' subsidiaries dance to their parents' tune, without regard for Canada, or find themselves susceptible to pressure from their parents' home governments? Given that Ottawa's thinkers regarded the market as a predatory power struggle, it was easy to sell the notion that the Canadian-based affiliates of Big Oil lacked "autonomy and bargaining power." Who would speak for the Canadian national interest?

In October 1973, the NDP introduced a motion calling for a national oil company and other measures "to ensure a continuity of supply at fair and just prices to all Canadian consumers." In fact, a state oil company was already in the works. Donald Macdonald had laid a little groundwork by pointing out in a parliamentary reply to the NDP that Venezuela was interested in negotiating a long-term contract, but wanted to deal with "a national government entity rather than an affiliate or affiliates of various corporations in Canada." Only a moment's reflection was needed to understand why this was so: Venezuela obviously thought it could get a better deal from a Canadian state concern than from the Sisters. An increasing bilateral fragmentation of the market — direct deals between individual buyers and sellers — could only work in favour of the producing countries, since it would make it much easier to apply direct pressure. Countries like Venezuela and later Mexico wanted to deal with a Canadian state entity not because that state entity was smart, but because it was likely to be dumb.

The great economist F.A. Hayek wrote in his classic work *The Road to Serfdom*: "It is one of the most fatal illusions that, by substituting negotiations between states or organized groups for competition for markets or for raw materials, international friction would be reduced. This would merely put a contest of force in the place of what can only metaphorically be called the 'struggle' of competition and would transfer to powerful and armed states, subject to no superior law, the rivalries which between individuals had to be decided without recourse to force."

Trudeaucrats wrote off such views as "simplistic," which is to say unanswerable. Petrocan, claimed Austin, was a "pragmatic" approach to an undeniable problem. If exporters wanted to deal directly with state companies, what were consuming governments to do? Also, the government needed to get a handle on things, find out what was going on. The big oil companies were considered to have a corner on information about reserves and other data, which they were believed to doctor in accordance with their immediate interests. Just look at Joe Greene's CPA-inspired speech and Bill Twaits's comments in Imperial's 1972 annual report.

A welter of economic jargon was produced to establish either that the market didn't work, or else that it worked against the "public interest." Big Oil was said to suffer from a "market bias"; it was constrained by the "exploration-production" nexus. The return that oil companies sought, the "private-sector rate of discount," was too high. This all led to "sub-optimal allocation of resources." A state company would pursue the government-mandated target of oil self-sufficiency by accelerating the timing of high-risk exploration and development, thus countering the alleged problem of market-biased "underinvestment."

As staunch nationalist and socialist academic Larry Pratt put it in a study written in 1981: "Because a Crown corporation could afford to use a lower rate of discount than a private enterprise, its investments in exploration and research could be undertaken without a commitment to the early production of discovered reserves. By thus severing the commercial link between exploration and production, it was hoped to increase the domestic reserves-to-production ratio, giving Canada an increased capacity to withstand a shortfall in world oil supply."

In fact, such a view disintegrated once it left the ivory tower. Like much of the logic of intervention, it turned the real world on its head. Reserves were built by companies who could make money selling their production, but Petrocan would build reserves out of good will and a sense of national purpose. It would spend lots on exploration but achieve little or nothing from sales. Nobody seemed to think through the financial implications of such an Alice in Wonderland view of the world. Severing the "exploration-production" nexus really meant severing the link with commercial or fiscal reality.

The concept of "market bias" might be compared to calling the desire not to step in front of an oncoming train "life bias." The notion of a state company accepting a lower "social" rate of discount that would serve the public interest better was wonderfully plausible theory, but had worrying real world implications. As Professor G. David Quirin of the University of Toronto pointed out in a 1976 paper: "The market is trying to tell us something when we perform economic calculations on a project and find it unattractive at a given discount rate. It is trying to tell us to wait, until higher prices or improved, cheaper technology make the investment attractive... If we interject into this scenario a public sector entrepreneur who thinks the social rate of discount is lower than the cost of capital to the private sector, we can be sure that a great many marginal prospects will suddenly become profitable."

Nevertheless, on December 6, two months after the Egyptian-Syrian attack on Israel, Pierre Trudeau rose in the House to announce a long list of new oil initiatives. Among them was the creation of a publicly owned oil company, "principally to expedite exploration and development." The company might choose to hold part of its reserves "for the long-term security of the Canadian market." Trudeau stressed that the company was not "intended in any way to displace the private sector."

Two weeks later, the OPEC ministers met in Tehran and doubled the oil price again, to US$11.65 a barrel.

Early in 1974, the Liberals called an election. They returned to power with a majority in July 1974. In October, the Petro-Canada bill, C-8, was introduced in the House. It declared: "The purpose of this Act is to establish within the energy industries in Canada a Crown owned company with authority to explore for hydrocarbon deposits, to negotiate for and acquire petroleum and petroleum products from abroad to assure a continuity of supply for the needs of Canada, to develop and exploit deposits of hydrocarbons within and without Canada in the interests of Canada, to carry out research and development projects in relation to hydrocarbons and other fuels, and to engage in exploration for, and the production, distribution, refining and marketing of, fuels."

The new entity would also have an imposing array of discretionary powers, giving it "a sweeping mandate for public intervention in the Canadian energy industries." But although Joel Bell had thrown everything into the mandate, nobody but those directly involved had any idea of the size to which Petrocan would grow, or how much it would cost. Pierre Trudeau had said it wouldn't compete with the private sector. Although refining and marketing was written into the legislation, few believed Petrocan had any place in that business.

. . .

In the course of the mounting OPEC crisis, a new rationale had presented itself to the Liberal government for having more control over oil: its increasingly bitter fight with Alberta.

The confrontation between the consuming countries and OPEC had been mirrored within Canada by a confrontation between Ottawa and the province that produced almost 90 per cent of the country's oil and gas. Alberta's premier, Peter Lougheed, was an aggressive young lawyer and former corporate executive who had revived the almost moribund provincial Conservative Party and led it to power in August 1971, displacing the fire-and-brimstone Social Credit Party that had controlled the province for thirty-six years. Lougheed chose energy as the battleground for provincial self-assertion. Soaring petroleum prices raised the stakes enormously.

Until the OPEC crisis, Canada's oil supplies east of the Ottawa Valley had been cheap imports, while those to the west had come from more expensive domestic oil. More expensive Alberta oil also found markets in the U.S. When OPEC prices rose above those of domestic oil, the Trudeau Liberals immediately restricted domestic increases, but decided to move U.S. exports to world prices, a move that caused outrage south of the border at first. What sparked the battle between Ottawa and the province was the Liberals' decision in September 1973 to cream off the windfall from charging world prices for exports. The spoils mounted sharply in the final quarter of 1973. Ottawa's concerns about Alberta acquiring huge new revenues were based on more than theoretical equity. Under the federal system of provincial income equalization, Ottawa would be liable to compensate the other provinces for Alberta's new wealth.

The issue was further confused by the huge profit increases

reported by the big oil companies for the final quarter of 1973, based largely on selling gasoline made from cheap inventory oil into a market where gasoline prices were soaring as motorists panicked. Not only did it appear that a group of Arab-led producers was holding the world to ransom, it seemed that Big Oil was in cahoots with them. The industry tried to explain that this was a one-time phenomenon, that it was all to do with first-in-first-out accounting and inventory profits, but eyes glazed over. The media found sensationalist headlines easier to print than explanations.

Public support to "do something" about these "unconscionable" profits grew. Both levels of government obliged. Alberta imposed a huge royalty increase; Ottawa declared the new royalties non-deductible for income tax purposes; the companies, hit with a double whammy, were left with next to nothing.

There was one final oil drama to be played out before the end of 1974. In December, Atlantic Richfield, one of the four partners in the proposed Syncrude tarsands plant at Fort McMurray in Alberta — a huge, almost science-fiction scheme to mine the heavy oil-saturated sands and process them into conventional crude — announced that it was forced to withdraw, leaving Imperial, Gulf Canada, and Cities Service Canada to make up its 30-per-cent stake. Following intense negotiations, the federal government and the provincial governments of Alberta and Ontario stepped in to take up the slack. Ottawa took 15 per cent of the project, Alberta 10 per cent, and Ontario 5 per cent. The agreement caused an uproar among left-wing nationalists, who claimed that governments had been duped by the multinationals into bailing them out. History proved the claims to be nonsense. Syncrude would prove both technologically frustrating and financially marginal.

Faced with hefty new taxes from both levels of government and political uncertainty, oil companies had cut back on exploration and other expenditures in 1974. This was now used as justification for Petrocan's creation. Donald Macdonald noted in March 1975: "The government does not feel assured that the private sector can be relied upon to mobilize all of the enormous amounts of capital which will be required to secure energy development consonant with Canadian needs over the longer term. Nor can it be certain that, faced with attractive investment opportunities and geological possibilities abroad, the private industry will be able to concentrate as much effort on our own petroleum prospective areas over the next decades as our needs require."

The Liberals had created a hostile and uncertain environment and were now accusing oil companies of not wanting to operate in it.

Macdonald said the state company's "most important function" would lie in oil and gas exploration and development, particularly in Canada's frontiers, where it would increase the Canadian presence. Joint ventures would be preferable, as in Panarctic Oils, but the company might carry out exploration on its own if commercial returns seemed too uncertain or distant to justify private investment.

"We have chosen to set the national petroleum company in a corporate business framework as a means to better achieve our goals. In its organization and business methods, the company will be subject to the basic disciplines of an operating statement and balance sheet. The corporation will be responsible to its shareholders, the people of Canada. I think the directors of the company may from time to time judge that short-term profit maximization is not in the interests of these shareholders, all of whom stand to be affected directly or indirectly by the corporation's actions. That criterion may properly be modified in the interests of long-term future energy supply for Canada, and in terms of job opportunities or the development of particular parts of Canada."

The underlying message was that oil companies were not to be trusted, that the market didn't work. But the notion of "properly modifying" the profit-maximizing "criterion" betrayed the government's overblown confidence in the insight of its advisors. Who would decide what was "proper"? The notion of the judicious abandonment of "short-term profit maximization" in the public interest implied the availability of a clairvoyant who could foretell the future. This was a typical, but ultimately enormously expensive, delusion. At the same time, the idea that Petro-Canada might be used to create regional job opportunities opened a potential sink-hole like the one at Italy's ENI.

Macdonald claimed the decision to go for a national oil company arose from the "radical and, for the most part, permanent" changes in world energy. These had "tipped the balance decisively in favour of federal entrepreneurship in the oil and gas industries." But this indicated a particular view of the way the world functioned. The well-worn reasons for avoiding "federal entrepreneurship" in the economy — a topic exhaustively covered by political economists going back to Adam Smith — have little to do with circumstances; they are based on the fact that it doesn't work.

Government organizations are slow to react because they need political approval for their actions; when they do not need political approval, they run out of control. "Broader" mandates sound fine in theory, but they end up becoming bogged down in political demands from every MP in whose riding the company has an interest, while the central government wants its "instrument" to carry out high-profile activities that help get it re-elected or serve other political purposes.

And what did the Trudeau government — or any government — know about the oil business? It claimed that Petrocan was to help inform its policy, but Petrocan's very mandate contained a number of sweeping — and naive — assumptions about the way the state oil company could operate. Most naive was the assumption that it could just take off for the frontiers and find out what was really there by drilling a few wells. Whether the needle is in the haystack cannot be decided by examining a mere handful of hay.

The unspoken rationale for the government's support — and Austin's particular backing — of Panarctic Oils in 1965 had been Cam Sproule's assertion that Big Oil was holding back, waiting for strikes to be made. A variant was that the majors knew where the frontier oil was, but weren't going to drill until foreign HQ found it convenient. Even then, however, if the price wasn't right, they wouldn't drill at all.

In fact, the whole exploration thrust of the major oil companies

in the late 1960s and early 1970s had been in the frontiers. The
Prudhoe Bay find in 1968 had spurred exploration in the
Mackenzie Delta to the east of Alaska's North Slope. Shell was
spending huge amounts of money off both the east and west
coasts. Other companies, like Mobil, were spending big bucks off
Nova Scotia and Newfoundland. Indeed, one of Peter Lougheed's
great concerns when he came to power in Alberta was that the oil
companies might be on the point of deserting Alberta altogether
in their search for big finds — hydrocarbon "elephants" — in the
frontiers. Wildcat drilling in Alberta had fallen by 40 per cent
between 1969 and 1971, while the province's share of exploration
expenditures had dropped from three-quarters of the Canadian
total in 1966 to little more than a half by 1970.

Nevertheless, although Big Oil had committed huge sums to
the frontiers, many in Ottawa didn't want big, foreign-owned oil
companies to make the frontier finds, because then Canada would
get its oil, but the major oil companies would get richer too.
Economic nationalists hated that idea. As usual, they wanted the
fruits of capitalism without its necessary processes.

Tory opposition to the Petrocan bill tended to dwell on valid
but vague criticisms that carried little weight with those who
didn't share the Tories' ideological assumptions. Getting to the
heart of why government direct intervention didn't work was a
complex matter. Tory MP and academic Jim Gillies told the
House: "This legislation will give power to the government to do
anything it wants in so far as the petroleum industry is concerned.
I think it is wrong in principle to pass legislation that gives this
sort of unlimited power to any government... The fact is that in
this legislation we are giving the power to the government which
will allow it, if it so desires, to move in and literally take over the
entire petroleum industry in Canada."

But what, the NDP and other Petrocan supporters might ask,
would be wrong with Petrocan taking over the entire petroleum
industry in Canada? Indeed, the NDP's concern had always been
that Petro-Canada would not go far enough. Tommy Douglas, for
his part, wondered if the company would wind up as a "bird dog

for the private sector," spending public money in order to make big oil companies' job easier. He still wanted to take over Imperial.

If the Liberals or NDP sought justifications for their policies, there were plenty of examples throughout the world. Big Oil was on the run everywhere. Senator Henry (Scoop) Jackson chaired hearings in 1974 before the U.S. Senate Permanent Subcommittee on Investigations. Senior executives of the majors were lined up in front of the politician who had coined the phrase "obscene profits" and made to testify under oath. In the atmosphere of a populist circus, they came across as "inept, insulated, self-satisfied, and out of touch," in Daniel Yergin's words.

"The American people," declared Jackson, "want to know if this so-called energy crisis is only a pretext; a cover to eliminate the major source of price competition — the independents, to raise prices, to repeal environmental laws, and to force adoption of new tax subsidies." Congress wanted to roll back oil prices and cap natural gas prices. Politicians pressed for divestiture. A "Rube Goldberg system of price controls, entitlements, and allocations" costing billions of dollars was set up. As Yergin wrote: "The entire regulatory campaign did less to boost the national weal than to cause a chronic migraine of immense proportions in the nation's politics. But such was the temper of the times."

The British government introduced a new oil tax and set up the British National Oil Corporation, with the right to buy 51 per cent of North Sea output. The head of one oil company remarked, "I don't see any difference any more between those OPEC countries and Britain." British Premier Harold Wilson said he hoped he might be chairman of OPEC by 1980, declaring: "We do have an interest in seeing that the price of oil doesn't fall too much."

Kuwait expropriated BP and Gulf. "We will just say thank you very much and goodbye," said the Kuwaiti oil minister, Abdel Mattaleb Kazemi. Gulf and BP asked for $2 billion in compensation. They received $50 million.

Venezuela had passed a "law of reversion" in 1971, which called for all concessions to start returning to the country in 1983. But in 1974 the politicians decided that 1983 was too long to wait. Juan Pablo Pérez Alfonzo, Venezuela's Walter Gordon, called for the nationalization not merely of the oil industry but of all foreign investment. The companies were realistic, almost fatalistic. For them, access to the oil was all important. A state holding company, Petroleos de Venezuela (PDVSA), was set up. Venezuela's nationalization would take place on January 1, 1976, the same day Petrocan established its bridgehead in Calgary.

The Saudis, too, had announced they would be taking over Aramco, the consortium of majors that had operated there for decades, although the American partners would continue to provide services and markets. According to Yergin, a Gulf senior executive compared the global withdrawal to the Romans' retreat from Hadrian's Wall. "There was this misunderstanding," he said. "Here was the conceit of the Americans that we were loved because we had done so much for these people. This was the American naiveté. We thought we had good relations. They saw it from a different point of view. They had always felt patronized. They remembered it. In all these relationships, there's this love-hate thing."

The "love-hate thing" was strong in Canada, but there was a big difference between Canada and oil-producing nations like Saudi Arabia or Venezuela. The Americans had operated in Canada alongside Canadians as equals under the law. There had been no "concession" system. Moreover, Canada did not produce huge amounts of cheap oil. Most of its potential consisted of high-cost reserves, in heavy oil, tarsands, or the frontiers. The majors would be necessary to develop these reserves, but they were hardly likely to do so under threat of expropriation.

. . .

How would Petrocan be monitored and controlled? It was all very well for Donald Macdonald to talk about Petrocan as a "profit maker" rather than a "profit maximizer," or for the bureaucrats to dance on the head of the sophistic pin with their "social rate of discount," but in reality the company would be run purely at someone's discretion. Petrocan — as an organization run by ambitious people with their own views of its mandate — would wind up doing whatever it could get away with. If Petrocan screwed up the bottom line, it could always say: "It's policy." If it didn't like a piece of policy, it could always plead: "Look what it'll do to the bottom line!"

In fact, the best hope for controlling Petro-Canada was through its chequebook. As long as Petro-Canada did lots of expensive frontier exploration with no production, it would have to keep coming back time and time again to the government for money. Naturally, therefore, management would seek to eliminate the financial leash from the start. Almost from the moment of its creation, Petrocan's management sought to take maximum advantage of Ottawa's coffers while avoiding direct control as far as possible.

According to the Petrocan legislation, there were to be three primary instruments of government control: Ottawa's approval of Petrocan's budget; direct orders from the Cabinet; and the government's appointment of the board and management. All three had serious shortcomings. For a start, just who was exercising the control? The budget was meant to be approved by the Departments of Finance and Energy and by the Treasury Board, which meant they would be examined by these departments' bureaucracies. In other words, if Ottawa's super-bureaucrats succeeded in taking control of Petrocan, they would be "controlled" by people they knew well, and with whom they shared many convictions.

On what basis would critical judgments about Petrocan's expenditures be made? Who in these departments had the expertise to say that an investment or exploration project was wise or not? The crucial factor in approval was likely to be not objective analysis, but the strength of the Ottawa networks of those running the state oil company. Since the budget would be presented by men like Bell and Hopper to other super-bureaucrats just like themselves, budget approval would become part of the cosy system of Ottawa insiderdom. At the political level, the amount of money lavished on the corporation would depend on its ratings in the opinion polls.

As for direct policy instructions, delivered in writing by the Governor-in-Council, this provision was meant to be a safeguard against any attempt by government at patronage-inspired "meddling." But again, that was not the way Ottawa worked. In theory, this provision gave Petrocan management the chance to "blow the whistle," but Petrocan's management was unlikely to do so. Power worked in more subtle ways. There would be favours that Petrocan management might need, so mutual back-scratching was a much more likely form of potential conflict resolution than whistle-blowing. Any manager of Petrocan knew who his real boss was: the government. Nods and winks were still very effective, whatever the formal channels of control.

The appointment of a board was to be the third instrument of control. What guarantees were there that powerful and independent board members were available, or would stay? Moreover, whose interests were they meant to be representing? Donald Macdonald had spoken of Canadians as the ultimate shareholders on whose behalf the board would be acting, but the shareholder under the legislation wound up being the minister of energy. When push came to shove, disputes would be settled between management and government. Seats on the board were likely to wind up as the usual patronage plums.

These "controls" turned out to mean virtually nothing. Petrocan's direction would be set through a process determined by the strength and resolve of its senior management in dealing with a government that either wanted it to grow for political reasons, or else had too many other things on its mind.

Third reading of the Petro-Canada bill took place on July 10, 1975. Royal assent was granted on July 30. Petrocan was set to come into existence, born of bureaucratic manipulation and Canadians' almost boundless faith in the ability of governments to solve their problems. It was created, according to academic Larry Pratt, as an *entreprise témoin,* "a bureaucratic device to witness what actually happened and why." But Pratt, like most well-meaning interventionists, missed another critical, although unspoken, benefit of its creation: the fact that it would be a powerful instrument offering high-paying jobs and executive perks. To ignore that fact, or to suggest that the bright men at EMR were unaware of the career potential in a state oil company, would be grossly naive. Austin had grandiose visions for his company. He wanted it to be involved in more than merely oil. He wanted a state energy company that would take over all the government's energy interests. But the interventionist thrust was whittled down, for the moment, to petroleum.

It all sounded so plausible. We couldn't trust Big Oil. It had done too well out of the OPEC crisis not to have been part of some "conspiracy." In any case, it was foreign-owned and thus didn't "put Canada first." We needed an instrument whose priority would be the "public interest," one that would provide a "window on the industry," both to keep an eye on the big boys and to help government make informed energy policy. One of Big Oil's problems was that it was too "bottom-line"; it served its own interests. How could we be sure that these interests coincided with those of Canada? Again, the assumption was that this was unlikely. Indeed, the view of the Walter Gordonites was that the interests of Big Oil were diametrically opposed to those of Canada.

Now Canada would have a champion, an instrument that would rectify these problems, correct for "market bias," boldly drill where no company had drilled before, tell us how the oil business really worked. Here was a new ship from the flotilla of state whose tiller could be guided towards Canada's best interests. The key question, once Petrocan had been given legislative life, was who would be the captain, the public-spirited man with his hand on the tiller of the good ship Petro-Canada.

Jack Austin had always seen himself in this role. After all, he was its progenitor; he had cultivated his idea in initially indifferent ground, then helped give it life. Of course, although he had had some business dealings, he had no experience as a corporate executive, but he realized that you could always hire professional staff. The important thing was to be up there at the highest policy level, to "take the big picture."

Austin had so impressed Trudeau that, in 1974, the prime

minister had invited him to run the Prime Minister's Office, which, along with the Privy Council Office, had become one of the twin command posts for Trudeau's rational revolution. Austin had secured Trudeau's commitment that he would be Petrocan's first chairman and chief executive. But in 1975, controversy blew up around Austin's former business dealings and allegations over conflicts of interest when he was deputy minister of EMR. Although nothing came of the allegations, Austin was tainted. Donald Macdonald told him it would be impossible to appoint him under the circumstances.

Macdonald had made informal approaches to a number of prominent oilmen. One of the first was to Jack Gallagher, the low-key but mesmerizingly charming head of Dome Petroleum, a still relatively small company Gallagher had founded, with U.S. backing, in 1950. Gallagher, already a regular visitor to Ottawa, had drilled the first well for Panarctic Oils. He had also agreed to sit on the board of the Gordon-inspired Canada Development Corporation, which had finally got off the ground in 1971, to the irritation of the business community. But when Macdonald approached him, Gallagher told him he just didn't believe in state oil companies (not that he minded a little government help for his own exploration visions, however).

Another candidate was Arne Nielsen, the stocky, amiable head of Mobil's Canadian subsidiary. Nielsen was universally popular in the oil patch; indeed, he was something of a local hero. As a geologist, he had discovered the huge Pembina field. Then he had gone on to become the first Canadian to head Mobil Canada. He also had Ottawa connections through his membership in NACOP, the organization set up by Joe Greene to consult with prominent oilmen. At the time, Nielsen was having problems with Mobil's New York head office. But he wasn't felt to be "political" enough. There was also a problem with salary.

Austin would subsequently imply that he had been sidelined because he offended the oil industry. "The oil industry is deeply ideological about itself," he said. "It's American in its thinking." But if, as Austin claims, the oil industry had somehow succeeded in sidelining him because he had offended its free-enterprise philosophy, they could hardly have been any happier with the man ultimately chosen as Petrocan's first chairman and chief executive. The successful candidate did not, in the end, come from the oil patch; in fact, one of the most intriguing things about him was that nobody was quite sure where he was "coming from." His name was put forward by the prime minister. He was Maurice Strong.

SIX

The Invasion of Calgary

WHERE MAURICE STRONG "came from," biographically and ideologically, and how he wound up in the top job at Petrocan were shrouded in mystery. Strong was stranger than fiction. His motivations had always been an object of fascination for those close to him, although it could be said without doubt that he was a firm believer in government intervention. Like Walter Gordon, he seemed to represent that self-contradictory strain of entrepreneurs with misgivings about free markets, torn between making a buck and espousing government intervention. Some believed there was no dichotomy, that Strong always had his eye on making a buck. But it was far more complicated than that. As for background, Strong didn't just come from the other side of the tracks from Gordon, he came from the other *end.*

Born in 1929 in Oak Lake, Manitoba, once the western terminus of the CNR, Maurice Strong was a prairie child of the Depression. The oldest of four, he — according to his own account — ran away from home when he was thirteen, falsified his birth certificate, and tried to join the armed forces. When he failed, he signed up as a cabin boy on a troop ship out of Vancouver. He returned to Oak Lake to finish high school, then spent a year with the Hudson's Bay Company at Chesterfield Inlet. He went on to dabble in prospecting and stock promotion, became a minor functionary with the new United Nations Organization at Lake Success in New York, and tried to join the Royal Canadian Air Force. Eventually he returned to Winnipeg to work for the brokers James Richardson & Sons; later he worked for the firm in Toronto as well.

Following the Leduc boom, Strong became Richardson's oil and gas analyst in Calgary. In 1951, he joined Jack Gallagher as Dome Petroleum's first employee. Strong was a hard worker and compulsively ambitious, but his restless search for a vocation soon took him off to see more of the world. He worked in Africa and travelled the Far East. When he returned, he tried to get a job helping underdeveloped nations, but he was turned down by External Affairs, the YMCA, and a number of foundations. Stung by the rejections, he returned to Dome to become vice-president of finance.

Perhaps Strong's most significant contribution at Dome was to hire a young lawyer from Manitoba named Bill Richards, who would eventually lead Dome into the frenzied expansion that would be its glory and ultimately its downfall. But at the time, Strong found Dome and Gallagher too cautious. Gallagher thought Strong too eager to expand.

In 1959, Strong founded his own company. With a talented oilman, Ed Galvin, he put together Canadian Industrial Gas & Oil. Within three years, he was on the move again, this time to become executive vice-president of Power Corporation in Montreal, which took over CIGOL. By 1964 he was president of Power and spinning off schemes for global expansion at a rate that made heads whirl at Power's board meetings.

For Strong, the world of business, whatever its riches and perks, was still inferior to that of government, with its heady mix of public service and naked power. From his position of corporate influence, he had cultivated political comers, including Pierre Trudeau and Peter Lougheed. He had also maintained his interest in the development field.

When a vacancy appeared at the top of the government's foreign aid program in 1966, Strong used his Ottawa network to lobby Paul Martin, then secretary of state for external affairs, for the job. Martin, with whom Strong had business and YMCA connections, was at first reluctant. He couldn't understand why a successful businessman should want a much lower-paying job as a bureaucrat. But Strong was eventually taken on, and he formed the Canadian International Development Agency. Like all the government interventions Strong helped promote, CIDA wound up being much more expansive than effective. But Strong always liked to put in the program, set up the institution, and move on.

Strong became increasingly influential in Liberal circles. He continued to spot likely young men, such as Jim Coutts, then a cherubic assistant in Lester Pearson's office, and Jack Austin, who was then working for Art Laing. He worked with Walter Gordon — the two had met while Strong was working at Power Corp. — to write legislation proposing the Canada Development Corporation.

A speech Strong gave to the Toronto Ticker Club in 1965 showed either his deep belief in the viability of government intervention, or that he had marshalled a great many plausible-sounding arguments for "a new kind of relationship between government and private enterprise," which would demonstrate a "positive Canadian nationalism." At the heart of his case was Walter Gordon's assertion that foreign investment and thus foreign ownership was a "problem" that had to be addressed. "No other major country has so much of its industry controlled by foreigners," said Strong, reciting the economic nationalists' credo. "Few would permit it," he intoned.

Strong claimed that Canadians were too conditioned by "U.S. thinking" about government-business relationships. He declared: "The United States is so wealthy and powerful that there is not the same need for business and government to work closely together to assure that American economic and political policies will not be compromised by the exercise of power from without the country."

Canada had to look to other nations for models, Strong said:

the U.K., France, the Scandinavian countries, Japan. Strangely, Canadian experience was not recommended as a field of study. Neither was it recognized or acknowledged that these other countries might have quite untransferable cultures or — as in the U.K. — might be engaged in interventionist experiments that would lead to the brink of disaster. Strong's bottom line was that the external threat, vague as it was, was so great that it justified the risk, if indeed there was any risk, of greater government intervention.

Strong added a strange and disturbing rider: "There is a very real possibility that if this generation does not act to ensure that there are a significant number of major Canadian-controlled and Canadian-managed enterprises with the size and ability to compete on a world scale, a future generation of Canadians may feel, rightly or wrongly, that socialism is the only means by which they can regain control of their own economic and political destiny."

"Rightly or wrongly." What an odd way to put it. Did Maurice Strong think a socialist grab for control was right or wrong? He never said. It wasn't clear if he was voicing a warning or making a threat. The logic was peculiar too, almost circular: Strong seemed to be saying that the only way to forestall socialism was to install some socialism, through state-ownership instruments like the CDC.

According to Strong, the CDC would be an instrument of government and yet beyond government interference, powerfully imbued with a sense of the public purpose, and endowed with superhuman business skills. Who would run it? Maurice Strong felt he might be a good candidate. Public purpose would blend with personal corporate power.

But by the time the CDC was finally created in 1971, Strong's wanderlust had taken him in new directions. Through CIDA contacts, he was invited to become secretary general of the first United Nations Conference on the Human Environment in Stockholm in 1972.

Strong enhanced his reputation enormously while organizing the conference from his headquarters in Geneva. He travelled the world for eighteen months, dining and conferring with scores of presidents, prime ministers, and potentates, even securing an audience with the Pope. His media apotheosis came in June 1972, with a long, adulatory article in the *New Yorker* that opened with the suggestion that "the survival of civilization in something like its present form" might depend significantly on Strong's efforts. The *New York Times* dubbed him "guardian of the planet." Following the conference, which was a great success, he moved to Nairobi for two years as executive director of the UN's environment program.

Considering his exotic, pinball career, Strong was an astonishingly low-key character. Slightly chubby, with a clipped moustache, he looked anything but a high-level political power broker and business wheeler-dealer. He dressed like a man with more important things to spend his money on than clothes and travelled economy class on the most gruelling of flights. He spoke in an apologetic mumble. Because of his asthma, he would often run out of breath at the end of sentences, like a man trying to deliver a message after running up a long flight of stairs. But there seemed to be an underlying purpose to Strong that belied his tendency to bounce all over the career map. Indeed, he got annoyed at those who accused him of inconsistency. He described the thread that ran through all his activities as dealing with "social problems in the business sphere."

With the creation of Petrocan, a golden opportunity appeared for Strong's brand of "positive nationalism" via direct government intervention. His old friend Jim Coutts had taken over from Austin as principal secretary in the PMO. Strong's experience in the oil patch, combined with his knowledge of Ottawa, gave him ideal qualifications. But many people still had misgivings. Donald Macdonald, for example, recognized Strong's merits, but he wanted somebody who would stay at the post for at least five years. He knew that Maurice Strong had never stayed anywhere for five years. Macdonald's misgivings were shared by his successor in the energy portfolio, Alastair Gillespie, a former partner in Walter Gordon's Cancorp. But Trudeau wanted Strong, so that was it. Strong began the search for staff.

Bill Hopper's skepticism about state oil companies had, according to Austin, declined with the approach of the company's creation and, cynics might say, the resultant job opportunities. But if anybody knew the potential pitfalls of a state oil company, it was Hopper. He was appointed Petro-Canada's vice-president of corporate planning. His relationship with Strong was not made in heaven. Two men with more different personalities could hardly be imagined. An Ottawa observer called them "nitro and glycerine." Hopper soon became convinced that he was a better and wiser oilman than Strong.

They were joined by David Scrim, yet another bright young bureaucrat who had done work on the *Phase 1* energy policy document. Joel Bell, the earnest young policy mercenary, also signed on full-time. Bell would embrace Petrocan as more than a job; it became a cause. He would prove very useful to Hopper because of his connections at the heart of Trudeau's super-bureaucracy. But Bell, too, would eventually find the organization too small for both himself and Hopper.

In the first week of January 1976, according to the corporate mythology, these four men sat down in a rented suite in the International Hotel in Calgary with nothing more than a typewriter, a taxi cab account, and an authorized capital of $1.5 billion, and began mulling over strategy. One obvious need was personnel, so Strong made the rounds of his old contacts from the industry, looking for executives.

Hostility to the state venture was high from the start among Calgary oilmen. Strong would have to take on staff by acquiring their companies or by poaching from the ranks of the disgruntled. Into that latter category came Don Axford and Don Wolcott.

Axford was described as a "wild-eyed explorationist," who, as it happened, had great faith in one of the areas where Petrocan was intended to boost activity: the East Coast. As Mobil Canada's head of exploration, Axford, like his boss, Arne Nielsen, was unhappy with head office in New York, which had slashed his budget during the Ottawa-Alberta pricing dispute of 1974 and was continuing to hold back on Canadian activity.

Mobil's actions, or rather the lack of them, appeared a prime example of why Petrocan had been set up: to make sure that foreign oil companies' global perspectives did not lead Canada to be neglected, and to compensate for the high-handed actions of those who did not "care" about Canada, but only watched their own bottom lines. In the eyes of those who made energy policy, Mobil fell into the category of those who sought "excessive" private-sector discounts. Petrocan could afford — or so said its creators — to pay a little more, persevere a little more, put up with a lower rate of return. After all, it had to pursue the "need to know."

The "need to know" view of exploration said a lot more about the mind of the technocrat than about the realities of oil finding. Once again, the conflict was between wishful thinking and reality. Petrocan's frontier expenditures would not necessarily satisfy a comprehensive "need to know" what was out there, any more than buying a thousand dollars' worth of lottery tickets would satisfy a "need to win." Mobil hadn't cut back on East Coast expenditures out of pique, although personalities could never be excluded from corporate decisions; it had reassessed the geological potential of the Sable Island area, about which Axford was particularly enthusiastic, and decided it had better prospects on which to spend its money elsewhere.

Axford was hired on as Petrocan's head of exploration. His first act was to go back to his old employer and offer to "farm in" on the acreage he had previously been exploring. Under a farm-in, a company agrees to drill one or more exploration wells on another company's land in return for a portion of the explored acreage, and thus a share of any subsequent oil production. Mobil was more than happy to help Petrocan achieve its lower "social rate of discount" by negotiating a very tough deal. Bill Hopper thought the verbal deal Axford had made with Mobil stank. He would later set about changing it.

The other unhappy senior employee hired away by Petrocan was Don Wolcott, one of Calgary's many characters. A great, bulky, sandy-haired bear of a man, Wolcott hid an extraordinary technical genius behind the image of a freshly scrubbed country bumpkin, straight off the farm. Wolcott had been the brains behind Dome Petroleum's success in extracting and transporting natural gas liquids from Alberta's natural gas flows using "straddle plants" and pipelines. Such schemes often involved legal and technical wrangling. Wolcott and Dome lawyer Bill Richards emerged as a double act at regulatory hearings. Richards's legal skills and killer instinct, combined with Wolcott's razor-sharp analysis, formed an almost unbeatable package. Their skill at getting their way and earning sweet financial deals earned them a grudging nickname from their opponents: Butch Cassidy and the Sundance Kid. But Wolcott felt that his contribution to Dome's earnings had never been fully recognized. Since he took a certain perverse delight in bucking the conventional wisdom, he decided to join the state oil company when Strong offered him a job.

A less disgruntled acquisition was Bob Meneley, a blunt, no-nonsense geologist who had spent fifteen years with Imperial Oil, then started a consultancy, then joined Panarctic. Petrocan had become the major shareholder in Panarctic when the federal government transferred Ottawa's share in the joint venture. Meneley would soon take over from Axford as head of exploration. An avowed nationalist, he became a true believer and accused the oil companies who did business with Petrocan while criticizing it on ideological grounds of being "hypocrites."

Petrocan still needed more operating ability. One of Strong's top priorities had been to draw up a list of companies for Petrocan to acquire. Strong, Hopper, and Bell had looked at wholly U.S.-owned companies like Mobil and Amoco, as well as majority U.S.-controlled concerns like Hudson's Bay Oil & Gas. But they had no desire to become involved in a hostile takeover, which might lead to U.S. political retaliation. They needed a company that was already on the block. The company that presented itself was Atlantic Richfield Canada, known as Arcan.

Part of Petrocan's capital had been taken up by the acquisition from the government of Ottawa's holdings in Panarctic Oils and Syncrude. With Syncrude came a hefty liability. Petrocan's contribution to the $2.1-billion expected cost of the plant, which would open in 1978, was around $315 million. But what more symmetric acquisition than the Canadian subsidiary of the company that had pulled out of Syncrude in 1974?

Atlantic Richfield had invested huge sums in Prudhoe Bay, inevitably draining cash from other parts of its empire. Arcan appeared to be another case of a parent company sacrificing the prospects of its Canadian subsidiary. After approaches by Strong to Robert O. Anderson, head of Atlantic Richfield and one of the great wildcatters and oil tycoons of the twentieth century, Hopper carried the brunt of the negotiations. Petrocan acquired Atlantic Richfield Canada for $342.4 million and transformed it into its principal operating subsidiary, Petro-Canada Exploration.

Arcan brought with it about 1,000 oil and natural gas wells dotted all over Alberta and northern B.C., pumping 28,000 barrels of oil and liquids, and 88 million cubic feet of gas daily. Petrocan instantly became a partner with hundreds of oil companies in major oil and gas fields across Alberta. Each field had been found through a combination of financial risk, sweat, perseverance, and luck. They had been developed with technical skills acquired and honed all over the world. Now, for many oilmen, they had been defiled by the sudden entry of a bunch of bureaucrats waving wads of taxpayers' money.

Arcan also brought 10.6 million acres of undeveloped oil and gas properties in Alberta, British Columbia, the Northwest Territories, the Arctic Islands, and Hudson Bay, and a one-third interest in 1.2 million acres of oilsands leases. Last but not least, it brought 300 less than enthusiastic staff. Around three-quarters of the senior executives would leave within a year. Nevertheless, with the executives acquired from elsewhere, Arcan's staff gave Petrocan the ability to act like an oil company.

By the end of its first year, Petro-Canada had participated in wells off the East Coast from Sable Island in the south to the mouth of the Hudson Strait in the north. It had committed itself to expensive drilling in the Arctic Islands. It had signed exploration agreements with other companies for acreage in the Northwest Territories and Yukon. It had also drilled a lot of very expensive dry holes.

Meanwhile things were going smoothly neither within nor without.

. . .

Petrocan was greeted in Calgary with all the enthusiasm that a communist occupation force might have attracted. Its alien nature was confirmed when those who phoned the organization were greeted with the words "Good morning, Petro-Canada, *bonjour.*" "What's that *bonjour* crap?" asked oilmen. It was official bilingualism, that's what. But Bill Hopper privately expressed sympathy with the oil patch's view.

Calgary looked with a mixture of distaste and amazement at the strange new lifeforms presented to it by the Crown corporation. Strong may have had oil patch experience, but that didn't seem to help. Indeed, he had left some hard feelings in his wake. Although Dome's Jack Gallagher was invariably polite, he still felt that Strong had deserted him all those years before. Now he was also considered to have "stolen" Don Wolcott.

Jack Gallagher would later tell a joke about Petrocan. Ann Landers had received a letter from a young man who had just become engaged. He was having trouble telling his fiancée about his family. His mother was a hooker, his father was a lush, his sister worked for his mother. He didn't mind telling his fiancée all that. *The problem was that his brother worked for Petrocan!* The story always produced roars of laughter and much side-slapping around the barbecue or at the Petroleum Club, where Petrocan employees were as welcome as a dry hole.

Strong's attempts to become part of the local community failed miserably. His style and his entourage would have looked much more at home at UN Plaza. Here they looked like a bunch of flakes. Strong, in the words of one insider, "played to his own caricature." Divorced from his first wife, he moved in his mystic

Buddhist Scandinavian mistress, Hanne Marstrand, and bought a ranch, an honour for which the locals considered sufficient cash not the most important qualification. He brought in consultants and advisors from the East, urbane individuals who made little secret of the fact that they regarded the locals as unsophisticated. Good God, they'd say, just *look* at Calgary compared with Montreal or Toronto.

As his executive assistant, Strong hired John Ralston Saul, a twenty-eight-year-old who positively oozed *savoir-faire* and *raffinement.* The son of a career officer in the Canadian Armed Forces, Ralston Saul had a PhD from the École libre des sciences politiques in Paris. Before making the jolting transition from Paris to Calgary, Ralston Saul had completed a novel based on six years of research. The result, *Mort d'un général,* published in English as *The Birds of Prey,* became a critical and popular success and a *cause célèbre* in France. It would make Ralston Saul famous.

A Petrocan insider reckons, "Ralston Saul provided the bilingualism, and background that Strong lacked." Strong's CV, which claimed among many other talents that Strong could speak Eskimo and Swahili and generally looked like an application form for the Renaissance Man Club, was easily interpreted as overcompensation for insecurity about his origins. Ralston Saul was all the things Strong was not.

Ralston Saul ran Strong's office, preparing briefs and speeches. Strong told writer David Macfarlane: "He was a facilitator, my right-hand man, and although he didn't know too much about the oil business to begin with, he learned, and I learned to pay a lot of attention to John's ideas."

Ralston Saul was not only a staunch Canadian nationalist, he also knew a great deal about the Third World, which put him very much on Strong's wavelength, although at an altogether more refined level. From Calgary's point of view, John Ralston Saul might as well have descended from Mars. Many regarded him as a monstrous poseur. Jokes were told in Ottawa about his pretensions. He was reported to have ordered a Campari and soda (typical poseur's drink), mixed it himself, then *sent it back.* Strong also brought along the diminutive, charming Albert Khazoom, to deal with such important details as catering and corporate art. Khazoom, nominally senior director of external affairs, was soon given the nickname "the Maître d'."

The company leased a red brick office block on the corner of Fourth Avenue and First Street. Locals named it "Red Square." The offices were decorated in apple green and hung with native art provided from the Glenbow Museum at the recommendation of Donald Harvie, Petrocan's deputy chairman and son of the great Calgary oilman and philanthropist Eric Harvie.

Perhaps ironically, the loudest indignation over Petrocan's arrival and mandate came not from the multinationals but from independent oilmen. The majors had seen it all before. Indeed, some of the heads of the big oil companies privately supported Petrocan's creation as a way of guarding against more extreme nationalist measures. But not all the big oil company heads — particularly the Canadian ones — judged Petrocan on a could-have-been-worse basis. Canada wasn't Venezuela or Iraq. American companies had always obeyed the rules. They had taken the risks. The notion that a "window on the industry" was needed to make sure they weren't ripping off Canada offended them deeply.

Nevertheless, in practical terms, if Petrocan was going to share the burden of frontier exploration, the big oil companies would be happy to take its money. Hell, the oil companies had signed deals with Lenin, so Maurice Strong wouldn't be a problem. The industry had always been based on shared risks, hunting in packs, swapping information, drilling on the other guy's lands in return for a piece of the action. Petrocan's money was as good as anybody else's. And since the company was starting from scratch without history or experience, there might be some sweet deals to be made. Mobil had apparently already made one.

What aroused industry outrage most was the proposal that Petrocan should be able to "back in" to exploration lands, just walk in and take a 25-per-cent interest *after* all the risks had been taken and work done. This prospect would significantly poison the atmosphere. The notion of carving off a piece of other people's efforts in the name of the nation sat easily in Ottawa. It wasn't so easy to sell elsewhere.

• • •

Strong, typically, soon showed signs of restlessness and became tired, in the words of one observer, of being "the skunk at the cocktail party." Government involvement in business looked fine on paper, but in practice it was beset with all sorts of difficulties. Strong found himself in conflict not merely with the industry but also with Ottawa and even his own board.

Like its executives, Petrocan's board was important in establishing its credibility. Energy Minister Alastair Gillespie wanted directors who would stand up to Strong, with whom he had an increasingly testy relationship. But Gillespie had found it difficult to get people with oil experience to accept board seats. The most experienced was Donald Harvie, who headed Petrofina Canada's Calgary-based exploration arm.

Donald Harvie's father, Eric Lafferty Harvie, QC, was a Calgary lawyer who, like many of his fellow Alberta barristers, had dabbled in oil leases all his life. That dabbling turned serious when Leduc was found on land he'd leased to Imperial Oil. He wound up accumulating more than $100 million. Stories about Harvie's frugality abounded. He drove dilapidated cars and never moved from the small bungalow in Mount Royal he had inhabited since he was a young lawyer. He reportedly pored over accounts, looking for minute irregularities. Such stories were eagerly recounted by those eager to peddle the Scrooge myth.

But the image ultimately didn't fit Harvie because he was perhaps the greatest of Western collectors and philanthropists. The 14,000 items he accumulated in his life ranged from the historically significant to the outright bizarre — from the drum that announced the battle of the Little Big Horn to a pair of Queen Victoria's bloomers. His Devonian and Glenbow Foundations were the driving force behind the Calgary Zoo and the Banff

School of Fine Arts, as well as research institutions and public parks from the Maritimes to British Columbia.

Petrofina had bought out Eric Harvie's main company, Western Leaseholds, and Don Harvie had remained a major shareholder in Petrofina, as well as a board member and executive. Don was low-key but, in the family tradition, had become involved in public-sector initiatives such as Heritage Canada. He was approached by Alastair Gillespie to take an executive position with Petro-Canada and finally agreed to be deputy chairman, with a salary based on the proportion of time he devoted to Petrocan. Like other private-sector directors, Harvie had misgivings about Petrocan, but he was persuaded that if it was going to happen, then it should be properly executed. Like many Canadians, he seemed to get the notions of public service and government intervention muddled, a trait of which Ottawa's interventionists took abundant advantage. In fact, it could be fairly said that the outside directors were seen by the Ottawa insiders as providing a cloak of legitimacy as much as a source of advice.

Apart from Strong and Hopper, the government was represented by three key deputy ministers: Tommy Shoyama from Finance, Gordon MacNabb from EMR, and Arthur Kroeger from Indian Affairs and Northern Development. To an outsider, this weight of super-bureaucrats might seem a stringent control mechanism, but deputy ministers are very busy men. This soon became apparent. If there was a board meeting in Ottawa, one or more of the DMs would invariably be called out to deal with more pressing business. They always had great trouble finding time to attend meetings in Calgary.

Shoyama was the most influential of the senior mandarins. Gentlemanly and erudite, Shoyama had cut his bureaucratic teeth in the CCF administration of Tommy Douglas in Saskatchewan. He was a socialist, and thus he obviously believed in government intervention. He had little or no business experience — almost a prerequisite for one of his ideological conviction — but he got on well with the private-sector members of the board.

A number of appointees had strong Liberal Party connections.

These included the prominent Toronto lawyer John Aird, David Mann, another lawyer from Halifax, and Claude Hébert, a Montreal business executive. Aird had Establishment connections that ran back, through his father, Sir John Aird, to the time of Laurier. He sat on a raft of big company boards. At one time he had been the chief national fundraiser for the Liberal Party.

Aird had been carefully cultivated by Jim Coutts, the arch-manipulator of Trudeau's PMO. He had moved away from the party because of disagreements over defence policy, but kept in touch. He had known Strong since Strong had been a messenger for Richardson's in Toronto. Like most Liberals, Aird took a pragmatic approach to life, which had enabled him to do quite well. In Aird's view, conflicts of interest were the inevitable challenges of a well-rounded career. Indeed, Aird once confided to a Petrocan executive, "Anybody who has never had to deal with conflicts of interest can't have amounted to much."

Hébert, independently wealthy, had been a war hero and was now chairman and chief executive of Montreal-based Bombardier. He was reckoned to be one of a dozen French Canadians who qualified for ranking in the national business establishment.

The strongest and most outspoken of the independent directors was Bud Willmot, chairman of Molson and a director of half a dozen other companies, including Texaco Canada, on whose board he'd sat for more than six years. Willmot said he didn't like the term "Establishment," but he admitted he was a member of it. Gillespie considered him a prize, both because of his status in the corporate community and because he was so skeptical about Crown corporations.

Despite his Texaco directorship, Willmot admitted that his knowledge of the oil business was slim. Nevertheless, during the OPEC crisis of the winter of 1973/74, when he and his wife had been at their vacation home in Florida, he had seen the gas station line-ups and witnessed the guard dogs and shotguns used to guard the pumps.

Willmot consulted with a number of senior oil executives about the invitation, especially the head of Texaco Canada, Andy

Farquharson, from whose board he knew he'd have to resign. He also spoke with the highly respected head of Gulf Canada, Jerry McAfee, with whom he sat on the board of the Bank of Nova Scotia. He called Bill Twaits, who had now retired from Imperial. They all agreed — whatever they thought of Petrocan — that the government needed business experience on the board. They'd all feel more comfortable if Willmot joined.

Willmot believed in the importance of a business-government dialogue. He was not a fan of government intervention, but he believed in public service. Like many businessmen, he also liked to believe he could "make a difference." Gillespie persuaded him that Petrocan was important for Canada. But Willmot found nothing at Petrocan that reduced his doubts about Crown corporations. Indeed, he discovered a lot that made him more skeptical than ever.

Strong wanted to be seen as an environmental statesman. This interest caused problems. Under Strong's influence, consultations were held with every group of environmental activists who presented themselves, as well as with academics and native groups. The result, according to the company's first annual report, was that "environmental and social impact assessments must be incorporated into every level of planning and day-to-day operations of Petro-Canada." A special department was set up to deal with environmental and social affairs.

The issue came to a head over exploration in Lancaster Sound in the High Arctic. Land had been acquired, but when the question of drilling came to the board, Strong started describing how environmentally sensitive the area was and explaining why there would be a long wait before drilling could be approved. Willmot sat and listened for a while with mounting incredulity, then called for a reality check. Just which hat was Strong meant to be wearing: that of Petrocan chairman or international environmentalist? Were they there to find oil or save the planet? They'd just spent several million dollars to get exploration rights, and now Strong was saying they shouldn't exercise them.

Fourteen years later, in an interview with the British newspaper the *Guardian*, Strong brought up this incident: "Once I had the whole board against me. It was a question of drilling in the Arctic. I said it was a vulnerable ecosystem where all kinds of species of life gathered and there would be no drilling. I put my job on the line." How Strong "put his job on the line" he didn't explain; certainly the board was in no position to remove him.

Willmot had much broader concerns about the board's lack of expertise in appraising the huge frontier proposals being put before them. Even with his Texaco experience, he realized he was in no position to analyze exploration plays. Again, this was the fundamental flaw of the "need to know" approach. No matter what the government *felt* it needed to know, what it found depended on the geological theories and strategies of its leading explorationists. How could Willmot or any of the others know if these theories made sense until they were drilled? Harvie was the most experienced oilman. He agreed with the notion of "elephant hunting," looking for very big finds, but it was still a very risky business.

Petrocan inevitably attracted policy groupies who smelled fat budgets and loose controls. To deal with public relations, Marie Choquette was hired on contract. Choquette, a relative by marriage of Bell Canada's powerful chief, Jean de Grandpré, was a woman around whom considerable mystery swirled. It was rumoured that she was *very* close to Pierre Trudeau, whose name she had reportedly dropped to Strong in order to get the job.

One of the greatest of Ottawa gravy trains was, and remains, the constant outpouring of expensive but largely ignored reports and studies on every subject known to humanity. Inevitably, it was suggested that part of Petrocan's role should be education of the public. Choquette appeared before the board with a proposal to make films, write reports, and hold meetings in communities from coast to coast in order to fill the nescient masses in on the realities of energy supply and demand. She wanted a budget of $6 million.

Now hold on, said Willmot. Surely films were available from Imperial Oil and others that could be used as aids or tools. There was no point in trying to reinvent the wheel. The board felt as Willmot did. Choquette was miffed, but returned with a new proposal costing $3 million. Willmot said it was still too much. "The trouble with you men," blurted Choquette, "is that you're too bottom-line-oriented!" Willmot was shocked. He had not come across this all-too-typical Ottawa mindset, so engorged with self-appointed public purpose that there was no room left for crass financial calculation. Eventually the board approved a budget of $600,000. Marie Choquette soon left.

Strong was frustrated by such squabbles, and his frustration was increased by his personal problems with Ottawa. Strong had no interest in formal chains of bureaucratic command. His *modus operandi* was the short circuit. He was meant to report to Alastair Gillespie, but when he wanted something, he called his old friend Jim Coutts directly in the PMO, or tried to get through to the prime minister. This understandably annoyed Gillespie.

Gillespie, by contrast, was impressed by Hopper, in particular when they travelled abroad seeking state-to-state oil deals. Heads of big state concerns such as Pemex and the Venezuelan oil company didn't just know Hopper, they treated him like an old friend. Hopper's status helped him in his bid to seize power at Petrocan.

In line with what would later be called the "Idi Amin complex," Strong had taken the title not only of chairman but also of president and chief executive. It was expected that he would eventually find somebody with operating expertise to take over the presidency. But Bill Hopper wanted titles too, and he went out of his way to take as much of Strong's burden as Strong was prepared to pass on. Strong still had misgivings about Hopper's lack of hands-on industry experience, but Hopper's impressive performance in Ottawa's eyes got him the posts of both president and chief executive. The morning the board was supposed to discuss Hopper's appointment, it was announced in the newspapers via a "leak." So much for the powers of the board. Strong was reportedly none too happy either.

Hopper had always been careful to cultivate people important to his career; he had an acute instinct for where power lay. When it came to the board, he saw that the man to win over was Willmot. Hopper went out of his way to court him, ask him for advice, tell him how much he appreciated his executive experience. Willmot's importance increased even further when he was selected to be chairman of the board's subcommittee on executive compensation.

Hopper soon approached Willmot with a problem. "Bud," he said, "we've got to do something about salaries." Willmot asked, "In what way?" Hopper said they were just too low. It wasn't so much his own salary that concerned him, but to attract top people, they were going to have to pay industry salaries, which were much higher than anything contemplated in government circles or paid to the heads of other Crown corporations. If there was a salary scale whose upper end was Hopper's present level, then they were going to have problems. There would be too much "compression." There was only one answer: Hopper's salary had to be boosted to make room for the talent that would have to be brought in beneath him. Other salaries had to be boosted too. Hopper presented a list of the sort of revised salaries he had in mind.

Willmot agreed wholeheartedly with Hopper's analysis of the problem, as did deputy chairman Don Harvie. But Willmot said they should hire outside consultants to set the scales. Hopper tried not to wrinkle his brow. How long would that take? He thought they should get on with paying higher salaries at once. So Willmot said that if Hopper was going to have a problem, then the revised salary schedules would be backdated. Hopper was delighted with this compromise. He really did appreciate the benefit of Willmot's experience.

Once Willmot was on side, higher salaries were easier to sell to the board, where the greatest source of possible discord was the three deputy ministers. Willmot found that they weren't really "open-minded" about the salary issue. Perhaps it had something to do with the fact that when he'd joined Petrocan, Hopper had been only an assistant deputy minister. Now he'd become president and was saying that a big pay increase was essential. Willmot declared that if they wanted to accomplish their mandate, they had to have the proper people. To get the proper people, they had to pay the right salaries. Hopper could only agree. The DMs weren't so sure.

Hopper also approached Alastair Gillespie with his "problem." He explained that salary wasn't a big problem with him, *personally*, although of course he had to have a salary that established his position as the head of a large oil company. At the same time, he didn't want to embarrass his friends in the bureaucracy. And if he had to pay a salary close to his own to hire a good executive, that didn't bother him, he said, although there would, of course, be this "compression" problem.

Gillespie sympathized, but it was difficult to get government to move on the issue. There was still a powerful ethic that senior bureaucrats, like politicians, should not be in it for the money. The Clerk of the Privy Council, Michael Pitfield, firmly believed in limits. Indeed, he would later express the opinion that nobody in Ottawa should earn more than $100,000.

So the Petrocan compensation committee cooked up a little scheme. Following the takeover of Arcan and its reconstitution as Petro-Canada Exploration, some executives, including Hopper, would be paid *two* salaries, one from each company. Among those who were not informed of this unusual procedure were most members of the Cabinet, who, claimed Don Johnston, one of their number, were thus "duped." Even Michael Pitfield may not have known the details. With subsequent takeovers, this process would become more widespread.

According to the 1976 annual report, direct remuneration for the ten senior officers totalled a mere $308,000, an average of $30,800. The following year, the aggregate for the top fifteen officers would be $810,000, an average of $54,000, an increase of 75 per cent. After its second annual report, Petrocan would stop reporting managers' salaries and directors' fees. A discreet curtain was drawn over that rather personal pane of the "window."

Willmot felt his involvement in this subterfuge was justifiable because of Ottawa's lack of knowledge of the way business worked. Part of his corporate philosophy had always been to pay senior executives well, giving them incentive for performance. The trouble was that it would be so difficult to judge Petrocan's performance.

By the end of year one, while the public image was of a tightly controlled company set up to serve the public interest in a hostile environment, the organization was already well on the way to becoming a hotbed of corporate intrigue whose various components played devious games with their Ottawa networks. Meanwhile, in certain respects, it had already slipped its shackles and was going its own way.

Once he had his coveted new job, Hopper was not afraid to distance himself publicly from some of Strong's more controversial suggestions, such as moving Petrocan into refining and marketing. "I don't see us turning into a huge integrated company," he said in an interview. "I don't think the company has to be enormous — that's probably one thing I disagree with Maurice on." That was what the industry wanted to hear.

. . .

Although Hopper was president and chief executive, he still had little or no operating experience. Moreover, he was still frequently hauled off by Pierre Trudeau or Alastair Gillespie to represent Canada at energy-related events or conferences around the world. Hopper never moved his family to Calgary. One of the reasons he gave was that one of his two sons was dyslexic and attended a special school in Ottawa. But he spent as much time in Ottawa as in Calgary, if not more. Both he and Joel Bell were acutely aware that the key to Petrocan's survival and success, not to mention their own, lay in preserving and building their Ottawa networks. And, like Austin, both were far more interested in the "big picture" than in the daily grind of running a company. Both kept Calgary apartments in London House, a low-rent high-rise close to Red Square.

Among the executives they had initially hired or acquired, Axford and Meneley were primarily explorationists; Wolcott was an ideas man; many of the senior executives of Arcan had left. Willmot and Aird stressed at board level how important it was to have somebody who could run things. The man they found, in 1977, was Andy Janisch.

Janisch had been born in Austria, then raised on the prairies. He had been trained as a civil engineer but decided to get into the oil business after seeing a John Wayne movie about fighting oil well blow-outs. It looked more exciting than building roads and bridges.

When he joined Gulf Canada he was so green he didn't even know what oil production facilities looked like. When the colleague driving him north to his first posting at Stettler, then Gulf's largest oil production operation in Canada, said they were driving through oilfields, he figured the guy was having him on. How could they be oilfields? Where were the derricks? When he got to Stettler, he met Kelly Gibson, the legendary Oklahoma-born oilman who would go on to head Pacific Petroleums. Gibson refused to shake his hand. He just said: "I don't like engineers."

Despite this inauspicious beginning, Janisch stayed with Gulf twenty-four years. He had just returned to Calgary from seven years in Toronto when he was approached by an executive search firm. Janisch didn't like travelling, and he knew that staying with Gulf would involve further moves. The advertised job was Calgary-based. When Janisch discovered it was with Petrocan, he had natural misgivings. Most of his friends had negative feelings about the state oil company. But Janisch took comfort in a conversation he had once had with Gulf's head, Jerry McAfee, whom Janisch, like most people in the oil patch, greatly admired. McAfee had said he had to be opposed to the creation of Petrocan, but he recognized that there were pressures in Canada that might one day result in the attempted nationalization of Gulf, Imperial, or Shell. McAfee felt any such move would have bad repercussions for Canada. He supported Petrocan as a safety valve. McAfee's successor, John Stoik, perhaps because he was Canadian, was much less sanguine about Janisch's move. Stoik was one of the very few heads of the major companies who had spoken out against Petrocan.

Janisch regarded himself as pragmatic. Petrocan was there and looked as if it would stay. He put ideology at the back of his mind and decided to take the job as a professional and managerial challenge. There were also opportunities in fields where he had special interests, such as building Canadian offshore drilling capability. He knew only too well that he was spending taxpayers' money, but he told himself he could help the country by spending it in the most efficient and effective way possible.

Janisch was taken on as head of operations and given a corner office in Red Square. His corporate ranking was roughly equivalent to that of Joel Bell, who had now taken over financial and administrative responsibilities. He settled in to come to grips with the job while office politics rumbled quietly and constantly in the background.

In April 1977, Strong made a speech to the Canadian Club in Toronto in which he gave vent to all his frustrations. He declared, "Some elements in the industry, principally a few large foreign-controlled companies, are waging an unrelenting underground campaign against Petro-Canada." He turned on the Canadian Petroleum Association, the representative body of the larger oil companies, and declared that it excluded Petro-Canada from membership while it admitted companies that were "controlled by foreign governments."

Strong claimed the industry's outcry against proposed preferential land rights for Petrocan was unjustified. He complained that Big Oil had for years had tax benefits from the U.S. government that were not available to Canadian companies. He made a thinly veiled threat to move into the refining and marketing end of the business. Finally, Strong made the nationalist case for further intervention: "It would be unwise for Canada to continue to rely solely on decisions made outside the country over which we have little control and may have little influence when the pressures mount during future periods of short supply."

Asked subsequently to identify just which foreign-controlled companies were waging this "unrelenting underground campaign," he declined. As for the charge that the Canadian Petroleum Association barred Petro-Canada from membership, a mystified spokesman said the state oil company had never applied. Jack Armstrong, the gruff oilman who had taken over from Bill Twaits at Imperial, when approached by the *Toronto Star*, professed himself "shocked" by Strong's remarks.

In fact, Armstrong was at the root of Strong's outburst. Strong had heard rumours that Armstrong had made derogatory remarks about Strong and his business dealings. Strong claimed that he had a showdown with Armstrong, then went to visit Armstrong's boss, Clifton Garvin, head of Exxon in New York, both to complain and to state that if Exxon ever wanted to sell Imperial, Petrocan would be a willing buyer. Strong, who had been on the board of the Rockefeller Trust — that ubiquitous Rockefeller name again — perhaps assumed that would give him clout with Garvin. It seems unlikely that it did. Strong later claimed that Armstrong was told to "mend fences." Jack Armstrong denied that it was "ever suggested, or directed, that I had fences to mend." Whatever the origins, or purpose, of Strong's outburst, it hardly helped relations with the oil community. There, Strong's habit of short-circuiting all the usual procedures was also putting noses out of joint.

An exploration group led by a prominent independent drilling and exploration company, Bow Valley Industries, had been negotiating for several years with the North Vietnamese government for drilling rights in the South China Sea. During a trip to Peking, Strong announced that he would be going on to Vietnam to discuss the drilling concessions on the group's behalf. When one of the consortium members, Bill Siebens, the tungsten-nosed head of Siebens Oil and Gas, read a report of the remarks, he blew his top. He called Bow Valley and asked if this "bullshit" was true. They said no. So all the partners then called Petrocan and raised hell. "Maurice," Siebens said later in disbelief, "had just decided to go and get himself into the middle of the deal."

Eventually the group met with Strong. Although he backed off, he certainly didn't apologize. His attitude appeared to be that the private sector should be grateful to have the helping hand of government, even if they'd never asked for it. Bill Siebens's attitudes, of course, could be written off as those of an unregenerate Stone Age capitalist.

These were political times. Some in the industry believed that the smart route to success was to link yourself with government objectives, or to persuade the government that your own objectives were synonymous with theirs. The two great proponents of these views were Bob Blair and Jack Gallagher, the chief executives of Alberta Gas Trunk Line (later Nova) and Dome Petroleum respectively. In 1977, each would achieve stunning successes by playing the patriot game. Each would in the process set itself up as a rival to Petrocan in the loudly proclaimed pursuit of the "national interest" against the power of the big oil companies. Each would seek to use Petrocan. All three companies would become involved in a titanic clash of egos.

• • •

Bob Blair was an enigma to his corporate colleagues and counterparts, but he inspired fierce loyalty in his staff, who would become — like Dome employees — caught up in something approaching a corporate religion. Blair's father, Sid, was a famous engineer who had been president of the Canadian arm of the giant engineering company Bechtel, where he was credited with much of the work on the feasibility of the Athabasca tarsands. Blair, a precocious youth, was born in Trinidad, where Sid was managing a refinery at the time. After attending exclusive preparatory schools, he went to Queen's University at age sixteen to study chemical engineering. After graduation, he worked for several years in pipeline construction, then joined Alberta & Southern Gas, a subsidiary of the giant San Francisco–based utility Pacific Gas and Electric. He spent ten years with A&S before moving, in 1969, to Alberta Gas Trunk Line, the natural gas gathering pipeline system within the province. AGTL had a political as well as a functional purpose: to assert Alberta's control over its natural gas.

When Peter Lougheed came to power, determined to bolster the province's status through energy, he found a firm ally in Blair. But Blair was also a very strong economic nationalist, a stance that had been strengthened by his years at Alberta & Southern, an

American-owned company. He sometimes talked about subordi-
nating corporate self-interest to higher, national goals. That sort of
talk made him an object of suspicion among his Calgary counterparts, with whom he rarely socialized. Sometimes, Blair seemed to
have assumed an almost Messianic mantle.

When Blair had joined AGTL, the pipeline system had appeared
to be in decline, since it was based on a low-priced, depleting
resource. He pursued twin strategies to reverse this decline. He
planned to revitalize the system by directing frontier gas through
the province; then he'd diversify beyond gas transmission, which
dovetailed with one of Lougheed's key objectives.

The crisis atmosphere of 1973/74 was replayed in the winter
of 1976/77 when the U.S. was hit by a natural gas shortage that
had a much more dramatic real impact than the oil shortages of
three years before. Factories, schools, and businesses were closed in
twenty states and more than 2 million workers were temporarily
laid off. Like the gas station line-ups of 1973, this crisis was largely the result of perverse legislation that controlled prices and
restricted movements of gas. Nevertheless, it led to demands for
frontier gas to be brought into the system.

Blair had been a member of the Arctic Gas consortium that
had planned to build a pipeline east from Prudhoe Bay to pick up
Canadian natural gas from the Mackenzie Delta and then pipe it
along the Mackenzie Valley to Alberta and the U.S. But then Blair
had formed his own group, with Vancouver-based Westcoast
Transmission and a U.S. company, Northwest Energy, which
eventually evolved a rival scheme to pipe Prudhoe Bay gas down
the route of the Alaska Highway, and to build a separate "Maple
Leaf" line down the Mackenzie Valley for Canadian gas.

In 1972, the federal Liberals had strongly supported the development of an "energy corridor" along the Mackenzie Valley as part
of a "northern vision." But in 1974, they had appointed Justice
Thomas Berger, an ardent socialist, environmentalist, and former
NDP member of the B.C. legislature, to carry out an environmental and social impact study of the proposed development. In retrospect, it seemed almost like an act of sabotage.

In May 1977, Berger delivered his bombshell report. It recommended that there be no pipeline across the Arctic National Wildlife Refuge, and that a Mackenzie Valley line be delayed for ten years. The National Energy Board delivered the death blow to Arctic Gas two months later when it declared a modified version of Blair's Alaska Highway (Alcan) line to be the "winner" of the pipeline contest. Bob Blair's flexible nationalism had triumphed over a Who's Who of the oil industry — a key member was, of course, Imperial Oil — that had spent five years and $140 million building a supposedly impregnable case for its pipeline.

Dome's Jack Gallagher could not have presented a greater contrast to Blair. He was an old-style promoter and visionary, a "riverboat man in a gambler's industry," who wanted to go down in history as a great oil finder. The exploration basin into which he had projected his dreams was beneath the frigid waters of the Beaufort Sea.

Following the huge find at Prudhoe Bay, there was a land rush in the Mackenzie Delta to the east. For a company like Dome, the only land available was offshore in the deeper water of the Beaufort, where drilling was correspondingly more expensive and difficult. The Beaufort was ice-bound most of the year, and there was only a brief summer window during which drillships could operate. Nobody had drilled in such circumstances before. In a bold move, Dome established a subsidiary called Canmar to build an offshore Arctic fleet, which came into operation in 1976. The rationale was not merely to make money by drilling for others, but to take part of the exploration play as part payment. By the end of the first year, it was clear Dome had overstretched. Drilling charges would not pay off the investment; Canmar could go broke. The solution that presented itself to Dome spoke volumes about the evolving energy environment: if the interplay of market forces was leading to trouble, persuade the government to rig the market.

Of course, it was in the government's power to declare higher prices for more expensive frontier oil, but price wasn't Dome's immediate concern; it was the demand for frontier drilling equipment. The solution hatched by Jack Gallagher and his corporate alter ego, Dome president Bill Richards, was to persuade Ottawa to introduce a tax regime that would encourage frontier drilling. In the national interest, of course.

One of the most important converts to Gallagher's vision of a Beaufort oil bonanza was Tommy Shoyama, the deputy minister of finance who sat on Petrocan's board. Shoyama had first become acquainted with Gallagher when Gallagher had accepted a seat on the board of the CDC, a move that at the time seemed almost daringly "public-spirited." Gallagher had cultivated Shoyama as Shoyama had risen through the Trudeaucracy, first as deputy minister of energy after Jack Austin had gone to the PMO, then as deputy minister of finance, a crucial position from Gallagher's point of view.

Shoyama was impressed by Gallagher's courtesy, both to himself and to his staff. The multinationals, by contrast, presented a much less appealing face. They had realized it was becoming more important to keep abreast of Ottawa's thinking, but their approach tended to be heavy-handed and sometimes self-righteous. By contrast, Gallagher's million-dollar smile and double handshake spoke warm concern. Still, Gallagher realized that charm was not the primary route to tax breaks; those required a public-interest rationale.

Gallagher used the same argument that had been put forward for Petrocan's creation: Canada needed to explore its frontier regions because there was a lot of oil up there. Gallagher's trademark became his presentation on the Beaufort's geological potential. For groups, he'd put on a "magic lantern show." For individuals, he'd pull out the maps he'd had specially prepared, spread them on the desk, and proceed to mesmerize his audience with his northern vision.

He'd point to the globular shapes of the forty or so potential oil-bearing structures that had been identified by seismic work. He'd explain how drilling offshore made more sense because in the great river delta oil-bearing regions of the world — the Mississippi, the Niger, parts of the Persian Gulf — the thickness of petroleum-bearing sediments increased as you moved offshore.

That was the way it looked in the Beaufort. But of course offshore Arctic drilling was very expensive, and the further offshore you got, the more expensive it became. But look at the potential rewards; look at Prudhoe Bay.

It seemed only reasonable that there should be some form of tax incentive to explore this hostile region, particularly when you remembered that exploration costs were such a small proportion of the enormous overall development costs of the Beaufort, which would in turn be just a small proportion of the huge revenues that would flow from Arctic oil. After all, came the visionary kicker, there were probably "one, maybe two, Middle Easts" up there. And a Middle East up there meant that Canada could be independent from the real, scary Middle East — not to mention Peter Lougheed.

Shoyama was helpful in obtaining a hearing for Gallagher with other super-bureaucrats and politicians. Michael Pitfield heard the dream and found it good. Donald Macdonald, now finance minister, and Alastair Gillespie were buttonholed and presented with Beaufort visions. So convinced did they become of the abundance and political value of Beaufort oil that in the 1977 budget, Macdonald introduced a "super-depletion" allowance, giving uniquely generous tax write-offs for wells costing more than $5 million. As it happened, Dome was just about the only company drilling wells costing more than $5 million, so the measure was quickly dubbed the "Gallagher amendment" in the "Dome Budget."

Bob Blair's pipeline victory and the "Dome Budget" were potent signs of the times. They clearly demonstrated a new environment in which the corporate executives who could most loudly trumpet the national interest, or develop powerful political and bureaucratic connections in Ottawa or Edmonton, would be the new stars. The name of the game was to win government concessions or approvals by establishing that your corporate ambitions were firmly aligned with the best interests of the nation. There was a widespread belief in the wake of the first OPEC crisis that politics now reigned over economics in oil and gas, that any government that controlled oil and gas reserves could call the tune.

AGTL and Dome became experts at whistling attractive tunes. But their schemes were either enormously expensive or dependent on finds that had not, as yet, been made.

Dome and AGTL would thus present themselves as rival "instruments" for the achievement of the national interest. As such, they were bound to trip over not only each other but Petro-Canada. Somehow, all those professions of national interest would get terribly mixed up with personal and corporate ambition.

Part of Petrocan's problem with Dome would be that Dome was so much more successful in arousing enthusiasm for the Beaufort than Petrocan was in stirring interest for the East Coast and the Arctic Islands. Each year, Dome would produce the exploration equivalent of the dance of the seven veils, flashing just enough hydrocarbon to keep enthusiasm going for another drilling season. Petrocan was just drilling dry holes.

The state oil company's second year of exploration was no more successful than its first. Petrocan participated in thirteen of the twenty-seven wells drilled in the frontiers in 1977. In two years, it had spent $77 million on frontier exploration. It would have spent more, but there was no drilling off Newfoundland and Labrador because of a jurisdictional dispute between the provincial and federal governments. For all its efforts, the only small successes the company had were on the Alberta lands acquired through Arcan.

Don Wolcott came up with an almost science-fiction scheme, the Arctic Pilot Project, to ship liquefied natural gas out of the Arctic Islands in reinforced supertankers. Blair became a partner. In turn, Petrocan became a partner in plans hatched by Blair to push Alberta gas beyond the existing eastern terminal of the TransCanada PipeLine in Montreal through a "Quebec & Maritimes" pipeline. Both these schemes had heavy undertones of corporate rivalry. In particular, they escalated Blair's ongoing corporate vendetta against TransCanada PipeLines, the giant Toronto-based gas transmission system that took Alberta's gas to its central Canadian and midwestern U.S. markets. The Arctic Pilot Project was clearly a rival to TCPL's proposed Polar Gas pipeline from the Arctic Islands. Meanwhile the Q&M system appeared to outflank TCPL both literally and figuratively, by extending TCPL's own system, and thus implying that it was not adventurous enough.

But while Dome, AGTL, and Petrocan were spinning off multi-billion-dollar schemes based on political appeal, the far more powerful economic impacts of higher oil and gas prices were beginning to show through in new conventional discoveries. It suddenly became clear that rumours of Alberta's decline as an oil and gas basin had been greatly exaggerated.

By the end of 1977, two Alberta discoveries were causing stock market frenzy. A company called Canadian Hunter had discovered a potentially huge gas field at Elmworth, while Chevron Canada, the 100-per-cent-owned Canadian subsidiary of Standard Oil of California, had made the biggest oil discovery in more than a decade at West Pembina. In the course of 1977, the Toronto Stock Exchange oil and gas share index had doubled. In the first week of December 1977, 28.6 million shares with a value of $209.7 million changed hands, a level of trading the TSE had not seen for eight years. One in three of those shares was an oil and gas share.

In its 1977 annual report, Petro-Canada came up with its first "independent" view on policy, the first fruits of the "window on the industry." It declared: "Petro-Canada believes that the potential for conventional oil and gas reserves in the Western Sedimentary Basin [i.e., primarily Alberta] exceeds official estimates."

This was hardly insider information.

• • •

By the middle of Petrocan's second year, Maurice Strong had had public run-ins with Big Oil, private run-ins with small oil, and spats with his board. Even in Ottawa, his short-circuit methods were about to backfire. Pierre Trudeau and the PMO had too many other problems to listen to those of Maurice Strong. Strong wanted to move on. In September 1977, a new appointment was orchestrated that would enable him to bow out from Petrocan gracefully. He became chairman of the International Development Research Centre, an organization he had created while head of CIDA. By a strange coincidence, the man moving out as president as Strong was moving in as chairman was D. William Hopper, Bill Hopper's older brother, who was moving to a post with the World Bank in Washington.

Quoted in the *Toronto Star,* Strong had some advice for his unnamed successor at Petrocan: "Don't work too hard." He said: "The chairman's role is supportive in terms of relations with Ottawa, with the Canadian public and with the energy community in general. A full-time chairman would impinge on the president's role."

Strong noted that some directors thought the next chairman should be from the private sector. "But," said Strong, "he will need to be a person with clout in Ottawa, someone to whom Ottawa will listen and who will listen to Ottawa."

Because Hopper had both private-sector and public-sector experience, Strong said, the chairman could also come from either sector. But Strong was clearly implying that it shouldn't be Hopper, even though Hopper "runs the company."

Strong's job was at an end. "I believe Petro-Canada is well established now." He gave the impression that he had decided to bustle on to bigger and better things. But his primary interest remained the public sphere, and power.

The IDRC post hardly represented a real job for Strong, and he soon announced that he was thinking about running in the coming federal election. There were rumours that Pierre Trudeau was going to resign. Strong saw an opening. In August 1978, he declared: "I tendered my resignation with Petrocan a year ago, but stayed on at the request of the prime minister. But my involvement there has been gradually downward and outward. This is the first time in the last several years that I have been in a position to take a serious look at the possibility [of running for Parliament]. Nothing is final at this point, but the matter has been placed before me." Just like Caesar's crown.

Who had "placed it before him" he didn't say.

SEVEN

Hopper Makes His Mark

BILL HOPPER had skillfully used his Ottawa network to cement his position as Petro-Canada's president and chief executive. He'd impressed the Cabinet during the energy crisis with his knowledge of the industry. He'd dazzled Alastair Gillespie with his international connections. He had made Pierre Trudeau laugh. He made bureaucrats and politicians feel they were "on the inside." Here, they thought, was a most valuable window. In the oil patch, meanwhile, he'd persuaded quite a few colleagues that he was a "free-enterpriser at heart," and that all those guys back on the Rideau just didn't know diddly.

Hopper had charisma. When he had to be, he would be charming. When it suited him, he could assume a down-home stumblebum image. When he needed to impress someone, he sought out his target's pet likes or hobbies — antique cars or stamp collecting — and brushed up on the subject. He was a great mimic and joke-teller, although of course he'd save his more racist jokes for Calgary. He did a great Jonathan Winters.

After becoming president and chief executive in mid-1976, Hopper acknowledged that there was a risk he'd become "bureaucratic," but he didn't think it likely. It was a strange remark coming from a former senior bureaucrat. Hopper was demonstrating a

Protean ability to run with the hare and hunt with the hounds. He even did it with his own family, sprinkled as they were throughout various public bureaucracies. "My family's full of fucking PhDs," he'd say, at once sporting a little background and separating himself from it. Hopper had a signed and framed photograph of Pierre Trudeau. When a visitor appeared from Ottawa, it stood prominently on his desk. When anybody from the industry came to call, Pierre wound up face down in the drawer. Whose side was Bill on? Hell, he was on *everybody's* side.

Beneath the amiable and flexible exterior lay a sharp mind and a burning ambition. Hopper wanted power, scope, and influence. He loved playing the Ottawa power game. He also wanted to take on Big Oil *mano a mano,* to be like Enrico Mattei thumbing his nose at the Sette Sorelle. The major companies talked a lot about competition, but in reality, Hopper believed, they acted like a herd of sheep, all moving in the same direction and taking pieces of each other's action. And of course, the main reason why business was booming was petroleum prices, not any genius of the industry. Hopper wanted to make his mark, and it wasn't the fuzzy, do-good, environment-friendly mark promoted by Maurice Strong; it was the mark of a corporate Zorro, Bill Hopper the Public Entrepreneur, carving his big B on the petroleum map of Canada.

But Bill Hopper had a problem; he was lumbered with an expensive mandate to drill in the frontiers while Alberta was going wild with new exploration plays. He was just itching to get some of the gravy. But first he needed to gain control. Like Strong before him, Hopper wanted all the titles.

Walter Gordon may have had a blind spot on foreign investment, but he understood corporate control. In a 1976 book titled *The Big Tough Expensive Job,* a collection of Exxonophobic essays by a group of rabid economic nationalists, Gordon wrote of Petrocan: "In an undertaking of this size and importance, I would like to see it headed by two men of different backgrounds, not by a single individual."

The problem with having one man as chairman and chief executive is that, as chairman, the top man funnels the information to the board upon which his performance as chief executive will be judged. Although many corporations bestow both titles on one individual, there is clear potential for conflict of interest. In the later words of a retired Petrocan director: "Any time you give the chairmanship and the CEO position to the same person, the board has lost control."

Strong's rapid departure from the chairmanship had come as a surprise to the Petrocan board. They had to find a replacement quickly. In May 1978, a press report claimed that deputy minister of finance Tommy Shoyama was expected to be Strong's successor; it was a rumour floated to tell Hopper he wasn't a shoo-in. But although officially appointed only "acting" chairman, by mid-1978 Hopper had all the titles.

The government had, after two years, shelled out $538.3 million of the authorized $1.5 billion to Petrocan, mostly in cash. In return, its window on the industry had let it into the secret that there was an oil and gas boom going on in Alberta. The company's frontier exploration had come up dry. The government's vague need to know, however, produced a very specific need for further exploration funds. Bill Hopper became concerned that going back to the trough year after year was a dangerous game.

Hopper knew that all the talk about government being able to take the long view or the big picture was bullshit. Government was fickle. Its attention span extended little beyond the next opinion poll. Petrocan's management wanted to remove itself from the vagaries of party politics and parliamentary debate, although they realized that they still had to maintain their links with the key Trudeaucrats.

A split had appeared in the board, the resolution of which was crucial to Hopper's plans. There was a "conservative" camp, led by Bud Willmot and the private-sector representatives, who said the company should confine itself to "national interest" functions and not compete with the private sector. After all, that's what Pierre Trudeau had promised in 1973; that's what Maurice Strong had reaffirmed as chairman. They believed the corporation could continue to be financed by government funds.

Hopper, leading the other camp, argued for an "entrepreneur-ial strategy," which meant developing a stronger and more inde-pendent financial base. Hopper summed up his views in an inter-view with Patrick Watson in 1979: "You know, the notion that we should go up and spend our total exploration budget on the fron-tier and go belly up in five years, and have people shooting at us because it's all red ink below, is just a lot of nonsense. We've got to concentrate as much as we can on the frontier, but at the same time develop the cash flow in order to fund that long-term fron-tier development. And that balance is a hard balance to fix on, but that basically is what my board has to fix on — and that's a pri-vate/public-sector board. And we have arguments about that every year. About how much we put on the frontier versus how much we dedicate to the plains."

Hopper made the board sound like a little more of a debating society than it actually was. But as chief executive, he wanted as little interference from the board, of which he was chairman, as possible. Within a year Willmot would be gone and Hopper's grip would tighten. Within a few years he would have complete con-trol of a troupe of Liberal patronage appointees.

Whatever Hopper wanted, Hopper got. And in 1978, after Strong left, Hopper wanted acquisitions. Despite all Hopper's talk about the board debating frontiers versus the conventional areas, on the really big expenditures, like takeovers, they had little or no input.

· · ·

On the morning of Tuesday, June 8, 1978, Bill Hopper received some bad news from the Toronto Stock Exchange. In the first twenty minutes of trading, the share price of Husky Oil had risen $4.75 to $35.75.

Hopper had been eyeing Husky, whose activities and share-holdings were split between the U.S. and Canada, as a potential takeover target for some time. The soaring oil prices of the early 1970s had greatly increased the value of Husky's 1.6 million acres of heavy oil lands, mostly in Saskatchewan. Heavy oil had always been less profitable to produce, for technical reasons, than the lighter, free-flowing crude. But higher prices suddenly gave it new economic charms, while also promising to promote Canadian self-sufficiency.

Petrocan had approached Husky soon after Hopper became president with a view to farming in on Husky lands. Gulf Canada had joined in three-way negotiations, but talks had become bogged down. Hopper decided to go for the whole ball of wax. Petrocan's rationale to its political masters was that heavy oil development would provide a "bridge" to longer-term frontier development without any commitment to new tarsands plants. Development would also be shifted to Saskatchewan, thus diversifying the nation's domestic oil sources beyond Alberta. It was also argued that an acquisition would reduce dependence on the public purse and "cross-subsidize" frontier exploration.

For financial advice, Hopper turned to two major Toronto brokerage houses, Wood Gundy and Pitfield, Mackay, Ross. They knew a lot about Husky; they were its investment advisors. Moreover, Ward Pitfield (brother of Clerk of the Privy Council Michael Pitfield) sat on the Husky board. The propriety of the investment dealers' ethics would be loudly questioned. Acting for a predator appeared a major conflict.

Hopper and his advisors were as shocked by the sudden share price movement as anyone. There had obviously been a leak of Hopper's intentions. But once the balloon had gone up, they had to act quickly. Gundy's chairman, Ted Medland, called Husky's president, Jim Nielson, and announced that Gundy and Pitfield were acting on behalf of a "reputable Canadian principal interested in visiting with Husky." He asked for a meeting at Husky's headquarters in Cody, Wyoming, the following Saturday morning, June 10.

Although Jim Nielson was Husky's president, it was his father, Glenn, Husky's founder, who called the shots. Nielson, a craggy-faced seventy-six-year-old, was a devout Mormon with a wry sense of humour. Behind the desk in his corner office in Husky's single-storey Cody headquarters, Nielson kept a plaque that read: "Lord Make Our Blunders Wise." In some quarters, the divine imprecation was seen as embodying Husky's management style. Many felt the company had become too complex and unwieldy, and that Jim was a weaker manager than his father.

One of the most frequent criticisms of the Nielsons was that they had steadfastly refused to move their headquarters from the little cowboy town where Glenn had founded the business forty years before. Cody was fifty miles from the main gates of Yellowstone National Park, set in the same rocky badlands as the Little Big Horn and the red bluffs where Butch Cassidy and the Sundance Kid hid out with the "Hole in the Wall Gang." Those famous forebears would provide appropriate analogies for what would happen: the Husky affair would start with an attempted hold-up and end with a massacre.

Medland could not name Petrocan when he spoke to Jim Nielson, and could not ask for a meeting right away, because although Hopper had received Cabinet approval for a takeover bid, he had not received the go-ahead from the Petrocan board. That approval was given at a hastily called meeting on Saturday morning. Then Hopper called Glenn Nielson, apologized for not having revealed himself before, and said he was boarding the Petrocan jet for Cody. Nielson suggested that they switch the meeting to Husky's Calgary office. Hopper agreed and contacted Medland and Pitfield, who were already in the air. The Wood Gundy jet banked towards Calgary.

When the two sides met at the Husky offices in Calgary, Hopper, who mistakenly believed that the Nielsons would be willing sellers, declared that the national oil company was prepared to offer $45 a share for Husky, valuing the company at $490 million and the Nielsons' 18-per-cent interest at around $90 million.

After Hopper had delivered his set piece, Dick Matthews, a prominent Calgary lawyer and Husky board member, turned to him and said: "You must have a commission from the U.S. government." Hopper looked puzzled. Matthews laid it out: "How much tax do you think the Nielsons will have to pay on that offer?" That was just one of the wrinkles that Hopper and his advisors had failed to think through.

Glenn Nielson had built the company from one refinery with nineteen employees to an integrated concern with revenues of more than $600 million. The thought of selling was painful; the thought of the U.S. taxman grabbing a big chunk of his life's work was more than he could bear. He was also deeply offended that Ward Pitfield should have shown up on the other side of the table.

The Husky side suggested alternatives. Why not plow the takeover money directly into heavy oil development? Hopper said no deal. He wanted the whole thing. Then what about splitting the company in two, so that the Nielsons could be left with control of the American interests and avoid taxes? Hopper and his advisors discussed this option but decided it would take too long, allowing rival suitors to mount bids. Petrocan's chief executive said he wanted Husky's answer the following day. Nielson said he couldn't get his board together that quickly. He was playing for time. He already had a plan in mind.

Following the meeting with Hopper and his advisors, Glenn Nielson called Armand Hammer in Los Angeles. The octogenarian Hammer operated out of a modest office in the Los Angeles suburb of Westwood, in a building that didn't even bear the name of his company, Occidental Petroleum. On a table behind his desk, among personally dedicated pictures of prime ministers, presidents, and potentates, was a photograph of a bald man with a Mephistophelean beard and penetrating eyes. The inscription on the photograph read: "To comrade Armand Hammer, from V.I. Ulianoff [Lenin]."

While in his twenties, Hammer had travelled to Russia, according to some accounts as a messenger for his father, who was a communist. There he met Lenin and obtained the first major concession to a Western businessman from the revolutionary government. He built Russia's first pencil factory and returned to the States loaded with Russian antiques. Hammer revolutionized the business of fine art selling, at one point marketing the treasures of William Randolph Hearst through department stores. King

Farouk of Egypt was a client, on one occasion sending Hammer a telex: "Send Lana Turner."

Hammer became a whisky distiller and leading cattle breeder. In his late fifties, when even he thought he was close to retirement, he began to "dabble" in the oil business. He gained concessions from the King of Libya and made finds that thrust Occidental into the Fortune 500. But he also, because of his dependence on Libya, found himself squeezed by Colonel Qadaffi into making the price concessions in the early 1970s that marked a key power shift from the oil companies towards OPEC.

Unknown to Petrocan, Hammer had been interested in Husky for a number of years. He knew Glenn Nielson through both oil and art. Hammer had negotiated with Nielson for the loan of paintings from Cody's Buffalo Bill Museum, which he had taken to the Soviet Union as part of a cultural exchange (Leonid Brezhnev was a great, if unlikely, fan of cowboys and Indians). When Glenn Nielson called Hammer and asked whether Hammer might be able to help him out, Hammer said, "Come on down."

On Sunday, June 11, Nielson struck a share-swap deal with Hammer worth around $49 per Husky share, $4 more than Petrocan's offer. The following morning, Monday, June 12, Petrocan released its offer, to a chorus of indignation from the industry, who already fiercely resented Petrocan's presence. That night, when the Petrocan and Husky groups sat down again, it was Nielson's turn to drop the bombshell of a rival bid. First Nielson stared at Ward Pitfield and said he was sorry to see old friends on the other side of the table. Pitfield blanched. Then Nielson announced the alternative offer from Occidental. Hopper was stunned. He said he needed time to consider. But he was not too worried. After all, Oxy's offer would need approval from Joel Bell's old friends at the Foreign Investment Review Agency.

The following morning, June 13, the Occidental-Husky deal went over the newswires. When Husky shares started trading again, they jumped $11.50, to close at $47.25. Almost 1 million shares changed hands. After board meetings in Toronto the following day, June 14, Petrocan increased its offer to $52 a share.

Occidental responded almost immediately with another share-swap offer worth $54.

Energy Minister Gillespie did not express open preference for Petrocan. He released a statement that Occidental's offer could be acceptable to the Canadian government if heavy oil development were to be "guaranteed in every way" and in accord with Canadian objectives.

After a week of excitement, observers speculated on the relative merits of the offers and the role that FIRA might play. Views ranged from stop-the-damned-Americans to stop-the-damned-government. But in the background, another bidder was girding for battle.

Bob Blair had also spotted Husky as a takeover candidate early in 1978, and had been secretly accumulating shares. When Petrocan was forced to show its hand, AGTL was close to the 5-per-cent holding that would require public disclosure. Early in the second week of the battle, Blair visited Ottawa and made the rounds of his own network, sounding out senior government officials. He met few objections to his joining the fray. From Ottawa's point of view, he was better than Occidental; from business's point of view, he was better than Petrocan.

The possibilities of furling himself in the twin flags of Canadian nationalism and free enterprise were not lost on Blair. On the one hand, he would appear to be fighting off the predatory eagle of U.S. economic imperialism; on the other, he was battling the ever-lengthening tentacles of government control. How could he emerge as anything but a hero?

Just before the close of trading on Thursday, June 22, heavy buying of Husky shares appeared in the Toronto and New York markets. It continued until the following Tuesday, by which time Blair had accumulated 35 per cent of Husky. On Wednesday and Thursday, trading was suspended. When it opened again on Friday, June 30, the battle for Husky ended as it had begun, with a great price swing, only now the shares were plummeting. Blair had seized minority control of Husky without making a takeover offer. The battle was over.

Blair's move caused consternation not only for Petrocan but for Ottawa and the Liberals generally. PMO officials had spent a lot of time trying to persuade Blair to run for the party in the West. They couldn't understand why he had torpedoed their chosen instrument. There were dark rumours that he'd been put up to it by Peter Lougheed.

For Hopper, the Husky affair was a bitter blow. First Hopper had had opprobrium heaped on him for assaulting the private sector; then derision had been piled on top for failing. Hopper had been keen to establish himself as big enough to fill Maurice Strong's shoes. Instead, he became known as the leader of the "gang that couldn't shoot straight." When he heard it was Blair who had blasted him, there were tears of rage and frustration in his eyes. Petrocan's relations with Blair and AGTL cooled to freezing point. But Hopper quickly demonstrated another of his key characteristics: the ability to bounce back.

· · ·

Shortly after Blair grabbed control of Husky, former Alberta energy minister Bill Dickie, who was on the Husky board, ran into Merrill Rasmussen, president and chief executive of Pacific Petroleums, at the Calgary Golf and Country Club. "We escaped Petrocan," joked Dickie, "but watch out, you might be next." Rasmussen had smiled, but inside he knew it was no joke. Indeed, he knew that Petrocan was very interested in Pacific.

In the fall of 1977, Kelly Gibson (the man who had refused to shake hands with the young Andy Janisch because he didn't like engineers) had run into Hopper at an informal gathering. Gibson, one of the toughest men in the oil business, had started as an oil-rig roustabout and climbed the corporate ladder to mastermind the growth of both Pacific Petroleums and its sister gas pipeline company, Westcoast Transmission.

Hopper had asked Gibson, by then retired but still a director of Pacific, whether the U.S. company that controlled Pacific and Westcoast, Phillips Petroleum, might be interested in selling.

Gibson had said he'd check it out. In November, Hopper had approached Rasmussen to express his interest in a takeover. But then Gibson had come back with the word that Phillips wasn't really interested in selling, although it was prepared to "meet and discuss the matter further." Hopper's attention had turned to Husky.

Although outside the ranks of the Seven Sisters, Phillips had been one of the most successful American oil companies in the 1970s. Its discovery of the huge Ekofisk oil field off Norway in the North Sea had made it enormously profitable. In 1977, its earnings had been US$517 million on sales of US$6.3 billion, making it far larger than any public company in Canada. Its 48-per-cent stake in Pacific dated back to joint ventures with Frank McMahon, one of the most colourful personalities to emerge in a colourful industry.

Frank McMahon was almost a caricature of the dream-driven oil and gas explorer. Born in 1902 in the small mining town of Moyie, B.C., the first of three sons of a local hotel owner, he attended Gonzaga College in Spokane, where he was a classmate of Bing Crosby and a star baseball player. In the 1920s, he worked as a labourer on the construction of the Golden Gate Bridge; then he worked briefly for Standard Oil of California before setting up a diamond drilling business. When the market crashed in 1929, so did McMahon. But he immediately bounced back. In 1930, he caught the petroleum bug in B.C.

McMahon's classic promotional technique was to acquire prospective exploration acreage, inject it into a company in return for shares, then sell more shares to raise the cash to drill. The process was long and hard, requiring considerable salesmanship. By 1936, McMahon had spent six years promoting wildcat wells with a lack of success exceptional even for an industry with an abysmal success rate. In that year, however, R.A. (Streetcar) Brown, father of Home Oil's Bobby Brown, brought in Turner Valley Royalties Number 1, thus sparking another Turner Valley oil boom.

After poring over local maps, McMahon found a lease less than a mile from Brown's well, owned by an employee of the

Canadian Pacific Railway who lived near Vancouver. McMahon quickly appeared on the CPR man's doorstep and forked over his last $100 for an option to purchase the lease for $20,000 plus an oil royalty. He then flushed out investors, bought the lease, and incorporated West Turner Petroleums. Despite the success of the Brown well, it took McMahon another eight months to raise the money to start drilling. Finally, on April 1, 1938, with a loan from an Imperial subsidiary called Royalite, McMahon brought in the proverbial gusher, 3,500 barrels a day. Two more successful wells were drilled on the lease, and the following year, West Turner was merged with another local leaseholder, British Pacific Oils, to form Pacific Petroleums, which McMahon then led on an exploration spree in B.C.

For the next eight years, luck eluded McMahon. But when Imperial Oil discovered Leduc in 1947, McMahon returned to Alberta to pursue his Turner Valley strategy, frantically searching for land close to the discovery well. He soon found 160 acres owned by a Scottish-born farmer. The first two wells on the acreage found oil, but the third, Atlantic Number 3, gushed wealth close to McMahon's wildest dreams. Roaring out of control, the well took six months to cap, spewing up to 10,000 barrels of oil and 100 million cubic feet of natural gas a day. Within two months, the well was surrounded by a forty-acre lake of oil.

Far from being a disaster, the black geyser became both a tourist attraction and a useful piece of provincial promotion. The gusher found its way onto cinema newsreels around the world. It also seeded other oil dreams. If it had not been for Atlantic Number 3, Bill Siebens would not have been mad at Maurice Strong thirty years later for trying to butt into his company's efforts in Vietnam. For if it had not been for Atlantic Number 3, Bill Siebens might not have become an oilman.

In 1948, Bill Siebens had come as a boy with his father, Harold, a wealthy owner of a sporting goods store and catalogue business from St. Louis, Missouri, on a family trip to northern Canada and Alaska. When the family's two trucks and trailers hit Edmonton, they camped on the grounds of the Legislative

Building. Alberta Premier Ernest Manning heard about their odyssey and spotted an opportunity to promote both provincial tourism and the booming provincial oil business. He arranged for the family to visit Atlantic Number 3, where, from a safe distance, they marvelled at the roaring black fountain as camera shutters clicked.

The holiday continued, but as Harold drove up the Alaska Highway, he couldn't shift that gusher, and its attendant possibilities, out of his mind. He returned to Calgary, set up an office, and became one of the industry's shrewdest land dealers. When Harold retired in 1959, son Bill took over and proved equally adept at making deals and money, and at spotting when the government was trying to butt into his business.

Frank McMahon eventually had Atlantic Number 3 capped. He had recovered and sold much of the oil lake, and used the money to regain control of Pacific, which had been taken over by more conservative managers. He took the company on another wildcat drilling binge, in northeast B.C. and northwest Alberta. Gas was found in abundance in the Peace River area, but McMahon needed a market, and a big one. He realized that to justify a "big inch" pipeline, he would have to look to the U.S. In a typically profane assessment of Vancouver's market potential, McMahon said: "There's no market for gas there except suicides." On April 30, 1949, Westcoast Transmission was incorporated to build a pipeline.

McMahon's hydrocarbon ambitions were flanked by the two themes of Canadian petroleum development: the inspiration provided by Imperial Oil, and the barriers to private enterprise erected by government in the name of the "public interest." What had inspired McMahon's belief in the potential of the Peace River area of B.C. was the flare from an abandoned Imperial gas discovery. But he had to overcome the perverse opposition of Liberal Premier Duff Pattullo, whose interventionist approach nearly scuttled the pipeline, only to be pressured by the *next* B.C. premier, W.A.C. (Wacky) Bennett, who told him he wasn't getting the line built fast enough.

McMahon had three problems: no export approval, no money, and no pipe. Somehow he persuaded the Royal Bank to lend him $19 million; then he dispatched his genial chief engineer, Charles Hetherington, to England to buy the pipe. Hetherington returned with about fifty miles of pipe and McMahon told him that, in order to keep Bennett happy, he'd better start "burying it." "Right," said Hetherington, "I'll get up to Fort St. John [the northern end of the proposed line] and start at once." "Hell no," Hetherington claims McMahon replied. "Put it down in the Fraser Valley where they can see you digging up the earth!"

Shortly after the gas started flowing down the Westcoast line, McMahon was accused of being a "robber baron." In fact, the Westcoast line was plagued by low prices for gas exports to which it had agreed in order to finance construction, and the gas supplies at Fort St. John rapidly ran out. Ironically, Westcoast was ultimately bailed out by the NDP government of Dave Barrett, which gave it regulated profits for the first time.

McMahon was always larger than life. His compulsive urge to gamble and build brought him great wealth. His homes included a French colonial mansion in Vancouver, a Spanish "cottage" in Palm Beach capable of seating 100 for dinner, and an apartment in New York. He owned a part share — along with Calgary entrepreneur Max Bell and Bing Crosby — in Meadow Court, a winner of the Irish Derby, the Epsom Derby, and the King George VI and Queen Elizabeth Stakes. McMahon also won the Kentucky Derby and Preakness with Majestic Prince. His many other investments included the smash-hit musical *The Pajama Game*.

The tale of Westcoast Transmission was one of constant twists and turns, of gas not being found where it should have been, of adaptations and corporate somersaults, of constant struggle for financing. The whole process was one of dedication, flexibility, originality, and salesmanship, based on the stick of going under and the carrot of personal riches. Eventually McMahon, burned out and ill, was unable to keep all the plates spinning. He always spent more than he earned. His motto was always, "If it's a good idea, the money doesn't matter." The federal government, in the shape of Petrocan, would take the same misguided notion to destructive conclusions.

McMahon drove Pacific into a hole from which Kelly Gibson, at Phillips's behest, had to extricate it. Gibson claimed, "I just worked country-boy style." But Gibson was a hard-driving manager who got results, even if he didn't make many friends in the process. It seemed strange that such a red-blooded free-enterpriser should be the go-between in a government takeover of the companies he'd helped build, but Kelly Gibson had always been obsessed with politics and politicians. He craved a Senate seat. Perhaps he thought guiding Pacific into the hands of Bill Hopper might help him get it.

Once Husky had fallen through, Hopper's gaze quickly turned back to Pacific, which meant further overtures to Gibson and Phillips. Negotiations began in earnest on August 17, 1978, when Hopper first met Phillips chairman Bill Martin. For two and a half months, the two sides hammered away on a price.

Following the Husky débâcle, a much tighter battle plan was adopted. Red Square's internal security was greatly increased; a paper shredder was added to the office equipment. The Petrocan and Phillips executives steered clear of each other's offices. The meeting between Hopper and Martin took place in Kansas City, and later meetings took place in Washington and other cities. Not even Pacific president Merrill Rasmussen knew that the talks had been reopened.

In what must have seemed like the replay of a nightmare, Hopper was horrified when Pacific's shares jumped $7 to $48 on September 26. When Hopper was approached, he flatly denied that Petrocan was doing any buying — the truth, as far as stock trading was concerned. By the beginning of November, the final touches were being put on the deal. Early on November 10, a surprised Rasmussen received a call from Phillips president Bill Douce, telling him the news. Later the same day, in Toronto, the media were summoned to a room in the Hotel Toronto where Alastair Gillespie, blinking into the portable television lights, told them that Petrocan had just bought Phillips's 48 per cent of

Pacific for $671 million and would be making a follow-up offer at the same price for the remainder. The price tag of $1.46 billion made this the biggest takeover in Canadian history to date, indeed one of the largest takeovers at that time in the world. Bill Hopper's corporate reputation had been refurbished, but whether the taxpayers of Canada had been well served was a different matter .

The deal would be financed through a US$1.25-billion issue of preferred shares in the Petrocan subsidiary, Petro-Canada Exploration. The subsidiary was used because preferred shares couldn't have been issued in the main company without parliamentary approval, with which neither Petrocan nor the Cabinet wanted to be bothered. Use of subsidiaries was a classic method for Crown corporations to evade government control, and Petrocan was quick to use it, albeit with Cabinet approval.

A new member of Petrocan's cast of characters who played a significant part in the financing for the Pacific deal was David O'Brien, a tall, measured, aristocratic lawyer from Montreal who had joined Petrocan at the beginning of 1978. O'Brien would go on to play a prominent role in the company for the next decade. Born and raised in Montreal, O'Brien was educated at Loyola College (now part of Concordia) and McGill, where he was a classmate, but not a close friend, of Joel Bell. He eventually joined the Montreal law firm of Ogilvy, Cope, Porteous, Hansard, Marlet, Montgomery & Renault, where another young lawyer named Brian Mulroney was also making a name for himself.

O'Brien had first had dealings with Petrocan during its takeover of Arcan, when he had acted for the Royal Bank of Canada, which had financed the deal. He had impressed Hopper. After ten years as a lawyer, O'Brien was becoming restless. He wanted to branch out into business, so when Petrocan offered him the job of general counsel, reporting to Joel Bell, he decided to take it.

O'Brien had no ideological problem with the Crown corporation. Being from Montreal, where many of the most prominent business organizations — such as Air Canada and CN — were Crown corporations, he accepted the notion of government being in business. The quite different mindset in Calgary, where free enterprise was mixed with Western alienation, came as a surprise to him.

O'Brien had become ill with an intestinal infection not long after he joined Petrocan and had perhaps been fortunate to be in hospital rather than in the middle of the Husky disaster. In the Pacific deal, his relationship with the Royal helped smooth the financing, which was of unprecedented size.

After the deal had been concluded with Phillips, O'Brien had gone to Bell's office and said: "We'd better call the banks now." Bell had replied, "Oh yes, I'll do that. I'll call the president down in Montreal." O'Brien, more attuned to the sensitivities of the business world, had cautioned, "No, it's probably better to call the local guy, and he'll line up the senior people down there."

"Of course," said Bell. He rang the local manager of the Royal and decided to have a little fun. When the manager came on the line, Bell said he'd like to arrange a financing.

"Certainly, Mr. Bell," came the reply. "How much?"

"One and a quarter," said Bell.

"One and a quarter, er," said the hesitant voice at the end of the line, not wishing to be so gauche as to ask "One and a quarter *what?*"

Then Bell unloaded: "One and a quarter billion dollars in U.S. funds."

There was silence at the end of the line. "I suppose you'll have to check that out with Montreal," said Bell, tongue in cheek. Oh the power. That weekend, he and O'Brien flew down to arrange what was then the largest corporate financing in Canadian history.

• • •

Pacific increased Petrocan's size and scope enormously. It made Petrocan the country's seventh-largest oil and liquids producer and its second-largest producer of natural gas. Through its holdings in West Pembina and Elmworth, it brought the state oil company into the heart of Alberta's most exciting exploration plays. Pacific also held extensive tarsands and heavy oil interests, and overseas acreage in the U.S., the Spanish Mediterranean, and the North Sea. It brought coal and uranium holdings, a 10-per-cent interest in a major liquids pipeline, and control of the large gas liquids plant at Empress, Alberta.

Pacific — as a result of the arrangements between McMahon and Phillips — held a 32-per-cent stake in Westcoast Transmission. Intriguingly, this made Petrocan Bob Blair's partner in his proposal to build the Alaska Highway gas pipeline. Taking control of a natural gas pipeline in B.C. appeared to have little to do with energy security, but Hopper's claim that he needed to acquire assets to produce cash flow meant that any business was fair game. B.C.'s premier, Bill Bennett, was strenuously opposed to Petrocan's taking control of Westcoast and tried to force Petrocan to sell its stake. But as usual, Bill Hopper outlasted his political opponents and got what he wanted.

Finally, Pacific brought around 1,100 employees to add to Petrocan's 850. Like the Arcan crew before them, the Pacific employees were none too happy. Those who left immediately included Pacific's top two executives, Merrill Rasmussen and Al McIntosh. Rasmussen went to head the American arm of AGTL-controlled Husky, McIntosh to take over at Consumers Gas–controlled Home Oil, by some strange symmetry, both companies that the government had tried and failed to take over.

During the parliamentary debate on Petrocan in 1974, it had been suggested that it might take ten to fifteen years for the Crown corporation to establish itself as a force in the industry. Instead, via the simple expedient of taxpayer-backed financing, it had taken just three. Moreover, the Crown corporation had now strayed a long way from the cooperative, non-competitive, frontier mandate that Pierre Trudeau had originally peddled. The Husky takeover could be justified as leading to the development of Canada's extensive heavy oil deposits, but where did the acquisition of Pacific fit in?

The answer, or at least the justification, appeared in Petrocan's 1978 annual report: "The fundamental goal of Petro-Canada in proceeding with the acquisition of Pacific Petroleums was to become a significant and balanced presence in Canada's oil and gas industry. The first three years of Petro-Canada's activity and expenditures have been predominantly and disproportionately oriented to high-risk, long-lead-time projects."

But it was Petrocan's mandate to be "disproportionately oriented" to the frontiers. Nowhere did its legislation say that Petrocan was meant to be a "balanced" presence, with, as the annual report declared, "less risky and profitable immediate returns." The Petrocan report tried to play both sides of the fence by stating: "This acquisition...provides a cash flow to help support the longer-term and higher risk frontier exploration and technology development projects which are important for Canada's future energy supplies."

There was an additional rationale for the Pacific takeover. A federal election was approaching, and Petrocan was keenly aware of the belligerent noises coming out of the Conservative Party about dismembering it. It was felt, although not publicly expressed, that one way of ensuring the state oil company's survival was to make it too large to disband; it would rely upon the principle of "survival of the fattest."

This rationale did not appear in an article that appeared in the *Financial Post* under Alastair Gillespie's name in the wake of the Pacific takeover. The article first outlined the extent of foreign ownership in Canada, although no conclusions were drawn from the fact that "91 per cent of the assets and 95 per cent of the sales" in the oil industry were foreign-controlled. The figures were presumed to be argument enough. Gillespie also pointed out that major European countries and Japan had national oil companies, but that the U.S. didn't, because, "after all, five of the seven companies named above are U.S.-controlled."

"How ludicrous it would be," declared the article, "if the Japanese national oil company, wanting to do business in Canada, had to seek as its partner not the national oil company of Canada but the national oil company of some other country." This ludicrousness was not expanded upon.

The key justification read: "If our national oil company is to be able to make a significant contribution to our future energy security, and do so within an industry largely foreign-controlled, then it must be big enough and financially strong enough to take on the kinds of projects that will be vital to our future."

The significance of the industry being "largely foreign-controlled" wasn't clear. How would a Canadian-controlled industry act differently? Also, the notion that Petrocan had to be "big enough and strong enough" to take on those "vital" big projects begged a number of questions. It seemed to assume that big projects were essential, but that they wouldn't be taken on by the foreign-owned oil companies. In fact, the foreign companies had rafts of big projects on the drawing board, and had just brought Syncrude into production.

"There are critics," declared Gillespie, "who have attacked this transaction as nationalization, or anti-free enterprise. I believe that true free enterprisers will reject that argument. They will recognize that it was Petro-Canada's participation in Syncrude, in Panarctic, in farm-ins in Saskatchewan heavy oil, Beaufort Sea drilling, joint ventures in drilling off Labrador and the East Coast, and pipeline studies that has helped to strengthen, not weaken, private enterprise; and with private enterprise to strengthen Canada."

These claims were questionable. Petrocan had merely taken over the stake in Syncrude acquired by Ottawa from the 1974 bail-out. It certainly was picking up more than its fair share of Panarctic's expenditures, but only because other oil companies were pulling out. Dome certainly didn't need Petrocan to promote the Beaufort, although it was more than glad to take its money. Petrocan had given a boost to the East Coast, but it only took taxpayers' money and a political mandate to do that. Whether the exploration actually made sense was quite another matter.

Gillespie declared that the Pacific takeover was "a commercial transaction that did not involve taxpayers' money." That was not true. Since the government guaranteed the financing, it ultimately remained on the hook. Moreover, to imagine that Petrocan's two acquisitions had made it "self-financing" was fantasy. Cash flow consists mostly of allowances against tax to rebuild the assets of a company as they are depleted. If the investment of the cash flow does not retain the overall value of assets, then any company is in the process of self-liquidation, burning the furniture to cook the next meal.

Meanwhile Petrocan had ignored corporate financial reality in presenting the economic rationale to Ottawa for the Pacific takeover. It was essential to suggest that the acquisition would not merely be self-financing, but would generate additional money for frontier exploration. But of course Pacific's financial needs as an ongoing company took no account of having to finance its own acquisition, much less of having to generate spare cash to go running off to the frontiers. The figures Petrocan put forward seriously underestimated Pacific's own cash needs, causing the appearance of "spare" cash. And the government went along.

Petrocan went in, under Hopper's leadership, bustling with self-confidence and convinced that it could make productive use of the assets it had acquired. Looked at in one way, Petrocan can be said to have been trying to save the government from Ottawa's short-sightedness. Hopper realized that Ottawa's interests were short-term. They would want to see results from frontier drilling, but frontier drilling was a long-term proposition. By *not* having to go back year after year for exploration cash, he was trying to get the long-term mandate fulfilled and avoid the possibility that Ottawa would lose interest.

But under a democratic system, whatever its faults, when the government loses interest in a publicly funded activity, that activity should stop. Nobody at Petrocan wanted that. Self-preservation and growth had now become the top priorities to achieve the aim of being a top player in the national energy game. Any government mandate was a constraint rather than a priority. Hopper and Bell had also discovered the fix of big-money power. As one executive said: "It's more fun to run a multi-billion-dollar corporation than a multi-million-dollar corporation."

That was certainly Bill Hopper's philosophy. And as for Joel Bell — well, he'd found that asking for "one and a quarter" provided quite a buzz.

Despite the rationalizations of Alastair Gillespie's article, free enterprise wasn't pacified. Bill Hopper later told a journalist: "People said isn't it *terrible, them* buying Pacific Pete, built on the sweat of good oil men. Well let me tell you, Pacific Pete *grew* on acquisitions." Bill Hopper was missing, or evading, the point. Pacific hadn't made its acquisitions with taxpayers' money. A Calgary entrepreneur perfectly summed up the feelings of the industry: "Pacific was acquired by a government that wouldn't have allowed Frank McMahon to build it in the first place."

EIGHT

Divine Intervention

A SENIOR BUREAUCRAT once suggested that Petro-Canada should have a large portrait of Joe Clark in its boardroom. "Without him," he said, chuckling at the delicious irony, "it might have ended up as just another medium-sized oil company."

Certainly, Clark's promise to dismantle the state oil company when he became prime minister in 1979 provoked a wave of public anguish, which helped convince the Liberals that Petrocan should be the centrepiece of a more interventionist oil policy. But such a policy would likely have emerged without the Clark government's bungling. What ultimately sank Joe Clark was his misfortune in coming to power at the same time as the Ayatollah Khomeini, the man who made the entire world feel in need of a security blanket.

The Shah of Iran had used the fruits of oil wealth to send his country hurtling down the path of Westernization and development. But by 1978, Iranians were losing patience with living in the midst of a corrupt construction site. The more things changed, the more attractive seemed the "old ways" of Islamic fundamentalism.

The thunder-browed Ayatollah Khomeini emerged as the focus of revolutionary sentiment. Expelled from neighbouring

Iraq in October 1978 at the Shah's request, he was given exile in France. There, this enemy of modernization used the telephone and smuggled audiocassettes to disseminate his uncompromising message. By Christmas, strikes had crippled oil production, slashing Iran's exports — once second only to Saudi Arabia's — from 4.5 million barrels a day to zero. "Spot" prices — that is, the price for instantly available oil not under long-term contract — in Europe surged 10 to 20 per cent above official prices. On January 16, 1979, the Shah left Tehran, and two weeks later, Khomeini returned. Shortly after, a cable was sent from the U.S. embassy: "Army surrenders; Khomeini wins. Destroying all classified."

The subsequent surge in oil prices was caused not so much by the withdrawal of Iranian oil as by sheer panic. With the cut-off of Iranian supplies, other producers boosted output, reducing the global shortfall to just 2 million barrels a day in the first quarter of 1979. But this shortfall increased to 5 million barrels a day amid a desperate scramble to build inventories. With the major oil companies no longer ruling global flows, the international system was reduced to a free-for-all.

Normally, a revolution half the world away would not affect Canadian politics, but price increases inevitably had a profound influence on a country that still subsidized the import of 450,000 barrels of oil a day. Canadian prices had been held below world prices since 1973, although they had been allowed to increase gradually. But the eastern part of the country still relied on imports. Before 1973, imported oil had been cheaper than domestic oil. But once OPEC came along, the imports were more expensive, so the government provided a subsidy, paying the oil companies to bring prices down to domestic level. When OPEC prices surged, so did the subsidy burden. Every increase of US$2 a barrel cost an extra $1 million a day. Moreover, the baleful stare of the Ayatollah, a man who was not economically "rational" in any comfortable Western sense, sent shivers down the spines of Canadian consumers.

Coverage of Joe Clark's election campaign in the spring of 1979, during which he flew and bussed across the country presenting his earnest message in schools and community halls, vied on the evening news and the nation's front pages with reports of fraying tempers outside U.S. gas stations. As in 1973/74, the queues were largely due to perverse U.S. government policies: because motorists could not fill their tanks, they went straight back to the end of the line after making their purchases; price controls stopped the higher prices that would have balanced the market; the government's allocation system prevented flexibility and the movement of supplies to where they were needed. But once again, the oil companies took the rap. Exxon's head, Clifton Garvin, appeared on the Phil Donahue show to explain petroleum logistics. Viewers' eyes glazed over.

In the week before and the two weeks after Clark's narrow election victory on May 22, the world spot price doubled. Soon after his victory, Clark himself became a sideshow in the great global oil drama: when Clark made a commitment to move the Canadian embassy in Israel to Jerusalem, the Iraqi National Oil Company threatened to cut off oil to Canada. Clark's backing away from that commitment marked his first painful lesson in the world of oil-fuelled politics. While the debate about Petrocan was meant to take place within the context of a fight against bloated governments and overextended bureaucracies, the electorate saw it as an attempt to disband the nation's only shield against the cold winds of international energy uncertainty.

Oil — and Petrocan — had played some part in the election. In the two weeks before the vote, the company had been conspicuously involved in two exploration successes, one at Sable Island off Nova Scotia and another at Whitefish in the Arctic Islands, which were declared to be of great potential. Tory guru Dalton Camp noted in his book *Points of Departure* that the High Arctic find was "a timely happenstance suggesting divine intervention." Or perhaps that of Jim Coutts.

Indeed, Hopper had been instructed to come up with a discovery in the Far North and had done so. An account of the background to Whitefish appeared in a book called *Quest: Canada's Search for Arctic Oil,* by a prominent Calgary journalist, Tom

Kennedy. Kennedy wrote: "On a whistle-stop tour of the West, Trudeau casually announced that Panarctic had scored the biggest-ever gas find in the Far North. In the bombshell dropped in Vancouver, Trudeau personally took credit for having financed the company through Petro-Canada.

"The prime ministerial insistence on a gas discovery came as a surprise to [Panarctic chief executive Charles] Hetherington. As importantly, it was news to Bill Hopper, by then vice-chairman of Panarctic's board... He was fighting Trudeau's election in the lion's den — in the heart of an antagonistic Canadian oil patch... The astute operator that he was, Hopper knew he had better come up with a gas discovery, and in a hurry. In an election campaign with the heat on down to the wire, and with the Conservatives in the lead, Hopper turned to Hetherington for a show-stopper. He was only obeying orders when Panarctic hurriedly designated ...Whitefish H-63 as the location which redeemed the prime ministerial boast."

In fact, Whitefish H-63 stood in six hundred feet of water, fifteen miles off the west coast of Lougheed Island, less than twelve hundred miles from the North Pole. Panarctic might as well have struck gas on the moon. Nevertheless, Hopper and Hetherington duly presented it to the media as a major gas discovery.

Does it seem the slightest bit plausible that Hopper was "only obeying orders"? Who would have told Trudeau in the first place that there was a find in the Arctic Islands? The Whitefish announcement was not merely obviously politically inspired, it highlighted one of the most fundamental flaws in the Crown corporate concept: in the real world, true national purpose would always and inevitably be subservient to short-term expediency. Hopper was more than a humble servant; he was a willing participant in a transparent scheme to win votes.

Another oil issue in the 1979 campaign was the "Exxon diversion," which enabled Energy Minister Alastair Gillespie to take a pot-shot at the old enemy, Imperial Oil. Following the cut-off of Iranian supplies, Exxon, on the basis of a rational "sharing of the misery," cut back its affiliates' supplies by 7 per cent. Since

Imperial produced three-quarters of its oil in Canada, the cutback amounted to a full quarter of its imports, all of which came from Venezuela, where there had been no supply disruptions.

"It's the principle I still object to," Gillespie told the *Financial Post*. "Imperial gets oil from Venezuela, which hasn't cut back at all. Why should Imperial suffer — why should Canada suffer — shortfalls when there's been no restriction from Venezuela?" Gillespie put heavy pressure on Imperial to deal directly with Venezuela.

Chairman Jack Armstrong, aware that he was walking in a minefield, pointed out: "It is true that Imperial does not receive any Iranian crude and that most of the supplies come from Venezuela. But supposing for a moment the shoe was on the other foot and that it was Venezuelan and not Iranian imports that were affected. If we were buying direct we'd be in real trouble... Exxon gets its supplies from a large number of producing countries, which is safer than relying on a single source."

Armstrong's point was valid, but, as usual, public opinion didn't care. It was easier to go along with the notion of a Big Oil conspiracy, with Petrocan as the Canadian champion — or, as the *Calgary Herald* put it, "an instrument of battle against the foreign-owned Imperial Oil whose parent company, Exxon, diverted Venezuelan oil from Canada after the Iranian crisis."

Hopper basked in the glow of being Canada's energy champion, even if he knew that Jack Armstrong was talking sense and Alastair Gillespie was talking politics. Bill Hopper wanted to preserve Petrocan, and in that he had a great deal of support, both from his more "political" colleagues in the Petrocan executive suite and from the more committed members of the bureaucracy back in Ottawa, who set about subverting the Tories' plans for Petrocan in the name of the public good and their own self-interest. The whole affair looked like a combination of a political Keystone Kops and the British television series *Yes, Minister*, in which the desires of elected politicians are systematically subverted by mandarins who believe they know better.

The Tories believed in laissez-faire and the power of the

market to solve problems. The bureaucrats considered this naive. The PhD economists who manned the upper reaches of the Department of Energy, Mines and Resources had been educated in the shortcomings of the market and believed that a better way was possible. They were concerned, indeed obsessed, by the market's side effects and by political rather than economic issues. They worried about "windfall profits" and "foreign domination." They fretted about Alberta getting richer.

In briefing papers to its new masters, EMR painted a picture of a predatory foreign-controlled oil sector muscling out smaller Canadian companies while spreading its tentacles through diversification. Big Oil's very success was treated as reprehensible. Its inevitable tendency not to move unless commercial conditions were right — as in negotiations over future oilsands plants — was treated as a form of blackmail.

Senior bureaucrats believed that the industry already had more than enough "incentives," so the only way to promote more activity was by direct government intervention. Given "considerable monopolization of supply options," declared a secret paper from EMR delivered in the summer of 1979, the only way to speed up development was through direct involvement or "chosen instruments." Which meant, of course, Petrocan.

The public seemed to agree. A Gallup poll taken in July 1979, two months after Clark's victory, showed that only 22 per cent of Canadians supported selling Petrocan shares; 48 per cent opposed the move. But part of the Tories' conviction as they came to power was that they were not going to be as poll-obsessed as their predecessors. Dalton Camp had called public opinion a "noxious phrase." Polling was regarded as the source of rule by public misconception. Bowing to the polls was seen as an indication of a lack of resolve, an absence of moral fibre. Which would have been admirable but for one fact: the Tories were a minority government. They didn't have the votes to pursue unpopular policies.

Allan Gregg, the Tories' brilliant but unlikely pollster, a man who wore jeans and sported long hair and an earring, warned the party of its potential problems with its Petrocan policy, as Jeffrey

Simpson pointed out in his book *Discipline of Power.* "Our action," he said, "is being presented through the opposition and the media as fuelling the uncertainties of the future. In other words, in the face of an impending 'energy crisis' and excessive profits by multinational companies, we are seen to be dismantling the only *Canadian* entity standing between the people and the problem. We must therefore, when explaining these changes to Petro-Canada, present something more than a knee-jerk commitment to free enterprise."

But shutting down Petrocan came to be seen increasingly as a test of the Tories' policy resolve as they were criticized for policy reversals elsewhere. Clark's inner Cabinet — Jim Gillies, Lowell Murray, and Bill Neville — also saw it as a test of their ability to overcome the resistance of the bureaucracy.

The Tories had known they would be faced by foot-dragging when they came to power, and they were determined to act decisively. Even before he had requested EMR and other departments to review "the immediate privatization of Petro-Canada," Ray Hnatyshyn, in one of his first acts as energy minister, sent a letter to Bill Hopper, instructing him to reverse the steps he had taken to absorb Pacific Petroleums.

The Tories could see that one of the unspoken rationales for buying Pacific had been to make Petrocan too large to disband. Petrocan had just informed Pacific's creditors that it had applied, under the Canada Business Corporations Act, to dissolve Pacific and fold it financially into Petro-Canada Exploration. The Tories wanted to stop the egg going into the omelette.

In fact, it wasn't that simple. The money for the acquisition had already been raised through the sale of preferred shares, which had to be serviced. To pay the dividends, Petrocan had to gain access to Pacific's cash flow. At this point, Pacific's absorption was a legal and financial requirement; it would not really affect whether Petrocan could be disbanded. Those most concerned by the Tories' instructions were the banks who had provided Petrocan with the money to buy Pacific.

The Tories wanted to put everything on hold, but it wasn't

possible to put running a company on hold. Pacific's senior executives had taken off. Andy Janisch had to go over secretly to Pacific's headquarters to review plans and sign expenditure authorizations. The Tories were reluctantly persuaded to allow the takeover to proceed. Nevertheless, on June 21, Clark's closest advisors asked EMR to undertake "an extensive and detailed review" of the immediate privatization of Petrocan. What they received two months later was a policy document telling them that such a move was, for a complex collection of legal, financial, and political reasons, impossible.

The study's author was David Scrim. Scrim was knowledgeable and had been one of Petrocan's first employees. He had returned to Ottawa because his wife didn't like Calgary. Scrim firmly believed in a national oil company. The paper he produced two months later was a masterpiece of tendentious reasoning, based on liberal-interventionist assumptions that in much of Ottawa were considered unquestionable. Sir Humphrey would have been proud.

It began by noting that Clark's policy was out of step with the rest of the world. "The role of state corporations," it declared, "has become an almost universal element of energy management both to combat the concentration of power in the hands of a relatively few multinationals as well as to provide an alternative to other more direct government stimulative action and to promote a better understanding of energy operations."

If the government wanted to accelerate heavy oil and tarsands development — the only way, the report claimed, to reach self-sufficiency by 1990 — then it could only do so through an instrument such as Petrocan. As for the frontiers, Petrocan had done a sterling job. It would be possible to provide further incentives to the private sector instead, but "with no control and without the benefits of future profits to compensate the initial risk undertaken."

With the exception of Alberta and B.C., continued the report, the provinces favoured Petrocan. The industry too, although its initial reaction was hostile, now "actually supports Petro-Canada on the grounds that they are an attractive partner for financing purposes and on the basis that if government is to be actively involved they prefer dealing with a corporate rather than a bureaucratic entity."

Then there was the public. "The general public tends to have a distrust of large multinational enterprises and a concern over the wealth distribution accruing to producing provinces. As a result it is almost certain that the concept of a government energy corporation has the general support of most Canadians. A recent Gallup poll indicated that Canadians were in favour of Petro-Canada being maintained by more than a two to one majority."

The "window on the industry" would be lost. "Petro-Canada's management and operating personnel have, on a number of occasions, provided timely and important advice on energy policy issues." The document didn't say which ones.

Scrim moved on to demolish the privatization alternatives. Selling to foreign interests would exacerbate the problem of foreign ownership. Restricting the sale to Canadian buyers would mean a lower price, and any purchaser would offset his costs against taxes, thus reducing the government "take." Moreover, a sale of assets would take place in a "fire sale atmosphere." The cash used to take over the company would be "diverted from the search for and development of new resources." (Just as the money used by Petrocan to buy Arcan and Pacific had been "diverted.")

A share sale? That avenue was blocked, according to the document, by a tangle of legal and financial problems. "It is clear that the pursuit of such an option would require a highly technical review of the existing corporate entities as well as the consultative assistance of financial intermediaries." Complexity, of course, is meat and drink to the bureaucrat, but in the case of a sale of Petrocan, it was just too much to contemplate. The issue would be too huge; the market would place a discount on the shares.

What about retaining Petrocan but cutting off its special status as a Crown corporation? No way. Then its government-backed debts of $1.7 billion might have to be repaid, with possible "serious financial implications for the government and/or the corporation."

What about a partial privatization? This alternative held some appeal for Scrim, in particular the notion of selling off some of Petrocan's assets. He suggested selling the pipelines, foreign producing properties, and refining and marketing assets acquired with Pacific. "None of these assets appear to have an essential function in terms of assisting Petro-Canada to fulfill its policy mandate."

Slipping into the language with which bureaucrats persuade their masters that their "servants'" ideas are their own, the document declared: "There seems no reason to question our party's commitment to privatize Petro-Canada. What this means specifically in terms of assets which go into the private sector and those which should be retained in some public body for strategic reasons is still a question."

But of course the Tories hadn't asked about which assets should be "retained" by the Crown corporation because they didn't want the Crown corporation retained. Nevertheless, Scrim's report implied that the retention of a "public body" was unquestionable. The document's suggested options all foresaw the sale of some assets but the continued existence of Petro-Canada.

When Clark's advisors saw the report, they blew their tops. They had asked for a review of privatization and received a recommendation to sell unnecessary assets. Petrocan's survival was regarded as beyond debate. The Tory inner Cabinet decided they had to show the bureaucrats who was boss.

When the full Tory Cabinet assembled at Jasper in August, they were told by pollster Gregg that the people thought they were not keeping their promises. Ironically, some took this as a sign to keep the one promise for which the people had no enthusiasm: the privatization of Petrocan. But opposition was growing within the Cabinet. Ray Hnatyshyn had been converted by his bureaucrats. John Crosbie and Flora MacDonald, having recently been exposed to the full blast of global energy concerns at a meeting of the OECD in Paris, now believed Petrocan was necessary. Others thought the poll's message about Petrocan's popularity more important than the call to stick to promises. But the Tories were determined to show their resolve. They appointed a task force.

• • •

If Joe Clark's portrait should be in the Petrocan boardroom, then the members of the Petro-Canada Task Force deserve at least miniatures. The chairman was Donald McDougall, who had recently left the presidency of Labatt's Breweries after a reported conflict with Labatt's chief executive Peter Widdrington. McDougall knew little about oil, but he was a businessman, a loyal Tory, and a friend of Clark advisor Lowell Murray. The other key members of the committee were Ross Sykes, a chartered accountant from Halifax and another devoted party worker; Roland Giroux, a powerful Quebec businessman with strong Tory connections; and Syd Kahanoff, a Calgary oilman who had built Voyageur Petroleums from nothing and reaped $55 million from its sale in 1978.

Investment houses Dominion Securities, Burns Fry, and McLeod, Young, Weir were signed up to give financial advice. Two other key figures were Paul Little, a business executive and party worker who acted as the group's executive director, and Ralph Hedlin, a Toronto-based oil consultant, who wrote most of the report.

The group had a big job — primarily to work out how to privatize Petrocan — and a short time to do it, but they started with an almost euphoric sense of purpose. McDougall even talked about getting out the report ahead of the deadline. The Petro-Canada Task Force set up twin headquarters at EMR's offices on Ottawa's Booth Street and in Red Square, where they were greeted with all the joy that the receivers would have attracted. Nevertheless, they were not treated with discourtesy. Indeed, some executives seemed positively glad to see them. Don Wolcott thought that Petrocan's internal politics and relations with Ottawa were so much bullshit, and said so. He thought ditching Hopper and Bell was a good idea. He thought he might make a good chief executive himself. Bill Hopper just bent over backwards to be obliging; he was very keen to keep his job whether Petrocan was in the public or private sector. Joel Bell's presentation to the task force on

Petrocan's achievements was considered a *tour de force.*

Some of the EMR bureaucrats were a little more outspoken in their views. They treated the task force to their opinions on the *important* energy questions: the structural side effects of higher prices — Big Oil and Alberta getting too rich. But these views cut little ice with men like Kahanoff, who understood the industry, understood markets, and above all understood the powerful positive role that foreign investment had played in developing Alberta.

When members of the task force met the Petrocan board, they noticed an inevitable chilliness. Tommy Shoyama couldn't contain himself. He didn't say that privatization was dumb, but he repeatedly questioned the whole concept. All Don McDougall could say was: "Well, that's not our mandate; we're not here to decide *whether* we should do it, we're here to see how we should do it." John Aird and Don Harvie, two of the "business" directors, smoothed things over and kept the temperature down, but the public servants could hardly contain their belief that the whole concept just hadn't been thought through properly. These Tories just didn't know what they were doing.

The task force offended the most powerful and independent board member, Bud Willmot, by its lack of consultation. Willmot believed the Clark government was primarily trying to find ways to embarrass its Liberal predecessors by uncovering examples of rash public spending. He also believed that privatizing the Crown corporation was ill-advised, not primarily for ideological reasons, but because it was so heavily in debt; it was unsaleable. But the task force could not consider any option but privatization.

Willmot took umbrage. He was no Liberal hack. He took his board responsibilities very seriously. If a board member was allowed no input, Willmot believed, then he had no place on the board, and so he resigned with effect from November 1979, sending stinging letters to the prime minister and other Cabinet members. Willmot thought the other directors should have resigned with him, or at least spoken out. In the event, Aird went off the board in December for unrelated reasons, but Mann and Hébert stayed on.

The task force met with a number of groups who couldn't wait for Petrocan to be broken up. B.C. Premier Bill Bennett was keen to acquire the stake in Westcoast Transmission, and Westcoast, for its part, was dying to get out from under Petrocan. Anthony Hampson, the independent-minded head of Walter Gordon's brainchild, the CDC, wanted to start rolling Petrocan into his organization straight away. Calgary entrepreneurs came forward to bid for Petrocan's gas stations.

But Petrocan also received support from some very unlikely quarters. Former Alberta premier Ernest Manning, now a senator, spoke out in its favour, as did Carl Nickle, long a spokesman of Canada's independent petroleum industry. Perhaps the most surprising support came from Jack Armstrong, the chairman of Imperial Oil, who declared he could live with Petrocan as it was. Some Conservatives considered that a stab in the back.

Oil companies, particularly the foreign-owned multinationals, saw Petrocan as a useful source of exploration financing. Bill Hopper had convinced them that he was educating Ottawa into the ways of the oil industry. Some began to see that having Petrocan as a partner in a project like Syncrude would make it easier to explain the project's difficulties to Ottawa. Perhaps Petrocan really could prove a useful "window." But the task force pressed on to write its report, its course already set.

The day before the report was due to be tabled in the House, it was leaked to NDP leader Ed Broadbent, who took it public. He portrayed it as a recommendation simply to destroy the nation's security blanket. That was all a public still spooked by the prospect of energy shortages needed to hear.

The report was couched in laissez-faire terms that seemed distinctly out of kilter with public perceptions of Big Oil conspiracies and madmen holding the world to ransom. Within a month, the U.S. embassy in Iran came under siege and the hostage crisis began. This did not appear to be a time to leave things to the market. Fine points about the non-viability of Petro-Canada's dual role as a profit maker and a policy instrument were too subtle for an electorate who thought Petrocan stood between them and fundamentalist bogeymen.

The task force's recommendation was for Petro-Canada to be split into two parts, one a private company called Petro-Canada, the other a government agency, which would essentially do the dirty work of frontier and technological development, and undertake the "non-commercial" parts of Petrocan's mandate. The broad sweep of the proposals was that everything likely to cause a cash drain should be dumped on the government and ultimately the taxpayer.

The report sought the worst of all worlds, since it maintained the notion that the government *should* continue to be directly involved in the energy business. As for the privatization of Petrocan's more attractive parts, that would be achieved simply by giving the company away to Canadian citizens.

The report was ridiculed by Ed Broadbent and publicly attacked by Ontario Premier Bill Davis. The mandarins quietly shook their heads. Don McDougall was dispatched to do a round of coast-to-coast talk shows to sell the concept. Ray Hnatyshyn and Michael Wilson were deputed to head a Cabinet committee to rescue something from the mess.

As it happened, the Clark government was defeated in the Commons and thrust into a new election campaign before it had time to stage its final *volte-face* on Petro-Canada. Ironically, according to a story in the *Financial Post,* on the afternoon of December 13, as Clark's government was facing a vote of no confidence, an Alberta member of Clark's caucus, renowned for his opposition to the Crown corporation, was visiting Red Square, where he was royally wined and dined. By the end of the afternoon, the MP was drunk and had missed his flight. Hopper offered him a ride on one of the corporate jets, but his arrival wasn't enough to save the Tories.

In the first week of the election campaign, Clark revealed his "final" Petro-Canada policy, a Frankenstein monster stitched together from ill-fitting limbs of public policy, political expediency, and a rump of obeisance to the market. Half its shares would be given away, another 20 per cent sold, and the remaining 30 per cent held by the government. The Tories would "contract" with the company to engage in country-to-country oil trade, non-commercial frontier exploration, and research and development. The monster would not only be as big and powerful as before, it would be even bigger.

The Tories had been nineteen points behind the Liberals in the polls even before the December budget that brought down the government. For the Conservatives, the combination of a minority government, a budget proposing an 18-cent-a-gallon increase in gasoline prices, and an electorate incapable of looking beyond its next visit to the gas pump proved disastrous. Those who understood energy knew that the 18-cent-a-gallon increase was due to the surge in world oil prices and the resultant much higher subsidies for Canadian import; but the Liberals brilliantly, and cynically, portrayed it as Tory heartlessness. They knew that all they had to do was go through the motions of a campaign and let the momentum of Clark's unpopularity carry him over the brink.

Pierre Trudeau, who had announced his resignation to a tearful Liberal caucus on November 21, 1979, was persuaded to return and lead the party once more. He maintained his personal political agenda of keeping Quebec within Confederation — an issue of growing importance as the 1980 referendum drew near—and patriating the Constitution. But those issues, as Trudeau's key advisors knew, were not "sexy" politics. The Liberals knew they had to have at least one specific policy in an area of widespread concern and interest. The choice was obvious: energy. Their thrust, in the wake of overwhelming support for Petrocan, also appeared clear: it was time for more economic nationalism.

NINE

The Fenestral Fallacy

THE CONCEPT of a "window on the industry" had been one of the most politically appealing rationales for Petro-Canada. The industry had had a reputation for secrecy extending back to the days of John D. Rockefeller and the muckrakers. In some ways, oil needed to be a secretive business. Exploration involved drilling and then keeping results under wraps for as long as possible while you accumulated acreage around any find. Land acquisition was often carried out through third parties so as not to arouse suspicion.

The tendency of the exploration branch of the industry to play its cards close to its vest fed a paranoid fear in Ottawa that the industry as a whole was manipulating information about Canada's reserves. In fact, the industry's intensely competitive nature meant that nothing stayed secret for long. Every company employed scouts to roam the oilfields, peering through binoculars at exploration sites, looking for telltale traces of oil or gas. The faintest whiff of petroleum always found its way to aggressive entrepreneurs. One man with enough chutzpah could always muscle his way into even the biggest company's exploration play, as Frank McMahon had done at Leduc. Nevertheless, a significant part of the supposed "need to know" was the belief that the *real* reserves picture, particularly about the frontiers, wasn't being revealed by Big Oil. You couldn't creep up on offshore rigs.

This belief was fed by the industry's visionaries and promoters, who muddied the reserve outlook with their claims of huge undiscovered deposits. Cam Sproule of Panarctic and Jack Gallagher of Dome conjured up alluring visions in order to pull in not just private investors and other companies but the federal government, through direct investment or tax breaks.

Cam Sproule had painted a picture of corporate conspiracy to willing Ottawa listeners like Jack Austin in the 1960s in order to gain public finance to drill the Arctic Islands. Jack Gallagher had used a more purely geological dream to persuade Ottawa to grant huge tax breaks for Beaufort drilling. Ironically, Petrocan didn't believe in Jack Gallagher's Beaufort dreams, but its views were discounted by Ottawa as sour grapes.

The fact that Ottawa wasn't prepared to listen to Petrocan's doubts about Dome raised critical questions about the window. It established that policy-makers only looked through it when they felt inclined, or saw the parts of the picture they found acceptable. Indeed, some of those who wanted the window, in particular the NDP, really desired an exercise in stained glass, with a colourful and dramatic portrayal of Petrocan as St. George, killing the many-headed conspiratorial dragon of Big Oil, sitting in its lair on a pile of windfall profits. What else was there to see?

The window analogy was deeply flawed. For a start, it assumed that you couldn't understand something without *being* it, or at least possessing it. Professor David Quirin of the University of Toronto had suggested in a 1976 paper that a sufficient understanding of the oil industry might be obtained with "sixty books of bus tickets to the Ottawa Public Library, and a few thousand dollars' book purchase grants to that worthy institution." He noted that since there were only twenty or thirty key policy-makers who needed to be "educated" about energy, Petrocan was "the most expensive educational program undertaken in Canada's history."

The fundamental flaw of the window analogy — what might

be called the "fenestral fallacy" — was the idea that a simple frame could in some way present a "real" and undistorted picture of a complex and changeable scene.

A person may decide that it would be nice to have a "window" on astrophysics or the Dutch language or skydiving. He hires people to read Stephen Hawking, study Linguaphone, and jump off hillsides. They will return, having learned to understand quarks, order a meal in Amsterdam, and experience an adrenaline rush. But unless they can explain what they have learned, in a way that allows others to absorb it themselves, the contractor will be none the wiser.

At least astrophysics, Dutch, and skydiving are essentially value-neutral. Imagine the results of hiring a "window on capitalism." There is no one simple "view" of such a complex topic. The view will depend on the window. An academic left-winger will return from his studies with a very different view from a businessman. There is no avoiding the filter of underlying beliefs.

With a window on the oil industry, there is enormous scope for bias, and an obvious danger of self-interest. Because the Crown corporation employed many people who shared the Trudeau government's interventionist mindset, businessmen would rightly complain that Petrocan's "view" had already been decided. On the other hand, Petrocan did operate in the real world, and as it absorbed the realities of doing business, its view moved towards that of its fellow oil companies. Then it became an object of suspicion in Ottawa.

Meanwhile, those in Ottawa receiving the "picture" could only view it with their own preconceptions or misconceptions. If they were shrewd, they would realize that Petrocan's strongest bias would be in favour of its own position. The window would first and foremost be concerned that it was well painted and maintained, expanded, and hung with the finest drapery.

In the end, the cosy notion of the clear "view" would turn into a constantly changing kaleidoscope that depended on the preconceptions and perceived self-interests both of Petrocan's senior management and of Ottawa's relevant politicians, policy advisors, and bureaucrats. The form and effectiveness of the window inevitably came down to the personalities and views of the individuals looking out or looking in.

The greatest test of the window — of Petrocan's effectiveness as a policy advisor — was the most significant energy initiative in Canadian history, the National Energy Program. The NEP was an unmitigated disaster. Its only beneficiary was Petro-Canada.

· · ·

Petrocan's year of uncertainty during the Clark government's brief reign coincided with a spectacular oil boom. With the great OPEC-induced price surge, oilmen's lives took on the aura of tabloid glamour. *Dallas's* J.R. Ewing replaced the benign image of Jed Clampett and the Beverly Hillbillies. In Calgary and the other great North American oil centres — Dallas, Houston, Denver, and Tulsa — real-life J.R.s sprang to prominence, riding to sudden wealth and glory. Some of them were real oil-finders, but the most important element in their wealth was the soaring value of the petroleum they already possessed or knew where to find. Many of them made their fortunes in natural gas.

In Canada, behind the politically "blessed triumvirate" of Petrocan, Dome, and AGTL, came a posse of entrepreneurs who were growing like crazy. They were less interested in politics than in the rush of the game, less in organization charts than in seismic maps, less in nationalism than in doing deals.

Most were hard-working and talented geologists or drillers or pipeliners who found themselves in the right place at the right time. They came in all shapes, sizes, and temperaments: big, wry Americans like J.C. Anderson at Anderson Exploration; swaggering Dutchmen like Gus Van Wielingen at Sulpetro; canny little Scotsmen like "Wee Bobby" Lamond at Czar Resources; reticent former Saskatchewan farmboys with vise-like handshakes like Daryl K. (Doc) Seaman and his brothers B.J. and Don at Bow Valley Industries; exploration and promotion "teams" like the cerebral American geologist John Masters and his dynamic alter ego Jim Gray at Canadian Hunter.

Calgary's petroleum entrepreneurs did not find the appellation "blue-eyed sheiks" offensive. During the 1970s, oil wealth had become more firmly associated than ever with the Arab burnoose, usually seen sweeping from Rolls-Royces to OPEC meetings in Vienna or Jedda. The most photographed burnoose belonged to Saudi oil minister Sheik Ahmed Zaki Yamani. Far from sinister, the urbane Yamani seemed the voice of reason: since petroleum was depleting, price increases could only be for our own good. It was a message Albertans liked to hear.

The balance sheets of the home-grown Alberta sheiks were still dwarfed by those of the Canadian subsidiaries of Big Oil, but most of Calgary's petroleum entrepreneurs were a lot richer personally than their corporate counterparts, and a whole lot more colourful. Moreover, it seemed, they were the shape of things to come. Dome, AGTL, and Petrocan in particular were governments' "chosen instruments" (Dome and Petrocan by Ottawa, AGTL by Edmonton). They saw themselves taking on the majors sooner rather than later.

Calgary seemed to be filled with men creating a mythology of success of which the whole nation — a nation badly in need of sustaining myths — could be proud. The denizens of Canada's oil and gas capital saw themselves as visionaries. After all, Toronto bankers came offering virtually open vaults; German tax money sat in a holding pattern above Calgary airport; drilling funds were just a phone call away. The majors, concerned by OPEC nationalizations and the belligerent noises of Third World countries, turned to Canada as a "safe" source of supply. The smaller sheiks had the pleasure of seeing charter members of the Seven Sisters come cap in hand to farm in to *their* properties. Such had been the experience of Canadian Hunter, which had been delighted to accept a huge chunk of exploration cash from Imperial Oil.

Between 1973 and 1980, the average wellhead price — that is, the price before transportation costs — for crude oil in western Canada had risen from $3.40 to $15.41 per barrel. The price of natural gas had risen even more spectacularly, from 17 cents a thousand cubic feet to $2.20. The impact on exploration was enormous. Total net cash expenditures of the petroleum industry in Alberta rose from $1.5 billion in 1973 to $11.5 billion in 1980. Bonus payments at the province's land sales rocketed from $76 million in 1973 to more than $1 billion in 1980. The number of wells drilled in western Canada, mostly in Alberta, more than doubled between 1973 and 1980.

With the second OPEC crisis, Canadian prices had fallen farther behind world prices than ever before. It seemed the process was about to start all over again: Canadian prices would follow world prices; Alberta and Canadian oil companies would enjoy a further surge of revenues and profits. Another tidal wave of wealth appeared headed for that bustling breed of explorationists and promoters who'd done so well out of the 1970s.

Moreover, as the Tories were going down to parliamentary defeat in December 1979, Calgary was abuzz with news of a major oil find off the East Coast at a location called Hibernia, on the Grand Banks, 200 miles northeast of St. John's, Newfoundland. The find seemed to confirm Petrocan's — and the Liberal government's — wisdom in promoting frontier exploration, despite the minor detail that the find had been made by Chevron Canada, the subsidiary of Standard Oil of California. Petrocan's 1979 annual report, which appeared after the Tories had tumbled to defeat and the Liberals had returned, declared: "In retrospect, 1979 may well be considered a turning point in Canadian frontier exploration." The Hibernia find appeared to put the icing on the cake.

But Sheik Yamani was deeply disturbed by the price increases of 1979 and 1980. He had always proposed small, regular increases in order to forestall huge, destabilizing ones. Indeed, in June 1978, while on a visit to Alberta, during which he appeared to speak to Premier Lougheed very much as one sheik to another, Yamani gave a scholarly dissertation to the Canadian Society of Petroleum Geologists in Calgary. He said that a world oversupply would continue to exert downward pressure on prices into the early 1980s. One of the reasons Yamani visited the Alberta tarsands was to learn more about their economics. He regarded them as a potentially huge source of supply, and thus a rival to his own oil. Yamani had always preached moderation because he knew that raising the OPEC price too high would simply encourage alternative sources of oil and other forms of energy.

Within eighteen months of Yamani's Calgary speech, the official price had doubled. Yamani's understanding of petroleum economics was sound, but unforeseen political events and panic buying had changed the timing. When OPEC met at Caracas in December 1979, Yamani said: "Political decisions cannot permanently negate the divine laws of supply and demand. Prices go up, and demand goes down, it's simple, it's A-B-C." Later he said: "There will be a glut in the market. It is coming."

Politics continued to overshadow economics. Gloom was heightened by the disastrous attempt to rescue the American hostages from Iran in April 1980. Yamani tried to restrain OPEC in June 1980 in Caracas, but to no avail. OPEC's Long Range Strategy Committee talked about plans for a 10-to-15-per-cent annual increase to bring the price to $60 a barrel within five years.

In the meantime, the lessons of the Tories' failed energy policy initiatives were not lost on the Liberals. They returned to power promising lower energy prices than the Tories, "Canadianization" of the oil business, and energy security through self-sufficiency. The promise of lower prices was quickly abandoned in the face of economic reality and bureaucratic advice. But the more general nationalist thrust and the strengthening of Petrocan were warmly embraced by the most powerful politicians, party policy-makers, and bureaucrats.

By the fall of 1980 these vague notions had been transformed, with the aid of a fiercely committed group of backroom policy advisors and public servants, into one of the most revolutionary policies in Canadian history. With the return of the Liberals, EMR became, once again, the "place to be" in Ottawa, just as it had been during those tense times in 1973, when policy was being made on the run in the face of the first OPEC crisis. Now the men at the top were even more forceful, and more cerebral, than they had been then. They could also be very persuasive.

The second coming of EMR could be traced to the arrival at the department in April 1978 of Marshall (Mickey) Cohen as deputy minister. A forty-three-year-old Toronto lawyer, Cohen had clearly established himself in Ottawa as a high flyer in the Department of Finance. He had practised law for ten years in Toronto when he was brought to Ottawa in 1970 to be a special tax advisor. In 1971, he had become the department's assistant deputy minister of tax policy. Three years later, he was given the responsibility for federal-provincial relations; he had played a key role in the heated negotiations with Alberta over oil pricing in 1974.

Both Pierre Trudeau and Michael Pitfield had been impressed by Cohen. It wasn't just his brain power. His unassuming and affable style enabled him to slip easily into the key policy group around the prime minister. He demonstrated an uncanny ability to handle bureaucratic egos and territorial jealousies, both within Ottawa and when dealing with the provinces. Smooth, brilliant, articulate, he was described by a colleague at Finance as "Trudeau's type of guy."

Cohen's move to EMR in 1978 had indicated that the department's policy star was once again in the ascendant. (He left briefly in 1979 to become deputy minister at Industry, Trade and Commerce, but the returning Liberals brought him back to EMR in 1980.) He brought from Finance many of the key players who would lay the groundwork for, and then write, the NEP. The most important of these was a man who would achieve almost demonic status for the oil patch, Edmund Clark. Of all the public servants connected with the NEP, none was to become better known than Clark. He was to be seen, particularly in Alberta, as the epitome of Ottawa's anti-business, interventionist bias.

Clark had studied economics at the University of Toronto, then gone to Harvard for his master's and PhD. During 1972 and 1973, he was a team leader of the University of Toronto Tanzania project. His doctoral thesis, "Public Investment and Socialist Development in Tanzania," became the best-known academic dissertation in the oil patch. In the wake of the NEP, photocopies appeared all over Calgary, with passages marked in yellow highlighter. "The study," read one such passage, "is seen as part of the larger effort by scholars everywhere to turn their attention to the issue of how to build socialist societies. It is my belief that socialist scholars in particular should devote more of their energy to analysing the problems of socialist societies and the problems of the transition to socialism, and somewhat less to criticizing capitalist societies. While anti-capitalist critiques can take us part way towards understanding how to build a socialist reality, they are not sufficient."

Such views and the desire to "build a socialist reality" were not particularly radical in the scholarly world at that time. Clark was a product of the post-Vietnam and Watergate era, when the espousal of left-wing "alternatives" flourished amid an academic community profoundly critical of the society that funded it. An active member of Harvard's Union for Radical Political Economists, Clark was remembered by colleagues as a forceful proponent of left-wing views who brooked no contradiction. His move to the Department of Finance in 1974 surprised some of his former academic colleagues, one of whom said: "I expected to find him leading a revolution somewhere in the jungle rather than sitting in an office in Finance." From the beginning, Clark impressed people. He had all the latest buzzwords and analytical concepts. Most of all, he had ideas, one of the currencies — the other being naked power — in which Ottawa counts a man's worth.

Clark first came to prominence in Ottawa at the time of the Anti-Inflation Board. The concept of wage and price controls — a key tenet of Galbraithian political economy — was easy enough; it was implementation that posed the problem. Clark came up with many of the answers as deputy director general of the Price and Profits Branch of the board, where he served during 1975 and part of 1976. Significantly, Joel Bell and Ian Stewart — from Jack Austin's original energy team — and Mickey Cohen had all been involved in the formulation and implementation of the AIB program. At that time, it was the place to be.

Clark returned to Finance in 1976 as director of the Long-Range and Structural Analysis Division. There, he got to know Cohen better. When Cohen moved to EMR, he brought Clark with him. When Cohen moved over to Industry, Trade and Commerce in 1979, the deputy ministership at EMR was taken over by Ian Stewart. Again, there was a powerful meeting of the minds between Clark and Stewart; both were brilliant academic economists, and both leaned heavily towards interventionism.

The analytical documents that emerged from Clark and Stewart's EMR during the Tory interregnum were very critical of previous Liberal policies. They implied that the Liberals had effectively given away the farm to Big Oil and Alberta. The bureaucrats had very firm ideas about energy policy, which happened to coincide now with the Liberals' more emotional predilections, in particular the economic nationalism of the Walter Gordon school, which had a number of staunch advocates in the Prime Minister's Office. The most important of these were Jim Coutts, the Harvard-trained Machiavelli who was regarded as the high priest of "pragmatic" poll-driven politics, and Tom Axworthy, who had followed Coutts as head of the PMO.

The political battering ram who would force through this policy was Energy Minister Marc Lalonde, an archetypical Trudeaucrat who combined cold logic with Gallic charm and a forceful personality. Lalonde was already the Liberals' energy critic when the Tories fell. If there was to be a new policy that required getting tough with both the industry and the producing provinces, then he was the man to implement it.

Lalonde's roots — ninth-generation farming stock from Île Perrot, west of Montreal — were very different from those of Pierre Trudeau, but he had had a long association with the prime minister. A lawyer by training, he had been a policy advisor to Lester Pearson and had helped persuade Trudeau to run for the leadership in 1968. After Trudeau had swept to power, Lalonde became principal secretary in the PMO. During his four years at the PMO he developed his skill and reputation as a political expediter, the man who could make things happen. He had entered Parliament in 1972 as the member for Outremont and had been at the heart of Trudeau's complex Cabinet committee system ever since.

Lalonde's relationship with Trudeau was not so much a

friendship as an alliance in a number of common causes: the fight against Quebec separatism, the promotion of "social justice," and the rule of reason. Lalonde shared with Trudeau a lack of sympathy with business, based on a sense of intellectual superiority and the anti-business liberal sentiments they had drunk in with their academic educations. As Richard Gwyn wrote in *The Northern Magus*: "Interventionism… came naturally to Trudeau because he has scant respect for the entrepreneurial ability of Canadian businessmen, and a great deal of respect for the ability of his government and himself."

Lalonde believed the government had made a mistake in taking as much notice of business's views as it had in the 1970s. In his opinion, this was part of the reason why the Liberals were looking back at eleven years without significant achievement. Petro-Canada was one of the few Liberal creations that had emerged as unqualified popular successes; and yet, if business had been listened to, the Crown corporation would never have been created. Lalonde favoured a strategy of choosing a course and then sticking to it, not listening to the carping self-interest of the business community.

Unlike Trudeau, whose intellect drove him to indecision, Lalonde was iron-willed once he had a task laid out before him. His years in the PMO had honed his skills as fixer to Trudeau the philosopher. Once he was convinced of the fundamental rightness of what he was doing, the combination of his charisma, his ego, and his knowledge of the Ottawa system formed a powerful mixed metaphor: a kamikaze juggernaut, prepared if necessary to sacrifice himself for the greater good of the nation and the party. Not surprisingly, his appointment to the energy portfolio made the more perceptive members of the Alberta government and the oil industry nervous.

Bill Hopper and Joel Bell went out of their way to oblige Lalonde. One of their more troubling offers was to put Lalonde's executive assistant, Michael Phelps, on the Crown corporation's payroll in June 1980, then immediately second him to the energy minister.

Phelps, a lawyer by training, had worked for Lalonde before in Justice. Bright and affable, Phelps was well regarded in both the bureaucracy and the oil industry. But taking a salary from Petrocan, as well as subsidized mortgages on his Ottawa house, appeared a very clear conflict of interest. As executive assistant to Lalonde, he had a constant stream of confidential information on oil companies coming across his desk. How could he keep this information from his "employer"?

When the details of the arrangement were dug up by *Globe and Mail* investigative reporter Peter Moon in October 1981, they provoked a good deal of negative comment. Canadian Hunter's Jim Gray called it "another horrible example of blatant abuse of power at the public's expense." Former energy minister Ray Hnatyshyn said, "The thing's a sham. It's obviously a subterfuge to get around the Treasury Board limitation on maximum salaries. If Lalonde would have us believe this is anything but hanky-panky, he'd have us believe in the tooth fairy." John Porter, managing director of the Independent Petroleum Association of Canada, said, "You know, Mike's a nice guy, but if he's never worked a day for Petro-Canada how can he be seconded to Lalonde's office?"

Phelps admitted that Bill Hopper had been involved in the arrangement, but Hopper "could not be reached for comment." Petrocan's public relations man, Bob Foulkes, declared, perhaps with more candour than he knew, that paying Phelps a salary and benefits was "a good investment." Phelps said, "I'm very excited about working for Petro-Canada... I regard this [job with Mr. Lalonde] as a Petro-Canada posting."

Phelps would indeed go to work for Petrocan, or rather its subsidiary Westcoast Transmission, but it was obvious that he could hardly take an objective view on policy towards an organization that was already paying his salary and where he would subsequently seek his career. It was all part of the subtle process by which Petrocan could use its control of funds to manipulate the policy process. And it knew there was a big policy in the works.

. . .

Ottawa's energy mandarins believed the federal side had come off the loser from the policies forged, in 1973 and 1974, in the heat of conflict with Peter Lougheed. The principal beneficiaries had been the province of Alberta and foreign-owned oil companies.

The very conspicuous symbol of Alberta's wealth was the Heritage Fund, set up to hold a portion of the province's energy revenues against the day when the petroleum ran out. By 1980, the fund was fast approaching $10 billion. As for the foreign-owned oil companies, said Ottawa's analysts, if the existing system was not changed, they would wind up owning an inordinate amount of the national wealth.

The Liberals had returned to power considering energy policy initiatives to be a matter of political expediency. EMR soon persuaded them that they were a matter of economic necessity. A new policy would have to make a bold grab for Alberta's petroleum revenues and provide a new fiscal system that would "help" Canadian companies and discriminate against their foreign counterparts.

In the past, the lack of growing Canadian private-sector companies had been cited as an argument for direct government involvement. Now the policy-makers turned that argument around: with the emergence of Dome, Nova (as AGTL renamed itself in September 1980), and the other smaller stars of the 1970s, Ottawa found discriminatory nationalism more viable because it had partners to whom it could "throw the ball." Petrocan appeared to confirm that view. It was operating in partnership with most of the other big companies in virtually every exploration province in the country, from the wheatfields of southern Alberta to the Arctic wastes of Baffin Island; it had acquired a professional staff; and it was a participant in the important Hibernia find.

Now, when the Liberals were about to make a radical energy policy, it seemed only appropriate to turn for advice to the entity they had set up for that very purpose. But Bill Hopper was a very shrewd man. He knew what was coming: a policy that was likely to favour Petrocan, discriminate against foreign oil, and stage a massive revenue grab by Ottawa. Hopper very deliberately distanced himself from the process in order to avoid the wrath of his private-sector buddies. At the same time, of course, he wanted as many advantages as possible from the policy, and so he sought real input. That input came from Joel Bell, a man who firmly believed in living on the "bridge" between policy and operations. In the run-up to the NEP, Joel Bell himself was Ottawa's "window on the industry."

For Bell, the Tory reign had been a nightmare. He had continued to advise the Liberals while Clark had been in power, helping Lalonde with the energy platform that would be presented in the 1980 election. For the bureaucracy to give advice to the opposition might have been illegal, but it was not illegal for an employee of a Crown corporation to do so. Advice on energy policy, however, might be considered somewhat irregular when the Crown corporation involved was Petro-Canada. But Joel Bell didn't see it as a conflict. When the Liberals returned, he moved to Petro-Canada's Ottawa office full-time. According to an insider, Bill Hopper had only one piece of advice for him: "Be careful."

Nineteen eighty was the *annus mirabilis* for policy-makers at the Department of Energy, Mines and Resources. Beneath EMR's black tower, on and around Dow's Lake, the skaters and ice sculptures of February gave way to the joggers and cyclists of spring, and then the little sailboats of summer, as the bureaucrats and policy advisors worked day after day, and late into each night, formulating their revolutionary new schemes for Canada's petroleum industry.

The more important the policy, the greater the power fix. Within EMR there was a feeling that this was the single most important and sweeping policy initiative on which most of them would ever work. It was a policy that would radically change both federal-provincial relationships and the whole structure of the Canadian oil industry in the name of "security, opportunity, and fairness."

157

Any interdepartmental jealousies that might have been created with the Department of Finance were alleviated by the fact that Ian Stewart had been moved to the Finance deputy ministership. Stewart had worked on much of the analysis at the heart of the new energy policy. A senior joint committee of bureaucrats from EMR and Finance was set up to review the evolution of the policy. It became known as the "Enfin" committee, a little bilingual in-joke. *Enfin*, in French, means "at last." In the committee's opinion, they were getting on with a job that had needed doing for a long time.

Consultations with the industry dropped to an all-time low. Even the Cabinet was frozen out of the consultation process. After all, what did politicians know? Pierre Trudeau, in any case, had other things on his mind. Liberal Cabinet minister Donald Johnston wrote in his book, *Up the Hill,* "Now many agenda items tended to founder, suffering, I believe, from the absence of his day-to-day attention.

"The National Energy Program (NEP) was one such example. Developed by Marc Lalonde and a small coterie of officials, it was accepted by Trudeau and [Finance Minister Allan] MacEachen and imposed upon the country as the centrepiece of Allan's first budget rather than as a Bill introduced by the Energy Minister. *Through this technique much of its content was hidden from the Cabinet until it was a fait accompli.* Certainly the tax implications belonged in the budget but hardly the entire program. Most of the measures should have gone to caucus for discussion given their significance. However worthy the ideas that underpinned the NEP, its glaring flaws caused enormous political damage" (italics added).

The policy, unveiled on October 28, 1980, was predicated on soaring, OPEC-driven world oil and gas prices, with Canadian prices in regulated pursuit. It featured heavy new taxes on petroleum production and a discriminatory system of exploration grants. All companies would suffer much higher taxes, but Canadian-owned companies would receive more from the government exploration hand-outs, the Petroleum Incentive Payments (PIPs), which defrayed up to 80 per cent of the costs of a Canadian-owned company drilling in the frontiers. The policy was not primarily concerned with finding more oil and gas — that was taken as given; it was designed to grab revenue from Alberta and, via direct and indirect means, to put more of the oil and gas industry not merely under Canadian control but under government control, and to direct more drilling towards the frontiers. "By ignoring the problem of foreign ownership in the past," declared the NEP, "Canadians have lost a significant share of the benefits of having a strong resource base. If we fail to act now, Canadians will lose once again."

Despite the NEP's tone of economic rationality, its heart was Walter Gordon's old xenophobic economic nationalism wrapped up in what might be called Ed Clark's Catch-22: foreign-owned companies were bad if they reinvested profits, because that would increase "foreign domination"; but if they didn't reinvest them, if they paid them out as dividends to their overseas shareholders, they were even *worse*. Such companies obviously had to be bought out immediately. "A further delay will put the value of companies in the industry so high as to make the cost prohibitive, leaving Canada with no choice but to accept a permanent foreign domination by these firms." Noting that seventeen of the top twenty-five Canadian oil companies were more than 50 per cent foreign controlled, the NEP declared indignantly: "This is a degree of foreign participation that would not be accepted — indeed, simply is not tolerated — by most other oil producing nations." The terminology was virtually the same as that used by Walter Gordon, Jack Austin, and Maurice Strong.

The NEP was very explicit about the Liberals' belief in a higher level of direct government ownership and control. "Direct public participation in this sector remains too low. By world standards, the degree of private investment in the Canadian oil industry is high. The industry owes much of its prosperity to cash flow and incentives provided by Canadian consumers and taxpayers, few of whom are in a position to share in the benefits of industry growth. For most Canadians, the only way to ensure that they do share in the wealth generated by oil, and to have a say in companies exploiting the resource, is to have more companies that are owned by all Canadians — more companies like Petro-Canada."

This was a tendentious analysis. To point out that the level of public ownership was relatively low by global standards, and to use this as a justification for further state ownership, was to ignore the fact that the world's largest oil producers were communist, Islamic fundamentalist, or military dictatorships. Were these the models we wished to follow?

Moreover, the notion of government ownership as a means of the public "sharing the wealth" or "having a say" was again super-ficially appealing but bogus. It was the language of socialism. Petrocan would emerge as a great destroyer of public wealth. As for "having a say," how would this "say" be exercised? Petro-Canada had no annual meetings; its annual report did not provide greater disclosure than others — indeed, it was a model of obfus-cation. Petrocan's "owners" could not even find out how much its executives earned, as Imperial Oil's owners could. The level of scrutiny from understaffed and overworked parliamentary com-mittees was superficial; that from central government agencies was shrouded in mystery. As Don Johnston pointed out, even Cabinet could be "duped."

Nevertheless, "Canadianization" sounded appealing, and many Canadians believed that government ownership was a valid means of achieving that objective. But what the NEP was really talking about was nationalization, through "an early increase in the share of the oil and gas sector owned by the Government of Canada." The NEP claimed: "The goal of the Government is to increase the proportion of the oil industry owned by Canadians, through their national government, by acquiring several of the large foreign-owned firms." The finances for the nationalization of companies would be provided through the Canadian Ownership Account, whereby funds would flow directly from the gas pump to Petro-Canada (or other companies "like" it).

The NEP also featured sweeping new regulations on federal exploration lands. Henceforth a 25-per-cent interest in every right on such lands would be reserved for Petro-Canada (or some other Crown corporation). In addition, a minimum of 50-per-cent Canadian ownership would be required before production would be allowed from such lands.

The NEP marked a major change in Petrocan's emphasis, from provider of security (which required skill and luck) to instrument of Canadianization (which merely needed money).

· · ·

The night the NEP was announced, a Dome executive, as he listened to the provisions unfold, scribbled down "NEP" on a piece of paper, then added after it the letters "-otism." There was no doubting the identity of the NEP's favourite son.

Still, it was obvious that there was some disquiet in Ottawa at the potentially enormous increase in Petrocan's size and power. The NEP boldly declared that it did not intend "to encourage monopoly in the public sector of the industry. To ensure competition in the public sector, the Government may establish one or more new Crown corporations to hold the assets acquired, rather than adding them all to Petro-Canada. Petro-Canada will remain a principal direct policy instrument of the Government of Canada in the energy sector, and it may be that some of the assets acquired will be transferred to Petro-Canada, to strengthen its capacity to perform this role. Nevertheless, it is the Government's view that if all the firms acquired were to be incorporated within Petro-Canada, its effectiveness as an instrument of Government policy would be reduced, rather than strengthened."

The concept of public-sector competition may have been considered an ideological breakthrough by the authors of the NEP. It opened vistas of numerous state oil companies all vying with one another, not according to squalid capitalist yardsticks like efficiency or profitability, but according to some altruistic definition of the public purpose.

According to the NEP, Petro-Canada would not be allowed to grow too large. "Petro-Canada will act as the agent of the Government of Canada to acquire the additional firms. Once significant progress has been made on the acquisition program, the Government will direct Petro-Canada as to the disposition of the assets acquired. There will likely be a small addition to Petro-Canada's asset base to round out the activities in which it is engaged, in order to ensure that Petro-Canada is involved in all aspects of Canada's oil and gas industry. Depending on the size and nature of the assets acquired, the remaining assets will form the basis for one or more new Crown corporations."

Bill Hopper had a word for the idea of public-sector competition, which he expressed to a magazine journalist. The word was "shit." The notion that Petrocan would acquire assets and then dispose of them was the height of naiveté. There would be no rival Petro-Canadas.

The NEP's new taxes and discriminatory grant system raised a storm of international protest. Under the headline "Wildcat Canada Resigns from the World," the British weekly the *Economist* declared: "Canada's new energy programme, the centrepiece of the Liberal government's first budget since it regained power, takes a giant leap away from the rest of the world." The *Wall Street Journal* noted: "This is the sort of program you'd expect to find south of the North-South dialog, rather than in a key democracy in the industrialized world. Canada is trotting out all the Third World arguments, asking oil companies to try to imagine how America would feel if 82 per cent of its oil and gas revenues were to go to foreign-controlled companies. But the key point is that 82 per cent of Canada's oil and gas revenues wouldn't have amounted to enough to put in your eye, hadn't foreign investors taken the risk and put their capital to work there."

In Canada, there were howls of outrage not merely from the multinationals but from the Canadian independents the policy was theoretically meant to help. Canadian Hunter's John Masters, the American head of a Canadian company, likened the NEP to Kristallnacht, when Nazi thugs broke the windows of Jewish businesses in Germany. The angriest reaction of all came from the province of Alberta, which considered the NEP the economic equivalent of Pearl Harbor. In response, Peter Lougheed announced oil supplies to domestic markets would be cut back, and approval for synthetic oil megaprojects would be held up. Astonishingly, the "oil weapon" was being used within Canada's own borders.

Intense negotiations between Ottawa and Alberta concluded at the beginning of September 1981 with a new revenue-sharing agreement. Like the NEP, the agreement assumed soaring oil prices and thus a huge petroleum revenue pie to be sliced up. But the figures agreed upon by the bureaucrats in their computer-generated world proved to be a fantasy. Once again, if Petrocan was giving advice, either it was very bad advice or it wasn't being listened to.

The crisis atmosphere in which the NEP was announced had been heightened by the beginning of the Iran-Iraq War, which had removed 4 million barrels a day from the world market, sending spot prices rocketing once more. But even as Saddam Hussein was indulging his megalomaniac desires, the market was weakening. The delayed impact of higher prices was at last being felt on both the demand and the supply sides of the equation. OPEC's output in 1981 would be 27 per cent lower than it had been in 1979, as non-OPEC producers cut their prices and captured markets.

The NEP had very deliberately painted a picture of OPEC's supposed power to override markets in order to justify putting more power in the Canadian government's hands. But in fact, as the NEP was announced, OPEC's power had reached its peak.

In October 1981, the Saudis agreed to raise the oil price from $32 to $34, while other OPEC members reduced prices to $34 from $36. The Saudi increase would be the last OPEC price rise for a decade. Far from soaring to $80 and beyond, as the NEP had forecast, the oil price would weaken, then collapse. The "divine laws of supply and demand" invoked by Sheik Yamani were already in motion. Perversely, driven by a logic that ignored Yamani's warnings, a nationalist-inspired feeding frenzy of acquisition was under way in Canada.

TEN

Other People's Money

O N JANUARY 29, 1981, while meeting in Edmonton with members of the Alberta government, Don Johnston, president of the Treasury Board, received a telephone call from the Privy Council Office in Ottawa. The caller was Bob Rabinovitch, a senior PCO official.

"Don," said Rabinovitch, "I called to tell you that there was a special meeting of Priorities and Planning this afternoon."

"Oh," answered Johnston in astonishment. He was a member of the Priorities and Planning Committee, but this was the first he'd heard of any special meeting. "On what subject?" he asked.

"On Petrofina," Rabinovitch replied. "We have acquired it."

There was a pause.

"We will be paying $1.7 billion," said Rabinovitch.

Johnston was dumbfounded that such a commitment should have been made without advance notice to ministers. "Good Lord," he thought to himself, "are my views irrelevant? Does the Cabinet no longer count?"

It seemed not. And who were the "we" who had acquired Petrofina for this huge sum of money? "We" were Petro-Canada.

The acquisition of Petrofina, and the method in which it had been made, indicated clearly the hell-for-leather approach now adopted by Marc Lalonde and his cohorts in the wake of the NEP. It also indicated a further transformation in Petro-Canada's mandate: it was now primarily an instrument for nationalizing the oil industry. In the case of Petrofina, the acquisition had an additional purpose: to show the national flag on Quebec gas stations.

Petrofina Canada was the Canadian subsidiary of the Belgian oil giant, Petrofina S.A. It had acquired many of its assets from Petrocan director Don Harvie's father, Eric Harvie, and had thus provided much of the cash for Harvie's subsequent philanthropies. (Don Harvie resigned from the Petrocan board at the time of the Petrofina acquisition.) But a major portion of its assets lay not in oil and gas production but in refining and marketing.

The first two ministers who had presided over Petrocan, Alastair Gillespie and Donald Macdonald, had both had grave misgivings about Petrocan being involved in the downstream. What did running gas stations have to do with making sure Canada had enough energy supplies? They could see the practical downside: ministers having to deal with complaints about gasoline prices and dirty washrooms.

Bill Hopper had said not long after taking over as president in 1976 that he didn't agree with Maurice Strong's notion of getting into refining and marketing. But all that had changed with the Pacific acquisition.

Pacific Petroleums had become involved in the downstream when it bought a little company, X-L Refineries, with a refinery at Dawson Creek and a few service stations on the Alaska Highway. Pacific had wanted an outlet for refined products for the processing plant it was building at Taylor, B.C., to handle natural gas out of the Peace River area. Pacific knew nothing about refining and marketing, and partner Phillips soon stepped in to take half ownership and run the business, changing the gas station signs first to Phillips 66, then to Pacific 66.

Like Macdonald and Gillespie, Hopper's board had misgivings about — or were outright opposed to — Petrocan moving into the downstream. At the first board meeting after the Pacific acquisition, Bud Willmot had said to Hopper: "Mr. Chairman, you'll be telling us soon what your plans are for disposing of the Pacific service stations." Hopper, taken aback, had said yes, sure, he'd be getting back to Willmot on that. But then the Tories had arrived, and Willmot had resigned, and something had happened that made Bill Hopper think twice about disposing of the gas stations. That is, if he'd ever thought about disposing of them at all.

"It wasn't part of any grand strategy," Hopper said later. "Pacific had just 300 stations in western Canada, scattered from the Lakehead to Victoria. So we had something like 2 to 4 per cent of the market. Other companies were interested in buying the downstream from us but we said, 'Let's reel the stations in and see if we do any good.'

"We had a little refinery up at Taylor, B.C. We put out Petro-Canada signs, and the sales went up. You could have knocked me over with a feather. You could have *killed* Bill Daniel [then head of Shell Canada]. We had a little advertising program: 'There's a new breeze in the West." And I said to myself, 'Jesus, we're not hated as much as we thought out here.' We just kind of stumbled into it."

A block from the Calgary Stampede grounds, station operators Violet and Jim Patterson were asked about the reaction to their switching to the Petrocan logo from that of Pacific 66. "I don't know if it's patriotism or what," said Violet, "but we are getting more customers."

The small success of Pacific enabled Hopper to convince Ottawa that he should move further into refining and marketing. Once again, part of the rationale was that acquiring assets would enable the company to provide cash flow for expensive frontier exploration. But another big part of the Petrofina acquisition was pure politics.

"It was at the height of the separatist movement," said Hopper, "and there was a feeling in the PMO and elsewhere that putting the Canadian flag up there was a good idea. So there was enthusiasm for us to do Fina. Gulf was there but it was considered too big. Fina was the right size and had marketing in Quebec. So we bought it and put the flag in and began to convert."

But who could possibly have brought to the politicians' notice the notion that state-owned gas stations in Quebec could be a factor in national unity? Hopper must have played a significant part in pushing it. This wasn't in any way unusual. Indeed, it was almost archetypical of the way Ottawa worked. Politicians were busy men looking for ideas and initiatives, which were provided by their advisors. If the advisor could find a way of doing himself good while serving the wishes of his masters, why not?

Petrocan paid an exorbitant price for Petrofina. The "official" price given to the public was $1.46 billion. But once finance and other charges were added in, the figure came closer to $1.7 billion. Several years later, Auditor General Kenneth Dye would put the cost, once all the tax wrinkles had been factored in, closer to $2.5 billion. The book value of acquired assets less assumed liabilities was only $562 million. The Liberals didn't really seem to care what Petrofina cost.

Further controversy erupted when it was discovered that Maurice Strong had been involved in the negotiations with the Belgian parent, and that a firm in which he held a stake had received a $1-million fee. In fact, Strong did have contacts that proved valuable in the transaction, and the fee — considering the size of the deal — was relatively low. Nevertheless, there were allegations that it was yet another example of the favoured few using Petrocan to feather their own nests.

There was also an outcry over alleged "insider trading" in Petrofina shares, which had soared in the months before the takeover, just like the shares of both Husky and Pacific. But Petrofina hardly amounted to a leak; it was more of a flood. The negotiations were one of the worst-kept secrets in Ottawa. At least two prominent journalists, Steve Duncan of the *Financial Post* and Geoff Carruthers of the *Globe and Mail*, had written about the talks. There were few secrets in Ottawa.

The reverberations of Petrofina's costs would continue for years. Auditor General Kenneth Dye made it a personal crusade to gain access to Cabinet documents in order to judge whether the Canadian public had received value for its money. But a large part of the answer was in Cabinet member Don Johnston's book: the full Cabinet had never had the Petrofina issue put before them. No analysis of the takeover was ever done by EMR. Even Pierre Nadeau, Petrofina's ardently free-enterprise president, said that Petrocan had paid an "outrageous" price for his company. The word was that Marc Lalonde had told Bill Hopper and Joel Bell to buy the company whatever the cost. Bill Hopper and Joel Bell were glad to oblige, but of course they couldn't do it out of the proceeds of that vaunted "cash flow" that was meant to make them independent. They'd have to go back to the trough for this one.

However bad a deal it was for the public, Petrofina was a wonderful deal for Petrocan, because it didn't cost the company anything except the issue of a few dividendless shares. According to Hopper, "I said to Marc: Look, we bought Atlantic Richfield and we borrowed $240 [million] and you gave us $100 [million]. We bought Pacific for $1.5 billion and we had to borrow it all. We were 65-per-cent debt and we were getting highly leveraged. We said we've got to put the money in or we're broke. We wouldn't have done Fina without equity. We said we're not going to go the CN or Air Canada route and build up lots of debt and then go back and ask it to be forgiven."

Bill Hopper made sure that the money was forgiven right at the beginning. In fact, it was Joel Bell who'd suggested to the Cabinet that they simply plug Petrocan straight into the gas pumps of the nation. Apparently, their eyes lit up. Why hadn't they thought of that?

One of the most self-serving provisions of the National Energy Program, from Petrocan's point of view, was its access to the Canadian Ownership Account, whose funds came from special gasoline and natural gas taxes. The COA had been thought up by Joel Bell. It was a masterstroke. But there was one problem with Bill Hopper's enthusiastic move into refining and marketing: he couldn't have entered the business at a worse time.

In the late 1960s and early 1970s, the Canadian refiners, principally the big four — Imperial, Gulf Canada, Shell Canada, and Texaco Canada — had seen opportunities in exporting refined products to the U.S., where environmental concerns had stalled refinery construction. New refineries had been built in eastern Canada to grab a share of this potentially profitable market. But OPEC price increases had blown demand projections to the winds. Not only did higher prices mean lower demand, but the Canadian government had erected barriers to refined exports on grounds of security. To maintain market share and keep their expensive facilities running at capacity, the majors slashed prices. Competition cut refining margins to the bone. In the first half of 1978, the year Petrocan acquired Pacific, the return on capital in the refining business dipped below 5 per cent. Intense competition had forced the closing of around 10,000 gas stations during the 1970s, but there was still a far higher proportion of stations per capita in Canada than in the U.S.

Refining and marketing was a cutthroat business, but Bill Hopper saw that Canadian consumers preferred to buy gas at Petrocan. He also liked the business because it gave him a chance to go head to head with the integrated multinationals. Hopper found the idea of beating Imperial, Gulf, Shell, and Texaco in the marketplace by waving the Canadian flag irresistible. And what the hell; Petrofina's 1,100 gas stations hadn't cost Petrocan anything anyway.

The root of the popularity of Petrocan's move into refining and marketing was partly naiveté and partly jingoism. Many people believed — and were led to believe by politicians, particularly the NDP — that the majors "ripped them off" at the gas pumps, but Petrocan, servant of the people, would be in a position to provide cheaper gas. The delusion persisted but the cheaper gas never arrived.

At the nationalistic end of the equation, there was what might be called the "Gulliver syndrome." The Walter Gordon crowd had successfully instilled in Canadians a belief that foreign capital was somehow a dangerous giant in the land. In fact, the giant, like Gulliver in the land of Lilliput, was bound by myriad strands of red tape, which gave him just enough leeway to do his work. Canadians were concerned about the giant, but deep in the national psyche, what many wanted was not merely to control the giant but to *be* the giant. Canadianization appeared to have bred a domestic Gulliver. The problem was that giants were different from us, and resembled one another. Moreover, ours would prove a very expensive giant indeed.

Petro-Canada's announcement of its takeover of Petrofina heralded a six-month buying spree of foreign oil companies by Canadians, puffed up with nationalism — real or feigned — and flush with the attentions of eager bankers. Typically, the biggest deal was made by Dome Petroleum. In what was perceived by Ottawa at the time as a brilliant corporate coup, Dome seized the 53 per cent of Hudson's Bay Oil & Gas owned by Conoco of Stanford, Connecticut, for $2 billion. That deal would mark the high-water line of NEP-induced folly.

· · ·

Dome's president, Bill Richards, an endearingly scruffy character with the air of a corporate James Cagney, was strutting around his office in the summer of 1981 so pleased he was almost hugging himself. He had pulled off not one but two major coups since the NEP. The first was the creation of a subsidiary, Dome Canada, to take advantage of government PIP grants and pipe taxpayers' funds into Dome Petroleum's exploration in the Beaufort. Dome Petroleum had a majority of foreign shareholders, so it did not have access to maximum PIPs. It created Dome Canada as a subsidiary and sold enough of its shares to Canadians to qualify it for 80-per-cent grants. Nevertheless, Dome Canada was completely under Dome Petroleum's control. Dome's second much-fêted move was the takeover of 53 per cent of HBOG. The deal had been pulled off just as Dome was entering another Beaufort drilling season, buoyed by seemingly limitless amounts of money.

With control of HBOG, Dome would leap past Petrocan to become the largest Canadian-controlled company, with combined oil and liquids production of more than 150,000 barrels a day, and natural gas production of over 700 million cubic feet a day. Richards strolled around the room, sucking on a huge Montecristo, as he expatiated on Petrocan. "Petrocan is becoming a kind of management-run company," he said. "Management-run companies don't give a shit for shareholders. You've got to have shareholders biting at your ass. That's what capitalism is all about. I sweat blood over our earnings per share. All they want to do is protect their ass and keep their minister out of trouble."

In retrospect, Richards ranks as one of the greatest examples of hubris in Canadian corporate history. At the root of his downfall was his success in persuading bankers that Dome had to grab all the oil and gas assets it could now because they would never be cheaper. This was not an aberrant view at the time; indeed, it was the conventional wisdom. Richards's misfortune was that he happened to be the theory's most aggressive and active proponent.

In fact, Richards wasn't so different from Bill Hopper. The main difference between Petro-Canada and Dome was that Dome made its post-NEP acquisition with borrowed money, whereas Petro-Canada bought Petrofina with "free" money donated involuntarily by taxpayers.

There had been no love lost between Petro-Canada and Dome from the very beginning, given the tensions that still existed between Jack Gallagher and his former first employee, Maurice Strong. Dome, pursuing its policy of employing "other people's money," had tried to interest Petrocan in some of its more grandiose and expensive schemes, like the world's largest icebreaker, but Hopper had been well aware that Dome was trying to use him. The sense of rivalry was heightened by the presence of former Dome employee Don Wolcott in the Petrocan executive suite.

Hopper and Bell believed Dome had succeeded in conning Ottawa in 1977 in gaining "super-depletion" tax allowances for frontier drilling. Part of the resentment grew from the fact that Petrocan was short of taxable income against which to use such allowances. But there was also a feeling that the potential of the Beaufort had been oversold by Gallagher.

Shortly after introduction of the NEP, Joel Bell had found himself on the same platform as Gallagher at an energy conference in Mexico. Gallagher had left his listeners dazzled with the potential of the Far North. At the intermission following Gallagher's talk, there was a buzz among the Mexican officials. Bell told them not to take everything they heard from Gallagher too literally. In fact, it was a lot of nonsense. Well, why don't you say that, they suggested. So Bell got up and said so. As Bell tore into the Beaufort, Gallagher moved from his seat to the front of the audience and attempted to vaporize the Petrocan executive with a laser stare. Bell was overstepping the bounds of acceptable corporate behaviour. You never dumped on anybody else's hydrocarbon dreams in public.

Other confrontations took place privately. The diminutive, paunchy figure of Bill Hopper once ran into the similarly short, stout shape of Bill Richards outside Marc Lalonde's office. Hopper, emerging from a meeting with the minister, said, with a smile, "Sorry, Bill, you're too late. I just got all the money." And Richards had to chuckle: "Well, I hope not," he said, "because we really need some too."

When Hopper, chairman of Ottawa's "window on the industry," tried to bring his concerns about Dome to the government, he was met with exasperation. Hopper almost exploded when Marc Lalonde would say to him, "Why don't you do good things like Dome?" Some of the most powerful deputy ministers on the Petrocan board — Tommy Shoyama, Mickey Cohen, Ian Stewart — all took Hopper to task for his negative attitude towards Dome and the Beaufort.

On his Ottawa sales tour in 1977, Gallagher had shown Pierre Trudeau and Michael Pitfield his special Beaufort maps, with their myriad dark blobs — "They look like a dose of acne," Hopper once said, sourly — and persuaded them that they were all brimming with oil. Pitfield called Hopper and expressed the opinion that Petrocan had "missed out" by not joining Dome in the Beaufort. "But we don't think there's anything there," Hopper had snapped. "Oh no," Pitfield had replied, "you're wrong. Jack Gallagher has shown us the pools." Hopper told Pitfield, "They're ripping you off."

But nobody in Ottawa was listening. That window was closed.

Ottawa was initially dazzled by the skill with which Dome appeared to have outmanoeuvred the giant Conoco to gain control of Conoco's stake in Hudson's Bay Oil & Gas. The Trudeau government took this, and the pile of Canadian bank-financed takeovers in the first six months of 1981, as evidence of the wisdom of its policy. But then, suddenly, it realized that things weren't as rosy as they seemed. The first impact was felt on the Canadian dollar.

The purchase of U.S. dollars to pay for the surge of foreign acquisitions in the first half of 1981, combined with the Canadian dollar sell-off induced by the NEP, caused the Canadian dollar to plummet. Between 1976 and 1978, the Canadian dollar had taken a hammering on international markets, falling from parity with the U.S. dollar to a value of around 85 cents U.S. It had shown some strength during the Clark government, but the rot had set in once again under the Liberals, particularly after the NEP. Between mid-1980 and mid-1981, the dollar slumped from 87 cents to 81 cents U.S. Finance Minister Allan MacEachen, alarmed, issued a directive to the banks to halt lending for foreign oil takeovers.

Marc Lalonde declared: "Canadianization has exceeded the government's most optimistic expectations. We're the victims of our own success." Nevertheless, continued Lalonde: "The message is still Canadianize. The Canadianization program has the full endorsement of the Cabinet and the minister of finance. It's a matter, over the next short while, of pacing ourselves a little bit better than we have in the last few months."

But the Canadian bankers and companies that had responded to the government's call for a holy takeover binge hadn't just been running too fast, they'd run all the way to the brink of destruction. Interest rates began to soar; the carrying costs of acquisitions became crippling; and both Ottawa and the banks began to panic. The greatest alarm bells rang over the Dome loans. Dome had spent $2 billion to acquire only *half* of HBOG, and didn't have access to HBOG's cash flow. The answer suggested by the Toronto-Dominion Bank's chairman, Dick Thomson, was that Dome should dump its HBOG holding onto Petrocan, thus saving the banks' hides at the expense of the Canadian taxpayer. This was both appalling and somewhat ironic, since Thomson had been one of Dome's most vociferous supporters. Indeed, a couple of years before, Thomson had accused Hopper of lack of "vision" with regard to Dome. Not surprisingly, Bill Hopper wanted nothing to do with such schemes. Dome had the makings of world-scale disaster. He wanted to be involved with it as little as possible.

The state oil company's only direct involvement came in June 1982, when Hopper took some delight in twisting the knife into his old rival. The Dome mess had now blossomed into a full-blown crisis. Dome was threatening to become the biggest bankruptcy in global corporate history. The company, now experiencing a massive cash-flow crisis, desperately needed the first PIP payments to be paid to Dome Canada, the subsidiary it had set up to take advantage of the NEP, so that Dome Petroleum could grab them to stay alive. The grants that had been touted as a brilliant innovation that would give Canadian companies an advantage over the bigger, wealthier foreign oil companies were now needed as a corporate life jacket. The problem was that the Tory opposition was holding up the relevant legislation in the Commons.

Lalonde and MacEachen met with Dome's senior bankers in Ottawa on Saint-Jean-Baptiste Day. They asked the bankers to lend money to Dome Canada against the forthcoming PIP payments. The government people knew the bankers would demand a guarantee, and asked Petrocan to provide it. Joel Bell, going back to the legislation he had written himself, refused to provide the guarantee without an Order-in-Council. The order was set in motion. Mickey Cohen, then deputy minister of finance, promised the bankers that he would have the Petrocan guarantee for them in Calgary the next day so they could advance the funds. They agreed to the loan. Both Hopper and Bell took delight in rubbing in the fact that they had been right about Dome, and the politicians and bureaucrats had been wrong.

Later on Saint-Jean-Baptiste Day, there was a conference call between Hopper, Richards, and other senior Petro-Canada, Dome, and bank officials. Hopper announced that he wanted collateral for the loan guarantee. This was *really* rubbing it in. Richards expressed annoyance. "You don't need collateral," he said. "Well, if that's the case," Hopper snapped back, "then why don't you just get the banks to loan you the money?" There was silence over the telephone lines. Richards agreed to pledge some TransCanada shares as security. But that wasn't enough for Hopper. "And what about a fee?" he asked. Twist, twist. Richards, fuming, agreed to $100,000. The next night, when the deal was signed in the Calgary offices of law firm Bennett Jones, Hopper made sure that he had the $100,000 cheque in his hand before he affixed his name to the dotted line.

The officials who had penned the NEP had attributed far too much power to OPEC. This was a common delusion around the world. The problem was that Canada had staked so much on the delusion. Within a little more than a year, the price projections of the NEP had proved to be a fantasy. Lower prices, combined with soaring interest rates, not merely sank the Canadian companies that had made expensive takeovers; they also pulled the rug out from under the megaprojects, which the Liberals had claimed would form the centrepiece of the country's industrial strategy in the 1980s and 1990s. Shell shelved its Alsands plant. Imperial cancelled a heavy oil recovery project at Cold Lake. An expansion of Syncrude was put on hold. Nova's Alaska Highway gas pipeline was proving unfinanceable. Petrocan's Arctic Pilot Project now looked like a financial as well as a technological fantasy.

By the spring of 1982, it was obvious even in Ottawa that the National Energy Program had played a major part in the worst economic crisis in postwar Canada. The flood of projected government revenues from petroleum had dried up. The federal government's deficit had doubled to $20 billion within a year. Astonishingly, the one entity that appeared to have emerged whole from the post-NEP débâcle was Petrocan.

ELEVEN

King of the Castle

ETROCAN WAS Bill Hopper's baby. Its success was his success. Its growth was his gratification. But Hopper had to grapple with his lack of legitimacy within the industry. Hopper was not an entrepreneur; neither had he spent the long years required on the corporate "fast track" to reach the pinnacle of any of the major companies. His funds didn't come from the market, they came from taxpayers, from the shifting policy priorities of the Ottawa system.

Hopper was particularly sensitive to accusations that he had been "born on third base," that he had not earned his position the hard way and was merely feathering his own corporate nest. To establish his status, Hopper sought to separate himself publicly from his Ottawa masters in regard to both policy and finances, and to ingratiate himself with the industry.

To separate himself financially from Ottawa, he promoted buying companies in order to "acquire cash flow." Hopper's desires were greatly helped by the NEP's boost to Canadianization, but ultimately, the process amounted to a kind of laundering operation. The mob launders stolen funds by buying assets, which then provide "legitimate" income; Petrocan, while doing nothing illegal, was using taxpayers' funds to buy assets that would distance it from its tax-funded origins. But Hopper's claim that he could effectively "buy cash flow" was at best ambitious, at worst grossly misguided.

Say Petro-Canada needed $200 million a year to carry out its mandate. As Hopper never tired of pointing out, the prospect of returning to Cabinet each year for this money raised the possibility that a government might change or might lose interest in the mandate. Of course, the government was *meant* to have responsibility for the fate of the mandate, but Petrocan sought to separate itself from the vagaries of politics. If Petro-Canada could persuade a government to give it $1 billion to buy a company that had a cash flow of $200 million, then it might seem Petrocan would have more than enough money to pursue its public purpose.

But the principal elements of cash flow are the depreciation, depletion, and amortization allowances available under Canadian tax law; these allowances provide the funds to replenish the assets of the business, not to go off in new corporate directions, although acquisitors usually believe extra funds will be generated by their superior management. Any acquired company, moreover, would have its own corporate expenditure plans already that would account for most or all of its projected "spare" cash flow. Finally, if the funds for acquisition had been borrowed, then the cash flow would have to service the additional debt too. There would be no "free cash flow."

Petrocan did not provide superior management of acquired assets. In fact, far from reducing Petrocan's requirements for government funds, the acquisitions left it more cash-strapped than ever. Yet Bill Hopper's ambitions grew with the size of his empire and the political opportunities presented to him. He used Petrocan's popularity to grab and spend as much cash as possible from the public purse.

In the five years from Petrocan's creation until 1980, Petrocan received just over $1 billion from the government in return for shares. In the four years from 1981 to 1984, it received more than $3 billion directly, and another $1.285 billion in PIP grants. Much of the increase is accounted for by acquisitions, in line with the new emphasis on Canadianization in its mandate. The more it spent, the more it needed. And it returned nothing to the public coffers. What this money did provide was a huge corporate fiefdom for Bill Hopper. Surprisingly, his laundering operation went almost unremarked upon, not merely by the public but even by the industry. That's because the industry began to think that Bill Hopper wasn't such a bad guy after all.

In the wake of the NEP, much of Calgary's outrage had been directed at Petrocan and its employees. Indeed, many of its own employees were outraged. Hopper made a speech at the company's 1980 Christmas party, just weeks after the NEP. "I want to thank you, and the government of Canada thanks you," he said. He was booed.

During the heated dispute between Edmonton and Ottawa in the wake of the first OPEC crisis in 1973/74, bumper stickers had appeared, declaring, "Let the Eastern Bastards Freeze in the Dark." Following the takeover of Pacific and its gas stations, a new legend showed up on rear fenders: "I'd rather push this car a mile than fill up at Petro-Canada!" Even the children of Petrocan's employees caught the heat. They were taunted with questions like "What does Petrocan stand for? Pierre Elliott Trudeau Rips Off Canada!"

In January 1981, three months after the NEP, the *Globe and Mail* declared Bill Hopper "Report on Business Man of the Year." A week later, the *Calgary Sun* labelled him "Public Enemy Number One." Calgary reporters started rifling through the garbage at the London House apartment complex where Bell and Hopper both had apartments, looking for empty liquor bottles. Wild stories, never substantiated, claimed Hopper was having wilder parties. Deeper conspiracies were hinted at. One piece suggested that Petrocan was shipping the Mexican crude it had acquired under a new, government-mandated contract via Soviet tankers! That story, too, was apocryphal.

The sniping came from the Petroleum Club and the other Calgary watering holes in a constant barrage. Hopper staged a high-profile resignation from the Independent Petroleum Association of Canada over IPAC's bitter criticisms. At a Calgary conference, he declared: "I find some of their statements excessive, radical, and, in some cases, intellectually dishonest, and I'm not going to pay $100,000 a year to an organization that beats me over the head with a baseball bat every day."

Calgary's frothing, Hopper suggested, was doing it no good in Ottawa. The petroleum industry's claims of "doom and gloom... just don't seem to get the reaction they used to get." He continued, "The National Energy Program is here. The government has clearly enunciated its goals, public support is overwhelming, and the sky has not fallen."

In fact, within six months, with the collapse of the megaprojects and the emergence of the Dome crisis, the sky *would* threaten to fall. But his Calgary colleagues knew Hopper had to make speeches in favour of the NEP, as if Ottawa had a gun to his back. Strangely, when the next barrage began, it was Big Oil that was under attack — and Bill Hopper was on *their* side.

The second OPEC crisis had led to another surge of inventory profits for the majors, creating more sensationalist headlines. Once again, the tired old hobbyhorse of Big Oil being in league with OPEC was led around the block. The most blatant attempt to manipulate public feeling against the majors came five months after the NEP, when Calgary's criticisms of the Liberals' energy policy were at their height.

A seven-volume report from Robert Bertrand, director of investigation and research under the Combines Investigation Act, was released late one afternoon, close to newspaper deadlines. It was accompanied by a sensational press release declaring that the major oil companies, led by Imperial, had ripped off the public to the tune of $12.1 billion between 1958 and 1973. These conclusions of *The State of Competition in the Canadian Petroleum Industry* were subsequently trumpeted in newspaper headlines and achieved top story status on television and radio news across the country. But the report was based on unrealistic assumptions and ignorance of the way the industry worked.

The $12.1-billion figure was concocted from three separate elements. Under the National Oil Policy of 1961, Canada west of the Ottawa Valley line was reserved for western Canadian oil, which was more expensive than the imported oil with which the majors supplied Quebec and the East. Bertrand claimed that the majors should have *ignored government policy* and put cheaper oil west over the line. This accounted for $3.1 billion of the "rip-off." Another $3.2 billion he claimed was siphoned off as a result of the difference between the price of international crude under long-term contracts and that available on the spot market. The security of long-term contracts and the relative scarcity of oil on the spot market in the period under examination — from 1958 to the first OPEC crisis — were ignored. Finally, $5.2 billion, the largest single element of the rip-off, was alleged to have been lost to "inefficiencies" in gasoline marketing. The figure was based primarily on the higher costs of running full-service gasoline stations as compared with the "no frills" stations run by independent retailers.

All the major oil companies, used to choosing their words carefully, reacted angrily to the report. Imperial said that it contained "errors and omissions" and in places showed either "complete ignorance" of oil industry realities or a "limitless willingness to distort fact and logic." A Shell Canada rebuttal declared: "Unable to document any real evidence of illegal and unethical activity, the Bertrand Report describes general industry practices and performances and then compares this information with completely unrealistic criteria based on an idealistic description of the market devised by the report's authors. [It] is distinctly unfair and biased. Its ill-founded conclusions are based entirely on its limited and selective 'analysis' of the evidence. The result has been to consider the industry guilty until proven innocent — a violation of all the principles which protect the rights of individuals and corporations in our society."

J.C. Phillips, Gulf Canada's chairman, laid the blame squarely at the door of Robert Bertrand: "He has long been known as a zealous advocate for change in Canadian competition law. As a public official, however, he has the duty to administer the law as it exists in an even-handed manner. The tone of the report and the method of its release clearly demonstrates that this perspective has been ignored completely. It has been supplanted by the desire to shock and inflame."

Socking it to Imperial:
Walter Gordon was the
patron saint of economic
nationalism. The business
community considered him
non compos mentis. Many
of his policies were
implemented. (CANAPRESS
PHOTO SERVICE)

Yes, Prime Minister: When
Pierre Trudeau appointed
Jack Austin deputy
minister of energy in 1970,
Austin was determined to
create a Canadian state
energy company. (CANAPRESS
PHOTO SERVICE)

The Commissar: Joel Bell (with Jack Austin in the background) considered Petrocan his baby, but Red Square wasn't big enough for him and Hopper.
(CANAPRESS PHOTO SERVICE)

Mystery man: Nobody was quite sure where Maurice Strong was "coming from" ideologically. His interests covered the spectrum from the environmental movement to corporate match-making. (CANAPRESS PHOTO SERVICE)

"Personal drive and ambition": When Bill Hopper went to Petro-Canada in 1975, he knew state oil companies were moulded by their chief executives. Sixteen years later, that notion would be far from flattering. (Petro-Canada)

"Money doesn't matter": Frank McMahon was a classic wildcatter. He took Pacific and Westcoast on a roller-coaster corporate ride. Petrocan would make the free-spending McMahon appear frugal. (WESTCOAST ENERGY INC.)

Hard man: Kelly Gibson, one of the toughest characters in the oil patch, cleaned up Pacific and Westcoast after McMahon left. He was instrumental in guiding Pacific into the hands of Petrocan.(WESTCOAST ENERGY INC.)

Commercial transaction: Energy Minister Alastair Gillespie said Petrocan's takeover of Pacific was a "commercial" transaction that wouldn't cost the taxpayer anything. He was wrong.

Joe Who? Joe Clark's misfortune was to come to power in 1979 around the same time as the Ayatollah Khomeini. That made his commitment to disband Petrocan appear suicidal to many Canadians.(CANAPRESS PHOTO SERVICE)

I love this guy: Hopper and Marc Lalonde at an OPEC seminar. Lalonde's National Energy Program was a disaster, but it plugged Petro-Canada directly into the gas pumps of the nation. It also funnelled $1.8 billion of PIP grants Petrocan's way. (CANAPRESS PHOTO SERVICE)

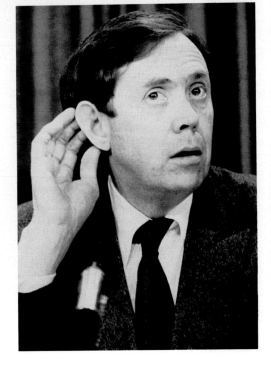

You've taken over what? Treasury Board President Don Johnston found out about the Petrofina takeover when a bureaucrat phoned him. He was not amused. He also believed the Cabinet had been "duped" over Petrocan salaries. (CANADA WIDE)

Out of the shadows: Auditor General Kenneth Dye tried for years to obtain details of the Petrofina takeover. But did we need details to know the Liberals had grossly overpaid? (WORKERS' COMPENSATION BOARD OF BRITISH COLUMBIA)

Showing the flag: Energy Minister Marc Lalonde loved the fact that Petrocan had a station directly in front of the offices of Quebec's Energy Ministry. (CANAPRESS PHOTO SERVICE)

From EA to CEO: Mike Phelps was paid a salary by Petrocan while he worked as executive assistant for Marc Lalonde. He would later become chief executive of Westcoast Energy, from which Bill Hopper received a healthy salary as chairman. (WESTCOAST ENERGY INC.)

Feet up: Former ambassador to the U.S. Peter Towe found Petro-Canada International Assistance Corporation gave him lots of opportunities for exotic travel as he doled out money for Third World exploration. (NEWSPHOTOS WORLDWIDE)

Warrior queen: Bill Hopper was concerned that Energy Minister Pat Carney might be hostile. Instead, she handed him Gulf Canada's downstream on a plate. (CANAPRESS PHOTO SERVICE)

Towering insult: Petrocan put the finishing touches on the twin towers of its Calgary head office just as the city's real estate market was collapsing. (PETRO-CANADA)

Torched: Prime Minister Brian Mulroney got into Petrocan's Olympic torch act, although the state oil company had caused his party nothing but trouble. (Petro-Canada)

Strategic mastermind: Olympia & York's Paul Reichmann was keen to have Petrocan take Gulf Canada's downstream operations. He knew Petrocan would pay more than anybody else. But the acquisition of Gulf couldn't have been worse timed. (Canapress Photo Service)

Jetsetter: Tory Minister Marcel Masse was one of the many Cabinet ministers Bill Hopper obliged with rides aboard one of the Petrocan jets.

Is this really happening? Bill
Hopper looks pensive as he sits
beside Energy Minister Jake Epp
and Privatization Minister John
McDermid at a February 1990
news conference following the
announcement of Petrocan's
privatization. (CANAPRESS PHOTO
SERVICE: CHUCK MITCHELL)

Watch the boondoggle! Prime
Minister Brian Mulroney and
Newfoundland Premier Brian
Peckford used the announcement
of Hibernia as a political photo
opportunity. When Gulf Canada
pulled out, Hibernia became a
severe political embarrassment.
(CANADA WIDE)

ILL

PER

Clean hands: Hopper under a barrage of questions at the company's May 1992 annual meeting. But in the end he played matador to a weak bull. The bull came second. (CALGARY HERALD)

But the headline stuck: "$12-Billion Rip-off."

The Bertrand case was a classic example of the oil companies' disadvantage in dealing with Ottawa, which knows how to manipulate the press. Imperial had known for weeks that a hostile report was about to emerge. It had cranked up its huge public affairs machine to set "communications objectives" and prepare position papers and briefing kits for senior management. When the report was released, senior executives granted more than thirty interviews to the media. Letters were sent to shareholders, employees, and agents. Brochures with "Not Guilty" emblazoned on the front were stuffed in with credit card bills. Within a few days, Jack Armstrong had taped a commercial denying the allegations and welcoming a public inquiry.

However, the ad was turned down by both the CBC and CTV as representing "advocacy," despite the fact that the networks' own newscasts had, without examination, featured the "$12-billion rip-off" as a lead item. In any case, as one observer noted, the Armstrong commercial made Imperial's big, blunt chief executive sound too much like Richard Nixon. And although Imperial was quicker off the mark than the other majors, by the time it had its responses out, the whole issue was dead. Just the mud was left sticking to the oil companies' already tarnished image.

It took more than five years after the Bertrand Report for Ottawa to set the record straight. In June 1986, the Restrictive Trade Practices Commission, after 200 days of hearings involving 200 witnesses and the review of thousands of documents, declared: "The director's allegation of $12.1-billion in overpayments by Canadian consumers is based on a series of assumptions that do not withstand close scrutiny." The commission found no proof of *any* measurable excess costs being passed on. It found "no evidence of collusion in any sector of the industry."

Here, at long last, was one positive side effect of the Petrofina acquisition. In future it would be much more difficult for a report like that of Robert Bertrand to appear unchallenged, because with Petrofina, Ottawa really had its own "window" on refining and marketing. That window, in the shape of Bill Hopper, took considerable pains over the next decade to tell Ottawa that refiners and marketers just didn't earn enough money.

Ian Smythe, president of the Canadian Petroleum Association through the late 1970s and the 1980s, later said, "When Petrocan was created, our members didn't want a state oil company at the table. It was the we/they attitude of the times. We didn't want our discussions going by pipeline straight into the minister's office. It never occurred to us that the pipeline could flow two ways and help us. After the NEP, Petrocan began to look more and more like any other company. Pretty soon, everybody in the industry was doing a deal with Petrocan somewhere somehow... [Hopper] attacked the NEP as vigorously as anyone. He was one of the guys."

In fact, Hopper was all things to all people. Ottawa thought he was one of *their* guys too. Hopper was a master of using the Ottawa network. He impressed politicians of both major parties with his abilities. Michael Wilson called him "a great politician." He was brilliant at handling his board of directors, having a lunch here, making a phone call there, ensuring that everybody was on side at directors' meetings, that there were no surprises.

Hopper endeared himself to a hostile industry by appearing outspoken with his political masters. Publicly, he'd defend the NEP, but then he'd give an interview to a reporter saying how he got so *tired* of making those speeches. "You know, spewing all that *pablum. Jesus.*"

Hopper cleverly used the old Canadian historical myths to justify his existence. An article in *Today* magazine in August 1981 noted: "He argues passionately in defence of his goals, recalling with dramatic anecdotes the role of similar projects in Canadian history: the CPR, TransCanada PipeLines, the Polymer Corporation (now Polysar Ltd.), which was created during the last war to manufacture vital synthetic rubber. 'When C.D. Howe set up that company there wasn't one voice raised against it. No one said, "No, let's argue about the wisdom of government intervention while our boys are dying."'"

In December 1982, an interview appeared in *Executive* magazine in which Hopper brought up the Polymer example again.

Hopper was quoted as saying: "My father worked for a time with C.D. Howe. During the war Canada needed to produce synthetic rubber because Malaysia was cut off. In the heat of the battle Howe set up Crown Polymer to make tires for the war effort. After the war, I recall my father telling me, there was an issue about whether we should sell Polymer. C.D. Howe was in favor of that but apparently some other people weren't and it wasn't sold.

"I would have taken the view that we shouldn't clutter up the government bureaucracy by owning and operating things in a commercial way unless we have some specific policy reason to do so."

In the one case, he was seeking to link Petrocan with the most heroic part of Canadian history — "while our boys are dying." In the other, he was saying it is important not to clutter up the bureaucracy once the battle has been won. In fact, Hopper was laying the groundwork for privatization. He had his big company now. All he had to do to complete the laundering process was separate himself from the Ottawa "mob."

Compared with his political masters, Hopper appeared a model of free-enterprise philosophy, even as he was sitting atop the greatest piece of government intervention since the war. As the *Today* article noted: "In one breath he is aloof from ideology; in another he is a white knight of the public interest, lancing the predatory dragons of big oil; in yet another he is Bottom-line Bill."

Hopper had an exceptional ability to benefit from policies even as he was deriding them and debunking the mythology on which Petrocan was based. He had been more enthusiastic than anyone about refining and marketing after the initial successes at the acquired Pacific gas stations. He had been keen to acquire Petrofina. Early in 1982, the company had launched a multimedia advertising binge, the principal theme of which was the Canadianness of the Crown corporation. "Petro-Canada," came the punchline at the end of the TV commercials, "it's *ours*." (Intriguingly, the Mexican nationalist cry that had roused the populace to the seizure of British and American oil interests in 1938 had been *"El petroleo es nuestro!"* "The oil is ours!" Nationalist political humbug has a universal pattern.) Billboards with gasoline nozzles levitating like a charmer's snake recommended: "Pump your money back into Canada."

But Hopper told *Executive* magazine: "I cringed when my advertising committee brought that slogan 'Pump your money back into Canada.' I cringed at its blatant nationalism and its implication that other companies don't pump their money back. Because many other companies do.

"When we talk about foreign multinationals in this country we tend to put them all in the same bag. That's wrong. Some multinationals operating in this country aren't very good citizens. They don't pump much money back into Canada. But there are others — Imperial and Shell and Gulf, to mention three — that reinvest very large sums in this country to the benefit of Canadians. I don't think Shell has ever taken any money out of the country... They are under attack and I think those I've mentioned and others are carrying a very bum rap."

Hopper also poured cold water on the notion that Canadian companies would somehow be better "corporate citizens" than foreign companies. "The notion that Canadian companies will somehow automatically act better is not really valid. Indeed, most foreign companies in Canada tend to be a little more careful about the way they operate than Canadian companies because they are in a 'host country.' Some Canadian companies say, 'We're untouchable. We're Canadian. We can do whatever we want.' Surely, there's no difference in the nature of greed — that's a very harsh word to characterize the private sector in which I spent most of my life — no difference in the 'quest for profit' between the two."

Hopper was also quick to shatter illusions that the Crown corporation could give Canadians a break at the gasoline pumps. There was a story that Hopper had educated Energy Minister Marc Lalonde in the realities of the gasoline marketplace by taking him to a self-serve Petrocan station in Ottawa and asking the man who ran it to lower the gasoline price by two cents. Then he sat Lalonde down and they waited. Within ninety minutes, the Imperial, BP, and Texaco stations in the vicinity all came down by two cents as well. Far from being uncompetitive — the persistent view about the oil "oligopoly" — the gasoline retail market was viciously competitive. All price-cutting did was to lower returns that were already well below those of other businesses.

Nevertheless, the belief that Petrocan should, and could, provide cheaper gasoline was among the most pervasive fantasies cherished by Petrocan's supporters. When Hopper would explain that his business was making very little money, and that lowering prices would just make it worse, their eyes would glaze over. They would go away convinced that, whatever the realities of the marketplace, Petrocan *should* give the consumer a break. In fact, because of the Canadian Ownership Account, Petrocan was responsible for gasoline being *more* expensive.

Bill Hopper undoubtedly spoke a lot of sense, but his one crucial bias lay in his commitment to Petrocan's survival and growth. "There's one thing you ought to understand about public sector corporations, particularly in the oil business, because I know them worldwide," he said in the 1982 interview with *Executive* magazine. "You can plot their mandate, you can describe their functions in economic terms and so on. But a great deal depends on the personal drive and ambitions of the people who run them. In the final analysis I want to be a winner. And that's kind of important."

Hopper was asked, "Would Petrocan see itself as 'a winner' as part of the industry or as part of the government?"

"It's both," he replied. "When I went to university I thought Milton Friedman and the whole Chicago School were great stuff. I was rather suspicious of the more 'liberal' colleges and some of the more left-wing notions that have come from there. I've mellowed a lot and matured and in some ways I don't think in the very long haul these things are going to make much difference. I've set some of that aside in my mind and now I want to achieve something. I'd like to look back and say, 'I built that. I did that.'"

Hopper was declaring himself the supreme pragmatist. Never mind the left and the right, the good and the bad, just get in there and make the most of it, using whatever means are at your disposal.

Hopper, in the words of a close observer, "liked to have all the air in the executive suite for himself. He wanted to suck it all in."

In other words, Hopper could bear no challenges to his authority. In the wake of the NEP, tensions inevitably mounted within the organization between Hopper and the man who felt himself at least as much, if not more, the architect of Canada's national oil company, Joel Bell.

. . .

Joel Bell rejoiced in being a policy entrepreneur. As Sandy Ross put it in a 1981 article in *Energy* magazine: "For nearly 15 years he has roamed at will in the uncharted waters where business and government intersect, looking for policy vacuums and finding ways to fill them." Petrocan was more than an assignment. Joel regarded it as his baby too. He had penned the legislation; he had crafted and delivered the presentations to Cabinet; he had arrived ahead of everybody else just after Christmas 1975, "in the manner of Cortez first setting foot in Mexico, to found an empire"; he had been at the heart of all the big deals; he had constantly shuttled back and forth between Calgary and Ottawa as the human "window," particularly in the formulation of the NEP.

The slim, ascetic-looking Bell, with his confident, death's-head, intellectual grin, relished the fix of big money and big policy power. He enjoyed the jetsetter lifestyle that his position as executive vice-president of Petrocan gave him. Although he had small apartments in both Calgary and Ottawa, Bell really didn't live anywhere. He was constantly on the move, ready at the drop of a hat to board Petrocan's $6-million Hawker-Siddeley DH-125 executive jet — when Hopper wasn't using it, that is — to do a deal, give a speech, or meet with senior politicians. He also found time for the social circuit, and could be seen at gala events for the National Ballet in New York or at the opera in Toronto.

But Bell was resented in some quarters. His free-floating status in Ottawa and his large consultancy fees had made him an object of both suspicion and envy among the bureaucrats. His work on the NEP had made him a lightning rod for an outraged industry in Calgary. When he addressed a group of corporate planners in

Calgary in mid-1981, the attitude towards him was almost openly hostile. Bell was telling the group that it was a fallacy to draw a distinction between national and corporate goals. The latter had to be fitted into the former. The responsibility for going behind public policies and understanding them, he said, lay with "us on the corporate side." But not too many people went along with the notion of Bell as one of "us"; Bell was very much one of "them." Moreover, Bell's assertion that corporate goals had to be fitted in with national goals held disquieting overtones. What penalties might a Bell-inclined government frame for those individuals and corporations who didn't want to go along with "national goals," who believed they were misguided or dangerous?

Bell was arrogant. He'd barge to the head of the line-up in Calgary's best restaurants, then send a bottle of Champagne over to those he'd cut in front of. Antagonism towards him took the form of subtle and not-so-subtle put-downs. First would come the compliments: a "Rolls-Royce mind"; "I absolutely respect his intelligence"; "a brilliant thinker." But then would come the barb: "But sometimes intelligence can be a handicap when you have to get things done quickly." "Of course, he's a lousy businessman." And then, the final low blow to the bottom line from an entrepreneur with oil under his fingernails: "Just ask Joel if he'd be a success in private life."

Bell could handle all this because he believed most of his critics were Neanderthals. He was pursuing a higher course. But his style continued to irritate people both inside and outside the company. By far the most dangerous was Bill Hopper. Hopper was not an intellectual and had no desire to pursue metaphysical issues. Sometimes, Hopper would wait until Bell was on the phone so he could slip out of Red Square. Also, Bell was always bugging Hopper for more power. In particular, Bell wanted badly to be on the board, but his appointment was always held up by somebody up there who didn't like him. Hopper increasingly couldn't stand him. On a flight from Calgary to Ottawa on the Petrocan jet, Hopper badmouthed Bell to a journalist the whole way. Of course, Hopper badmouthed everybody, including his ministers, but Bell was now really getting under his skin. When a photographer turned up from *Saturday Night* magazine in the summer of 1981, Hopper refused to be photographed with Bell.

The contrast — and tension — between the two men showed up at parliamentary committee hearings in the spring of 1982 over the NEP legislation. Bell swept in with an air almost of celebrity, surrounded by Petrocan underlings and leaving CBC cameras bobbing in his wake. He handled the slim challenges thrown at him by the committee's Tory MPs with aplomb, dancing around allegations of unfair advantage, expressing a degree of self-righteous indignation at the notion of conflict of interest.

He noted the "importance of control and accountability," spoke of Petrocan's staff as being "second to none," pointed out that the company's record was "very comparable with the industry," and boasted that its frontier exploration performance had been "enviable." Bell's vision of sensitive capitalism appeared to offer the best of all possible worlds: "hard-nosed commercial standards while promoting Canadian interests."

For Calgary Tory MP Harvie Andre, who sat across from Bell, chain-smoking and interjecting barbed remarks about profiting from takeover leaks, it was all so much bullshit. But it was so hard to tie Bell down. To the outside observer, Andre, with his lantern jaw, five-o'clock shadow, and charmless bulk, came across as the epitome of the unacceptable face of capitalism. Bell, by contrast, looking as if he'd just returned from a jog along the Rideau, projected an image of competence and concern, the very model of a guardian of the public purpose. Bell described himself as a "pragmatic idealist" — that is, an interventionist ideologue under a more acceptable name.

Arguing with Bell about the legitimacy and performance of Petro-Canada was like arguing with a true believer about the existence of God. If Bell found himself on the defensive, he could always retreat to the position that Petro-Canada was ultimately an article of faith, an entity whose very existence coincided with the national interest.

Bill Hopper, by contrast, realized the dangers of being too

publicly linked with Ottawa. He wanted a written mandate, an arm's-length relationship, the minimum of government "interference," and, of course, every penny he could squeeze out of the Treasury. When he turned up after Bell at the same parliamentary committee in April 1982, the atmosphere was quite different. Before the session started, Hopper sat joking with Tory MP Jim Hawkes about the French version of a Petrocan submission. Hawkes said he had only two further lessons to go on his own French course. "Well, that's good," said Hopper, smiling. "Then you'll be bilingual. You'll be able to be a bureaucrat."

When somebody made reference to testimony previously given by Bell, Hopper said he hadn't read the transcript. "I have to read enough of what Mr. Bell writes." Bell's inside track as an advisor on the NEP had been enormously useful to Petrocan and Hopper, but now Bell was becoming a liability. Hopper was as adept as Bell — indeed more adept — at cultivating his Ottawa network, but he was a good deal more subtle about it.

Within Petrocan, meanwhile, Bell's style was also earning him few friends. It was generally agreed that he was a lousy manager and administrator. As one former executive put it: "Policy people don't have any experience in managing. You can't run a company like a brainstorming session, and what Bell ran was a series of brainstorming sessions. You have to give people roles and responsibilities and let them do their thing within levels. But that just wasn't Joel's style. He was tough on people because in those days he was unmarried and work was also his hobby, and I think he expected the people who worked for him to devote their whole lives to work. He constantly had people waiting outside his office to see him, often for a couple of hours. It was a mix of politics and business. Joel was always going to fix problems by buying things. We were having a problem with TransCanada? Let's buy it. There was a very strong interventionist, I'm-more-clever-than-the-market attitude, and if I can control it then it will do the right thing."

Bell was difficult to work with and sometimes impossible to work for. He had been frustrated by the fact that he was never appointed to the board; he had been deeply disappointed when Ed

Lakusta was brought in as president after Andy Janisch left. From Bill Hopper's point of view, Ed Lakusta was the perfect man to operate the company. Lakusta, a former Gulf executive, was described by a former Petrocan executive as "an oilman's oilman in the worst possible sense." When he wasn't dealing with the specific problem in hand, his recreation consisted of heading for the hills and blasting off at God's creatures. A director discussing the relative merits of four-wheel-drive vehicles discovered that Lakusta's favourite was the one with the greatest armament-carrying potential. Cultural activity for Lakusta was flipping flapjacks at the Calgary Stampede. His international perspective was revealed when he was receiving a briefing on the operations of Petro-Canada International Assistance Corporation, the aid affiliate set up by the NEP in Nepal. "Nepal," he said. "Isn't that the place where Union Carbide had that big gas disaster?" He couldn't tell Nepal from Bhopal.

With the way to the top barred, Bell left in November 1982 for what seemed bigger and better things. In Liberal backrooms, the popular success of Petrocan and the NEP led to sweeping plans for a similar industrial policy. Once again, the men at the centre of the plans were Jack Austin, who had been appointed to the Trudeau Cabinet from the Senate, and Maurice Strong. The government attempted to implant Strong as chairman of the Canada Development Corporation, Walter Gordon's old creation, but was met by fierce resistance from the board. The attempt was seen as the height of political bad faith and sleaziness.

One of the conditions of CDC's creation and subsequent share sale to the public had been that the government would not seek to influence the company's strategic direction. When this form of pressure failed, a new entity was created, the Canada Development Investment Corporation, to hold both the government's stake in CDC and a number of other government industrial interests, such as Canadair and de Havilland. Although the rationale for the CDIC was that of management and disposition of government assets, Austin and Strong saw it as another interventionist instrument. And who better to be its president than Joel Bell? Bell's departure from Red Square was greeted with a good deal of executive relief.

TWELVE

Hopper's Navy

IBERNIA FEVER swept Newfoundland in 1979. Wealth at last. An end to dependence. The bars of George Street in St. John's and the offices of the Confederation Building filled with the elaboration of expansive dreams. Speculative fever ran through the town's little clapboard houses. The seagulls hovered over a real estate boom. Trawlers cut under Signal Hill, where Marconi had received his famous message, into a town that had only one topic on its mind: oil.

Just as the North Sea had spurred the claims of the Scottish nationalists, so the East Coast stirred the aspirations of Newfoundland. A history of dependence since Confederation made provincial self-assertion all the more strident. That self-assertion was embodied in the form of Newfoundland's premier, Brian Peckford.

Because it had joined Confederation in 1949 as a sovereign nation, Newfoundland had always claimed a right to ownership of offshore resources. In 1964, Premier Joey Smallwood, the little man with the big ideas who had led Newfoundland into both Confederation and a raft of disastrous development programs, had dispatched divers to deposit a plaque on the ocean floor, 200 miles from the coast, asserting Newfoundland's claim to the riches of the ocean and what lay beneath it.

In 1977, the Liberal government of Pierre Trudeau had offered the Atlantic provinces resource revenues in return for ceding control of development to Ottawa. Newfoundland's Conservative premier, Frank Moores, had refused even to meet with the federal Liberals on the issue. Moores was supported by a group of young, aggressive politicians and public servants — the first generation of university-educated Newfoundlanders to have grown up within Confederation — determined to wield the oil weapon against a distant and much-resented Ottawa. Chief among them was Peckford, a feisty former schoolteacher who became the province's petroleum champion, Newfoundland's answer to Peter Lougheed.

Peckford was mindful of Smallwood's development failures. Nevertheless, raised on the myths of the rapacious merchants of St. John's Water Street — the men who sent the Newfoundlanders whaling, sealing, and sometimes to their deaths — and the realities of Smallwood's giveaways to private companies, Peckford was obsessed with government "management." This wasn't just a fight about revenue sharing, it was a fight about self-respect and self-determination, about provincial destiny.

In 1977, Peckford, then energy minister, introduced legislation to ensure local job and contract preference. He and his team had made a detailed analysis of North Sea development policies and had concluded that they favoured the Norwegian model of tight control and insistence on local content rather than the full-speed-ahead approach of the British. Like their counterparts in Ottawa, they had profound faith in their ability to seize the "tiller of society" for the public good.

During the brief reign of Joe Clark's Tories in 1979/80, the pendulum appeared to swing in the Atlantic provinces' favour, just as the Hibernia find, and the 1979 gas find by Petrocan at the Venture site on Sable Island, off Nova Scotia, were upping the stakes. The Tories had been supplanted by a Liberal government determined to assert itself in energy, but Pierre Trudeau's return did nothing to dampen optimism about the East Coast.

The political rhetoric grew more heated as the fruits of success appeared greater. Despite the jurisdictional dispute, the NEP promised to put turbo thrusters on the East Coast bonanza. Even though Newfoundland officials had spoken of fighting a "legal guerrilla war" against Ottawa, geophysical and drilling activity reached record levels all along the East Coast in 1980. Although Newfoundland also declared it would fight Petrocan's back-in rights, the state oil company drilled on in the vicinity of Hibernia.

Mobil, the operator of Hibernia, adopted a more guarded approach. It announced in the wake of the NEP that it would take the jurisdictional issue to court, and would not develop Hibernia until it was settled.

But Hopper's attitude towards Mobil was ambivalent. Mobil was both a significant partner and his biggest rival. At the start, Hopper had tried to seize the operatorship of Hibernia so that he could dictate the pace of development. He badly wanted to be "out in front." Peckford was then in a race for the leadership of the provincial Tory party, and although Hopper lobbied him successfully for support, Ottawa, much to Hopper's frustration, backed Mobil. Peckford was aware that Hopper was keen to maintain his support, and he wasn't slow to take advantage of that situation. The arena in which Peckford chose to put pressure on Hopper was the most outstanding of Joey Smallwood's failed attempts at "forced growth": the refinery at Come By Chance.

Come By Chance had been built, largely with taxpayers' money, by John Shaheen, a New York–based promoter who mesmerized Smallwood with visions of industrial development. Smallwood showered Shaheen with concessions, and together they hatched a plan for a 100,000-barrel-per-day plant that would not only produce premium jet fuel for New York's Kennedy Airport but also anchor a huge petrochemical complex. The deal cratered amid political uproar over unsecured loans by the government to Shaheen. As a result, John Crosbie, then a provincial Liberal, crossed the floor of the Newfoundland legislature and joined the Tories. Ironically, it was the Tory government of Frank Moores that, having defeated Smallwood, revived the scheme.

Shaheen celebrated Come By Chance's opening in 1973 by hiring the *Queen Elizabeth 2* out of New York, filling it with bankers, politicians, engineers, and socialites, and steaming up to his gleaming new venture. The Champagne soon went flat; the refinery, beset by technical problems, never worked. By 1976, the year of Petrocan's creation, Come By Chance had piled up debts of $550 million and was losing $12 million a month. Creditors were closing in. Who better to examine the outlook for the refinery — that is, take over responsibility for the dog — than the new national oil company? But Maurice Strong stated clearly that although the Crown corporation, at the government's suggestion, was studying the refinery, it was "the last thing I would want to take on at this time."

The plant was mothballed but remained an issue. It nagged at Newfoundlanders: how could all that equipment, all that investment, not provide jobs? Reputable and less-than-reputable businessmen, including Shaheen and a handful of shady jetsetters who could smell government subsidies an ocean away, came by the premier's office with plans to revive the plant.

With the Hibernia find in 1979, interest in the refinery was renewed. Surely Hibernia oil would be processed there? But Hibernia's waxy crude was unsuitable for the refinery, even if the refinery could be made to work, and making it work would cost a lot of money.

Peckford pressured the Clark Tories, then the returning Trudeau Liberals, to have Petrocan take over the plant. In March 1980, a month after the Tories' election defeat, Petrocan announced it had "succeeded" in "negotiating an option" to buy Come By Chance.

Petrocan's attitude hadn't changed since the days of Maurice Strong: it was the last thing the company wanted to do. Hopper left neither Peckford nor his Ottawa masters in any doubt about what he thought of Come By Chance: it was crazy; it would never work. And although he never declared in public that he had been forced into the deal, he did say that there was only a "30-per-cent chance" of the refinery reopening. He claimed that it would cost between $150 million and $250 million to reopen the plant, a figure much higher than that projected by others.

As Petrocan's interests in refining and marketing increased, it became even less inclined to open Come By Chance and thus aggravate the problems of surplus capacity. The costs of keeping Come By Chance out of commission, on the other hand, were relatively small. Hopper was prepared to take on the mothballing costs because he had other big things to do off the East Coast. And the NEP gave him both the status and the funds to do them.

The NEP pointed to an East Coast boom; a boom would inevitably lead to shortages of equipment. Even before the NEP became public, Petrocan studies had estimated that the rig count off Newfoundland and Nova Scotia could increase from eleven in the latter half of 1980 to thirty by 1985, with Petrocan operating as many as a dozen itself. But the problem, declared Bill Hopper at a conference in St. John's in September 1980, "is that we doubt very much whether we will be able to get twelve rigs from the international market by that time. The rigs we now have on contract will barely satisfy Petro-Canada's needs until 1983. The obvious conclusion is that like any other major offshore operator, Petro-Canada will have to gain long-term control over a fleet of offshore rigs."

Thus was born what was later dubbed "Hopper's navy." By 1980, Petrocan had already put four dynamically positioned drill-ships on contract. It had also contracted a semi-submersible drilling rig, the *Bredford Dolphin*, owned by a British-based subsidiary of Norwegian shipping magnate Fred Olsen. But none of these facilities was Canadian, and that, in the eyes of the authors of the NEP, was a problem that should, and could, be put straight.

The NEP declared offshore drilling a focus for the development of Canadian expertise. "In Western Canada," it read, "the oil service industry is largely Canadian owned, and it is a dynamic and profitable industry. Offshore drilling, however, has thus far tended to be dominated by foreign firms. This type of drilling requires large equipment and more sophisticated technology. Also, the offshore production facilities that would be required will be at the leading edge of technology. Canadians should be in the forefront in this effort. Canadians have the ability to capture these opportunities, and the government wishes to support Canadian firms wishing to do so... The government will use its regulatory power, too, in support of an expanded Canadian presence across the spectrum of industrial activities related to the petroleum boom."

Bill Hopper thought this was all naive.

Petro-Canada had declared before the NEP that it wanted to construct one or more semi-submersible drilling rigs. Given the thrust of the NEP, Petrocan should have shown preference for a Canadian drilling contractor, using Canadian shipbuilding facilities. But Bill Hopper was not happy with the notion of bringing "industrial and employment benefits" to Canadians. He wanted to get on with the job, not hold the hands of a lot of inexperienced Canadian companies.

Hopper tended to be cynical about those who wrapped themselves in the flag. He knew their motivations; he was one of them. He had always spoken out about the danger that Canadian companies might see the state oil company as a "soft touch" for contracts. He was also acutely aware that he could only encourage development of Canadian expertise at the expense of his own bottom line, which was already far more desperate than its accounts revealed. Hopper was reluctant to link up with either inexperienced Canadian contractors or Canadian shipyards, whose costs were higher and who were reluctant in any case to take on rig construction.

In September 1982, when Petrocan brought the rig *Vinland* from Norway to work off Nova Scotia, Halifax politicians complained that it was not staffed with local people. This was seen as just one example of Hopper's reluctance to indulge "Canadian preference." Nova Scotia's development minister, Roland Thornhill, said: "I'm only asking Petro-Canada to do what foreign oil companies have shown themselves quite willing to do, which is to spend the benefits of the offshore among Canadians, among Nova Scotians." But Hopper knew that the politicians had no concept of the realities of economic development; they understood form but not substance. To them a worker was a worker, a refinery was a refinery, a rig was a rig. They did not understand the subtleties and importance of experience and function; they believed taxpayers' money could take care of all that.

When Petrocan announced its first semi-submersible construction joint venture, the partner was Sedco Inc. of Dallas, acknowledged as the world leader in offshore drilling. Petrocan entered into a 50-per-cent joint venture with Sedco to construct a dynamically positioned semi-submersible at a cost of $125 million.

This arrangement caused considerable grumbling among the Canadian drilling community, various members of which felt that they were capable of building a semi-submersible in Canada. In response to political pressures, therefore, Petrocan also invited proposals from private Canadian drilling contractors for the design, construction, and operation of a second semi-submersible. A deal with Calgary-based Bawden Drilling fell through, but another Calgary firm with international experience stepped into the breach.

Bow Valley Industries had never been considered a "political" company in the style of either Jack Gallagher's Dome or Bob Blair's Nova. Its founder, Doc Seaman, was a shrewd, self-made entrepreneur from rural Saskatchewan who, with his two brothers, B.J. and Don, had built an impressive drilling and exploration company. Bow Valley had extensive international interests for a company of its size. It knew all about dealing with "government priorities" and "national objectives." Bow Valley had seen legislation at least as punitive as the NEP in other countries. It had endured the British Labour government and its overzealous bureaucrats in the North Sea. It had coped with the hair-tearing frustrations of doing business in Vietnam and Indonesia. For once, Bow Valley appeared to be on the winning side of nationalist legislation.

Faced with Petrocan's reluctance to contract with a Canadian company, Bow Valley decided to force its way into the East Coast offshore. It bought the *Bredford Dolphin,* the rig Petrocan had already contracted, and renamed it *Bow Drill 1.*

One of more than 250 semi-submersibles either already in service or under construction around the world, the *Bow Drill 1* was a steel behemoth. The rig was 355 feet long, 220 feet wide, and the height of a thirty-storey building. Each of its eight anchors weighed 30,000 pounds and was hooked to 4,000 feet of chain. Powered by two huge Siemens engines, which between them generated 7,000 horsepower, the vessel could make eight knots and accommodate almost 100 people. It could also drill to 26,000 feet in water depths up to a quarter of a mile.

By the time the rig reached Halifax in November 1981, Bow Valley's commitment to offshore drilling had taken another mighty leap, in concert with Bill Hopper's old rival, Bob Blair. Bow Valley and Nova's oil subsidiary, Husky, agreed to build two semi-submersible drilling rigs, a fleet of state-of-the-art supply boats, and extensive shore-based facilities in St. John's and Halifax.

Doc Seaman and Bob Blair realized that PIP grants would cause a boom in demand for drilling equipment, but they also believed they could use commitments to build parts of the new drilling fleet in Canada as a bargaining tool to obtain exploration permits from Ottawa. Both wanted to build a semi-submersible in Canada. The problem was in arousing the interest of Canadian yards. Offshore rigs had been built in Canada before but had always run into cost problems.

There was no doubt that a Canadian rig would be more expensive than a rig built abroad, so Bow Valley and Husky sought government subsidies for a Canadian-built rig. They suggested cheap financing through Ottawa's Export Development Corporation. The EDC turned them down; the rig was not for export. The partners thus turned to Norway for their first rig. Once Ottawa heard about this contract, it stepped in. The Cabinet overrode the EDC board. A dummy corporation was set up in Bermuda so the rig could be "exported." The manoeuvre was clearly against the spirit of international trade agreements, but Ottawa was gripped by nationalist fervour. The ends justified the means. Trade rules could go by the board.

The only Canadian yard prepared to build a rig was New Brunswick's Saint John Shipbuilding & Dry Dock, which belonged to the Irving family and badly needed the work. But it had no experience of such vessels, and its dry dock was not suited for the construction of most semi-submersible designs. Even when

Bow Valley and Husky found a design that could be built there, the rig had to be built in two halves, then welded together. Nevertheless, a contract was signed. *Bow Drill 2* would be built in Norway, *Bow Drill 3* at Saint John. Four of the fleet's six supply ships would be built by Hyundai in Korea, two by West Coast shipyards in Canada.

By early 1982, work was under way at both Saint John and the Norwegian yard, Framnaes. Framnaes soon pulled ahead. Saint John had problems with parts suppliers and with inexperienced management and workers. Delays were compounded by the zeal of officials from the EDC. If they were going to finance a Canadian-built rig, they wanted to make sure that it was Canadian-built. They sat like commissars, demanding to see dockets and bills. An additional problem loomed: the workers at the Saint John yard realized that when the *Bow Drill 3* left, so did their jobs. Work slowed to a crawl. Sabotage led to further delays. The partners were desperate to get the rig out of the yard, even though it wasn't completed.

On November 26, 1983, in a howling storm, the ceremonial honours were performed and *Bow Drill 3* was launched and quickly moved to Halifax for its final fitting. The rig finally cost around 30 per cent, or $40 million, more than its Norwegian counterpart. The support boats built in Canada were 50-per-cent more expensive than their Korean sister vessels. The *Bow Drill 3* didn't move into service until March 1984. By then, the NEP had been shown to be disastrously misguided. The petroleum world was falling apart, just as Sheik Yamani had predicted.

As in the 1920s and 1940s, fears of shortage had led to higher prices, and in turn to more exploration, new technology, and eventually surplus. American oil production began to rise again in the first half of the 1980s. Alaska, Mexico, and the North Sea all sent major new streams of oil into world markets. New exporters appeared. Between 1979 and 1983, non-OPEC production increased by 4 million barrels a day. High prices affected demand too, spurring both alternative energy development and conservation efforts. By 1985, the U.S. would be 25 per cent more energy-efficient and 32 per cent more oil-efficient than it had been in 1973. Over the same period Japan would become 31 per cent more energy-efficient and 51 per cent more oil-efficient. The result was that oil's share of the total market for energy would drop from 53 per cent in 1978 to 43 per cent in 1985.

The increase in non-OPEC supply, the global decline in demand, and inventory dumping led to a stunning reduction in demand for OPEC oil. The Iranian Revolution and then the Iran-Iraq War had slashed exports, but instead of a shortage, the market was facing a massive glut.

Only in March 1982 did OPEC begin to act like a real cartel, cutting production in order to maintain price. The required cut was severe. In 1979, OPEC had produced 31 million barrels a day. In March 1982, it set an output limit for the group of 18 million barrels per day, with individual quotas for each country. Members complained about each other's cheating, but there was — after all — no cheating the market. A year later, at a meeting in London, OPEC slashed its prices by about 15 per cent, to $29 a barrel, and set the quota at 17.5 million barrels a day. Saudi Arabia agreed to act as the "swing producer," opening or closing the taps to keep supply in balance — as long as its fellow members didn't cheat.

OPEC's power had proved to be much exaggerated. The organization now appeared like a gold-plated semi-submersible, hugely impressive but ultimately just bobbing on a tide of market forces, which had surged in 1973 with such vehemence only because the majors had succeeded in holding the world price down for so long. Just as the multinationals' system had been broken, now OPEC appeared broken too. Half the world's oil had moved onto the spot market or was being traded at spot market–related prices. In 1983, West Texas intermediate crude started trading on the New York Mercantile Exchange. Oil had become "just another commodity." But in Canada, it was still seen as being inextricably, if vaguely, linked with the national psyche and with federal and provincial self-assertion. Just like the Mexicans, we seemed to think that national pride might somehow be able to stand up to market forces.

Perversely, the NEP was causing an unprecedented surge of exploration in the frontiers when economics dictated that companies should have been scaling down or pulling out. Ottawa realized its mistake, but it was too late: the program was in place, the commitments had been made, and the money was hemorrhaging from federal coffers. Petro-Canada's PIP grant receipts said it all. The company received $138 million in 1981, $299 million in 1982, and $468 million in 1983. Perhaps the most ridiculous waste was in the Arctic Islands. Even though most of Petrocan's partners had dropped out, Panarctic nevertheless signed a mind-numbingly expensive series of agreements with federal authorities to spend $500 million.

Now federal energy officials, in a panic, set about bolting the stable door. The stark realization that the horse had taken off came first not from the East Coast, or the Arctic Islands, but from the Beaufort.

. . .

Jack Gallagher's "Beaufort dream," and his success in selling it, had been instrumental in persuading the Liberal government that the frontiers contained the motherlode that would free them from the threats of both OPEC and Alberta. First had come the generous tax allowances of super-depletion in 1977, then the NEP's PIP grants in 1980, both of which were aimed at promoting the drilling of expensive offshore wells. But the potential for abuse was obvious, particularly after Dome Petroleum stumbled into financial crisis. PIP grants became essential to the Canmar fleet's profits, which were in turn essential to Dome Petroleum's corporate survival. Dome subsidiary Dome Canada quickly became the top recipient of PIP grants, pulling in a record $486 million from the program in the period up to March 1983 (it would later be overtaken by Petrocan). That month, Dome Petroleum announced a five-year, $1-billion exploration program for the Beaufort. Three-quarters of that sum would come from Dome Canada. Eighty per cent of Dome Canada's costs would come from the Canadian taxpayer. At around the same time, Gulf Canada announced another agreement. It was this agreement that set off the alarm bells in Ottawa. The Gulf agreement was only for $150 million — but then it was only for one well.

Gulf Canada also had extensive Beaufort interests that it was keen to explore. The problem was that the only offshore drilling facilities belonged to Dome's Canmar. Dome always negotiated tough terms, not merely on "day rates," the daily charges for the fleet, but also by demanding a piece of the exploration action. One of Dome's disgruntled partners referred to them as "pirates." Gulf decided it wasn't going to take it any more; it would build its own Arctic fleet. It committed $674 million to two massive drilling units and a fleet of support vessels that included the two most powerful privately owned icebreakers in the world.

Although Gulf wasn't eligible for the highest level of PIP grants, Canadian partners who drilled on Gulf lands using Gulf's drilling equipment would be. Thus Gulf, like Dome Petroleum, would obtain indirect advantages. Nevertheless, Gulf executives bristled at the suggestion that the fleet was constructed to take advantage of the much-hated NEP. It was predicated, they would say, on their evaluation of their Beaufort acreage *in spite of* the NEP.

The Gulf fleet needed high day rates to cover its huge capital costs. When the government saw those rates — most of which, they realized, they would have to pay out in PIPs — they were horrified. Moreover, even though they had to find only 20 per cent of the costs, the Canadian partners were horrified too. As drilling costs all over the world were dropping, those in the Canadian frontiers were skyrocketing. The federal government stepped in to jaw down Gulf's rates. Nevertheless, Gulf lost some of its partners, who began to see that drilling $150-million wells in remote regions while world oil prices were sagging, even if the government covered 80 per cent of your costs, was a horrendously wasteful proposition.

In his 1983 report, Kenneth Dye, the auditor general who was still chasing details of Petrocan's Petrofina purchase, slammed PIP grants, which he estimated would cost more than $8 billion by

1987, with no guarantee of return. He censured the government for failing to monitor the expenditures, although by then public servants were busily trying to haul down rates by monitoring wells costing more than $50 million. Which was suddenly an awful lot of wells. The alarm bells were ringing off the East Coast too.

The Bow Valley–Husky team found itself in the same position as Gulf, only more so. Because the *Bow Drill 3* and two of the supply boats had been built in Canada, their costs, and thus their day rates, were relatively high. Bow Valley and Husky had sacrificed economics in order to accommodate "national" objectives of promoting Canadian offshore expertise. Since the resultant higher costs were incurred in pursuing the federal government's objectives, it did not seem unreasonable that the federal government should pay up via PIPs. PIP administrators thought otherwise. They ruled that rates for equipment had to be broadly "competitive." As a result, part of the costs of the Bow Valley–Husky East Coast equipment was declared "non-PIPable." The government had effectively said: "Do the Canadian thing and we'll look after you." Now, horrified by the unforeseen costs of the program, it was backing down on the deal.

Petrocan's "buy foreign" policy had not turned out well either. The *Sedco 710*, built in Japan, fitted out with German equipment, and declared to be "the most sophisticated rig in the world," had turned into a nightmare. In St. John's, it was dubbed "Petro-Canada's hard-luck rig." Instead of anchors (although it also possessed them as a back-up), the rig used thrusters to maintain its position. But when it arrived at its Labrador drill site in the spring of 1983, six of its eight thrusters were misfiring. The rig had to be taken back to port for repairs. All its anchor chains then had to be replaced. While at Marystown for repairs, one of its cranes — among the few rig components that were Canadian-made — collapsed. Its second crane was found to have welding flaws. One of its two supply vessels capsized and sank.

For taxpayers, the most appalling aspect of the *Sedco 710* affair was that they got stuck with most of the $340,000 daily charge for the crippled rig to sit in port. Federal Tory energy critic Pat

Carney declared: "This is an example of the financial nightmare that PIP grants are all about. It's appalling. Who's accountable for this mess and why should taxpayers pay the dough for a rig that isn't working?"

THIRTEEN

The Man from Petrocan

I N THE period from the introduction of the NEP in 1980 until early 1983, Petro-Canada went on a spending spree. It put up a giant new office tower in Calgary. It made yet another major downstream takeover, buying — for the first time but not the last — assets from one of the Seven Sisters. It staged expensive staff raids on other oil companies.

For Calgary, the new Petro-Canada headquarters was the final insult. The twin towers began to take shape towards the end of 1982, as business was falling apart and office space came tumbling onto the market, driving down rents. Not only was one of the towers — at fifty-two stories — the largest building in the West, but Petrocan chose to clad the development in red granite, as if to rub the local community's nose in the "Red Square" label. Worse, from an economic nationalist's point of view, everything you could see from the outside was foreign-made. Although it had solicited bids from Canadian quarries, the company declared that none was able to supply the "quantity and quality" of granite required. So the buildings were covered with Taivassalo granite from Finland, cut and polished in Italy. Since "no Canadian manufacturer could supply coated reflective glass to meet our specifications," Petrocan turned to Pittsburgh Plate Glass of the U.S.

The larger of the two towers soon acquired a nickname:

"Pierre's Finger." Allan Fotheringham declared in *Maclean's*: "Ottawa wanted to leave its mark on Calgary the way the Mafia leaves a dead fish on the doorstep, the way a Prussian student wants to leave a duelling scar on your cheek."

When the company began moving employees into the building towards the end of 1983, it still held leases on more than a dozen properties around the city. Early in 1982, it had rented the 232,000-square-foot Hanover Building for around $18,000 a day. It would remain empty for years.

Hopper skated through all criticism. He continued to play his political advantages to the hilt. While PIP funding fuelled the East Coast drilling boom, Hopper used the popular success of Petrocan's downstream to build his refining and marketing empire despite the misgivings of his political masters.

By the end of 1982, the Liberals were in trouble with the electorate. The economy was in recession. The party's bold interventionist thrust had come unstuck. PIP grants in particular had proved a much bigger and more unpredictable drain than expected. When the Liberals announced spending cuts in October 1982, two years after the NEP, to cope with a soaring budget deficit, Petrocan was earmarked for restraint. The government announced its capital budgets would be cut by $290 million over the following three years. Petrocan blew off this frail financial lid almost immediately.

Don Johnston, the Cabinet minister who had been appalled at the Petrofina takeover, was now paraded before the nation's television cameras as the new rising star of the party, proof of Liberal "pragmatism" and renewed dedication to free enterprise. Not only had Johnston criticized the Petrofina deal, he had now emerged as a strong opponent of Petrocan's expansion into refining and marketing. But his real power relative to that of Bill Hopper was revealed when Petrocan announced, soon after the budget, that it would be taking over the downstream assets of British Petroleum: another 1,640 gasoline stations and two refineries. Hopper had persuaded the new energy minister, Jean Chrétien, and Marc Lalonde, who remained a powerful force as minister of finance, that Petrocan "needed" the refining and marketing assets of BP, which had come up for sale in 1982, to "round out" his empire.

Gasoline is the classic "distress purchase": you buy it when the needle nears empty. Petrocan appeared to be changing that pattern. Hopper pointed out that the public was responding positively to the Petrocan logo. The spiky Maple Leaf symbol was pulling in drivers prepared to "pump their money back into Canada." In the first eight months of 1982, Petrocan's retail sales in Ontario were up 19 per cent over the same period in 1981, while sales in the industry as a whole had dropped by 6 per cent. In Quebec, the company's sales had risen 6 per cent while those of the industry had slumped 14 per cent.

Just look, said Hopper, at how popular Petrocan is. And the BP takeover was Canadianization, which was still government policy. Moreover, he told the uneasy Liberal ministers, this wouldn't cost them a *thing*. He'd finance the deal commercially, and then the BP stations would throw off cash flow to deal with his real mandate, in the frontiers.

To make the takeover a little more palatable, Petrocan obligingly minimized the costs in its public announcement. The price was given as $347.6 million. Once BP's inventories and other obligations had been taken into account, the acquisition cost was closer to $600 million. Omitting the cost of inventory — that is, the gasoline in the refineries and gas stations — was the equivalent of quoting the price of an automobile without the engine. It was, to put it mildly, cosmetic accounting.

Now Petrocan had almost 3,000 stations coast-to-coast. Hopper, it seemed, wanted to be no less than a mirror image of Imperial Oil, his old employer and the nationalists' nemesis. Nevertheless, according to a press release: "Petro-Canada indicated that this acquisition would complete its refining and marketing business."

The notion of a "complete" refining and marketing network was a long way from the company's original mandate as understood by its Liberal creators. Petrocan's "non-competitive" status had also been defenestrated. Petrocan's success at the gas pump could only be bought at the expense of the other gasoline retailers. It might be popular with Canadians, but it certainly wasn't going to make them drive farther. Gasoline retailing is a zero-sum game.

And was it truly "complete"? Since all BP's stations were in Ontario and Quebec, when Bill Hopper looked at his coast-to-coast network, it seemed to him… well, a little *light* in the West.

• • •

Bill Hopper continued to betray an extraordinary sense of self-satisfaction with his achievements. He was unafraid of a high profile. Indeed, he rejoiced in publicity. In 1982, the National Film Board decided to shoot a documentary on Hopper. Petrocan's chairman agreed to allow a film crew to follow him as he jetted to Europe and South America for meetings with Petrocan executives, oil ministers, and heads of other national oil companies.

Nationalist academic Larry Pratt was hired as the film's writer. Pratt, more than most, was fully aware that organizations such as Petrocan tended to go off in pursuit of their own mandates. He had written in 1981: "Whether this ambitious venture in state capitalism will use its position to promote Canadian national interests as well as its own interests is another question entirely." Nevertheless, Bill Hopper clearly charmed the pants off everybody associated with the project. When the CBC was shown an early version of the film, it rejected it as too pro-Petrocan. Paul Wright, executive producer of television documentaries for CBC current affairs, told the *Toronto Star*'s Diane Francis: "It made Bill Hopper look like the saviour of Western civilization."

The Man from Petrocan finally aired in March 1984, showing Hopper in the no-bullshit, international-oilman-guru mode that he so relished. Big-time Hopper aboard his jet, bathing in the gentle light of the stratosphere, expounding on other countries' attitudes towards Canadian energy: "They say, 'What's the matter with you guys? Can't you get it together?'" Hard-hat Hopper, explaining directional drilling aboard an offshore rig in the sunny Mediterranean. Hopper in the office, deriding the Canadian language commissioner over an acute accent in the French version of the company's name. Hopper standing over Calgary, dumping on job applicants who came looking for security. Hopper at a meeting of South American state oil producing companies (wrong geography, right attitudes), comparing the size of Canada's megaprojects. Hopper scuttling through an airport with a model of an offshore rig he was having built in Norway, chortling: "You can tell the men from the boys by the size of their toys."

While Hopper played to the camera, saying things like "I wanna be out front," the solemn voice of economic nationalism intoned its chorus of support for Petrocan and its criticism of Big Oil: "Hopper's aim is to get new technology for use in Canada." "He began to build the company that would guarantee Canadian energy security." Hopper "must find middle ground between profits and the national interest." The East Coast was described as "the stage on which his struggle with the multinationals will be acted out."

Towards the end of the film, Hopper was seen making the trek up Parliament Hill with his trusty PR man, Bob Foulkes. They were going to discuss the East Coast with Marc Lalonde, then still energy minister. In the minister's office, Hopper attempted a stunning on-camera power play with an obviously uncomfortable Lalonde to shove Mobil aside as the operator of the most important East Coast discoveries. With the camera rolling, he put it to Lalonde: "The gut issue here is whether Mobil in New York will spend at the rate we want to spend." Hopper had cleverly slipped in the name of Gotham, the nationalist trump card: "Mobil *in New York*." But Lalonde told him Mobil would continue as operator. "Hopper has overplayed his hand," came the off-camera chorus, somewhat sadly. "Lalonde had backed the multinationals. The government fears a fight with the Americans."

Back at the office, meanwhile, Petrocan was on an aggressive recruiting drive, raiding many of its corporate rivals. Gulf was particularly hard hit. In addition to Ed Lakusta, Petrocan had also lured away several other Gulf executives. "We were royally pissed off," said a Gulf official. Bill West, head of Imperial's refining and marketing side, was persuaded to jump ship and join the Petrocan crew as vice-president of the products division in 1982.

Petrocan needed all the executive help it could get. It had made four takeovers in nine years. In the wake of the BP acquisition, it had gas stations sitting across from each other at intersections all over Ontario and Quebec. And while it needed senior executives, it had too many staff, the result of taking over so many parallel organizations. Also, despite the huge influx of PIP grants, its even more massive expenditures meant it was strapped for cash. In February 1983, with world oil prices headed down but Canadian prices still held below them, Hopper asked the federal government to move to world prices as quickly as possible. This was not the message that economic nationalists had hoped would emerge from their champion.

Petrocan's period of rapid growth was now declared to be over. "We are on the second wave," Hopper said. "Now we are wrestling with the problems of integration, effective management, and getting things to work better than they are." A policy of belt-tightening was announced to the world. Ed Lakusta declared that the company had cut back on perks such as club memberships and company cars. The practice of giving workers "Golden Fridays," that is, two out of every three off, was ended. "We all work a thirty-nine-hour week now," said Lakusta.

With increasing popular unease about the economy and about the huge expenditures of the NEP, Petrocan's star appeared on the wane. A Gallup poll taken in March 1983 and released the following month showed that 45 per cent of Canadians thought Petro-Canada should be sold, as opposed to 34 per cent who opposed such a sale — almost the reverse of the percentages polled at the height of the second OPEC crisis.

Once again, a Tory government loomed on the political horizon, although the Tories were in the midst of a damaging internal leadership battle. One of the more outspoken candidates, Newfoundland's John Crosbie, had declared in Calgary that if he became prime minister he would turn Red Square into "Black and Blue Square."

The victor in the June 1983 leadership race, Brian Mulroney, had no discernible ideology. Senior Petrocan executive David O'Brien had practised law with Mulroney and was among his circle of friends in Montreal. Shortly before Mulroney came to power, O'Brien had run into his old colleague in the street. Mulroney had told O'Brien he had no intention of dismantling Petrocan, but that at some stage he might privatize it. For Petrocan, that was no problem. Indeed, it was what Bill Hopper wanted.

Mulroney and the Tories were wary of their former nemesis, the entity that had helped bury them in 1979/80. Although the Tories claimed to be in favour of a policy of privatization, party policy did not link the program with Petrocan. Not only were the Tories circumspect about Hopper and Petrocan, but they had more important energy priorities. They wished to install a new, comprehensive, market-based energy policy, and make petroleum peace with Alberta and the Atlantic provinces. The issue of Petrocan — and thus the fate of Bill Hopper — was on the back burner.

Not that Hopper wasn't worried; he worked at strengthening his links both with the industry and with his new masters. Among the Crown corporation's new hirings in 1983 and 1984 were a number of executives with close Tory ties, at both the federal and the provincial level. Tory MP Harvie Andre, who still glowered at the mention of the state oil company, grumbled that "an oil company should be looking for oil, not political support in Ottawa." Hopper was accused of "Tory-shopping." Meanwhile, Hopper was developing a relationship with Frank Moores. Moores, former premier of Newfoundland, was very close to Mulroney. The men were soulmates. Just as Moores had helped Mulroney from the fit of depression that had followed Mulroney's loss at the 1976 Tory leadership convention, so Mulroney had helped Moores after his exit from the provincial premiership in 1979. Moores had been deeply grateful and was reckoned to have been the "godfather" of the Ottawa plotting that later supplanted Joe Clark as Tory leader.

In December 1985, Petrocan was revealed to have hired Moores's lobbying company, Government Consultants International. By then, Moores had become the most controversial consultant in Ottawa, embroiled in allegations of influence peddling and conflict of interest. Although Petrocan claimed it had hired Moores to give advice on energy issues involving the Atlantic provinces, many doubted it. As John Sawatsky wrote in his study of Ottawa lobbying, *The Insiders*, "Everybody knew that Mulroney and Moores were cronies who kept in touch, and that reality alone enhanced GCI's value in the marketplace... Whether the image was justified or not, Frank Moores symbolized the quick-fix school of lobbying. Nobody produced evidence of influence-peddling, but everybody suspected it."

One observer noted: "Bill Hopper was just doing what any other corporate executive in his position would have done." But Petrocan wasn't meant to be like any other corporation. Nothing so clearly demonstrated the naiveté of those who imagined Petrocan to be a disinterested servant of the vaguely defined "public interest" as the Crown corporation's hiring of Ottawa consultants to influence the policy process and ensure its own survival. This practice would later expand enormously.

To move closer to the industry, Petro-Canada joined the Canadian Petroleum Association, the lobbying group most identified with Big Oil in Canada. This move came as no surprise to those who understood the workings of the industry and the independent survival instincts of political creations such as Petro-Canada. But of course, Petro-Canada had been created by those who didn't understand either the oil industry or institutional realities. They had claimed they wanted an "independent" voice. Now Petrocan was joining the industry chorus.

In April 1984, Petro-Canada joined its integrated colleagues in pouring scorn on proposals by Ottawa's anti-trust watchdog — the director of combines investigations, Lawson Hunter — to the Restrictive Trade Practices Commission about reforming the downstream end of the business. At the time, the commission was well on its way to establishing that the allegations of one of Lawson's predecessors, Robert Bertrand, regarding the multinationals' "$12-billion rip-off" were nonsense. Nevertheless, Hunter asserted that the industry restricted competition and kept prices artificially high. Hunter proposed that gasoline stations be permitted to sell rival brands. A Petrocan response declared: "The recommendation gives no consideration to the investment in facilities and brand promotion, and proprietary rights are disregarded in a way that amounts to nothing less than expropriation without compensation."

Here, at last, the window on the industry was explaining to Ottawa the way the world worked, puncturing the balloons of the capital's theorists. But did the taxpayers really need to buy 3,000 gas stations before we could get the goods? Commenting on the CPA membership, a Petrocan spokesman declared, perhaps tongue in cheek: "We'll become directly involved and have a window on the industry. We'll know what the rest of the industry is doing."

· · ·

People tended to compare Pat Carney — the new energy minister in Brian Mulroney's Tory government, which was elected in September 1984 — to mythic female figures. She had been likened to Boadicea, the British warrior-queen who fought the Romans. She had been described as "Valkyrian." And indeed her statuesque form did seem to beg for a sword, spear, and pointed helmet to complete the ensemble. There was also a little of the warrior-queen in her temperament. Bill Hopper was particularly uneasy with the notion of her as a Valkyrie, because Valkyries were "choosers of the doomed," who led slain warriors from the battlefield to Valhalla. Bill Hopper wasn't ready for Valhalla yet. He dispatched Petrocan executives with Tory connections to Ottawa to sound out the level of animosity against him. "Jeez," he said, "that woman *hates* me. She's going to *get* me." He was comforted to learn, however, that he did not appear on the hit list. Indeed, as it turned out, Pat Carney would prove perhaps the most surprising and valuable of all Bill Hopper's benefactors.

Pat Carney was born in Shanghai. She returned with her parents to B.C., where her father became a government veterinarian. After graduating from the University of British Columbia, she became a business journalist. When she wrote in praise of Imperial Oil for its exploration in the Northwest Territories, she was not ashamed to have the headline "God Bless Imperial Oil Co." above her story. In the late 1960s, she became fascinated by energy and the North. She visited Prudhoe Bay and the Panarctic Oils drill site on Melville Island, a vision for the roughnecks in her pink pant suit and Elizabeth Arden makeup. She moved to Yellowknife, capital of the Northwest Territories, and wrote a report on the social and economic benefits of a proposed Mackenzie Valley gas pipeline, a report for which she was roundly criticized by the anti-development social scientists and environmentalists who had descended on northern issues.

Persuaded by Joe Clark to run for the Tories, Carney won a seat in Vancouver Centre in 1980. Although it was Clark who had brought her into politics, she remained neutral during the 1983 leadership struggle, and after Mulroney won, he made her energy critic. Carney came to the post with a sense of the "romance of energy." She believed that frontier energy projects and other megaschemes, such as heavy oil and tarsands plants, could prove an engine of growth. The Liberals had held the same vision and been rudely disillusioned in 1982. Nevertheless, although OPEC appeared weak, there was some consensus that prices would start rising again by the early 1990s. Carney — and the party — remained captivated by the notion of energy developments from St. John's to Vancouver. But the first steps in achieving such a vision were to dump the National Energy Program, return to market prices, and make peace with the provinces. Petrocan could be dealt with later.

Before the 1984 election, Hopper expressed dissatisfaction with all the uncertainty. "I just wish it was all over with," he told the *Globe and Mail*. "Then the federal government could set its goals for Petrocan and we could get on with our jobs." Nevertheless, he began singing songs he knew the Tories — indeed everybody — wanted to hear: "My preference is for a financially sound corporation — one with a manageable level of debt." Hardly going out on a limb.

He must have suffered a little frisson of dread when his salary was revealed, along with a list of other Crown corporation heads' incomes, by the Tories in October. The intriguing aspect of Hopper's income was how it was constituted — a regular salary of $114,000, but another $300,000 in income from Petrocan's subsidiaries, the device used to evade Ottawa salary ceilings. Prime Minister Mulroney noted at the time, "Those are pretty handsome numbers for anyone running a corporation that doesn't have to declare a profit." But Mulroney didn't say he thought Hopper was overpaid; he always liked to take a balanced view.

After the election, Hopper began doing the rounds of the newspapers and magazines, preaching a bottom-line mandate. "We're changing in a totally new direction now," he told the *Financial Times of Canada.* "What we're now doing basically is shifting very much away from the mandated national interest stuff into commercial bottom-line considerations. The need to know, as far as we're concerned, is finished. Now's the time for commercial bottom-line development of those fields we found. We're pretty healthy right now and we're generating substantial cash flow."

Elsewhere, Hopper pushed the desire to privatize. He told the *Globe and Mail* that there would be no conflict between a sale of shares to investors and the objectives of Petrocan, "because for the last two or three years, Petrocan has been putting bottom-line commercial considerations ahead of political objectives."

In December, Hopper was reappointed as head of Petrocan by Mulroney, who described him as "an excellent manager." Mulroney also relieved Hopper of any blame in the Petrofina deal, declaring that Petrocan's chief had simply been following the orders of Liberal Energy Minister Marc Lalonde. To exonerate Hopper seemed strange, given that the Tories' inquiry into Petrofina — including a study by accountants Ernst & Whinney — was only just beginning.

But if the Tories didn't want to make Hopper an issue, they were pretty keen to clear out the board, which was replete with Liberal Party appointees. At the end of a three-hour meeting at the company's Ottawa office on November 22, Hopper handed out resignation letters to most directors. Some were visibly upset.

Robert Laxer, the rabid economic nationalist who had been appointed earlier in the year, was beside himself. Here he was, close to the dream, and now it was being taken away from him.

Even among those experienced members who'd expected it, there was an undoubted sense of loss. For those who had been there since the beginning, businessman Claude Hébert and lawyer David Mann, there was sadness. They had shared a sense of camaraderie that had been skillfully nurtured by Bill Hopper. Long-serving public servants, like Ian Stewart, were hardly surprised to be going but had genuine concerns about the fate of the entity for which they felt strong personal responsibility.

The Tories appointed a new board. Most were lawyers with strong party connections, like Jean Bazin from Montreal, Rudy Bratty and Peggy Dubin from Toronto, Roy Deyell from Calgary, and Bill Elliott from Regina. Robin Abercrombie was a former employee at Nova with connections to Pat Carney. John Lundrigan was a former politician from St. John's. Ed Barroll, a former Mobil employee, was the only oilman on the board. Jocelynne Pelchat-Johnson was a corporate executive and wife of prominent Quebec Liberal Daniel Johnson, Jr. David Read was a strong Tory and McDonald's franchisee from Dartmouth, Nova Scotia. James Robertson was a businessman from Inuvik who, like Abercrombie, knew Carney from her northern days. Of the old board, only businessman Harrison McCain and energy deputy minister Paul Tellier survived.

These people all took their new appointments seriously. Bill Hopper and Petrocan were symbols of things they didn't like. They were going to tell the company to shape up. They were going to stop it getting away with anything.

Hopper's first meeting with the new board was at La Chaudière, a new hotel across the river from Ottawa in Hull. When he walked in, he knew only a couple of the people present. The antagonism was almost electric. The meeting was tense. But within a couple of months, Hopper had them all won over. Hopper was masterful. He got in touch with each board member after the meeting, and made sure he stayed in touch. He catered to their wishes, made sure there were always little gifts in their hotel rooms when they came to Ottawa or went elsewhere for board meetings. He held meetings in the board members' various home towns, with a Petrocan-funded cocktail party to which the board member could invite all his or her friends and associates.

A new "mandate" for Petrocan appeared in Petro-Canada's 1984 annual report. "In the first nine years," it declared, "Petro-Canada was directed to work towards Canada's energy security effectively and efficiently, without overriding concern for profitability. The Corporation has now been given a new mandate by its shareholder — to operate in a commercial, private sector fashion, with emphasis on profitability and the need to maximize the return on the Government of Canada's investment. In this regard, Petro-Canada is not to be perceived in the future as an instrument in the pursuit of the Government's policy objectives. However, the Government maintains the right as a shareholder to formally direct Petro-Canada to carry out certain activities in the national interest." The final two sentences were contradictory: the company was not to be a policy instrument, unless the government wanted it to be. The wording seemed to speak volumes about the government's ambiguity towards Petrocan; but perhaps the most intriguing aspect of the "commercial mandate" was that it was inserted not at the insistence of Pat Carney but at the suggestion of Bill Hopper.

The "commercial mandate" was part of Hopper's ongoing effort to separate himself from political influence. But the thorny issue of using Petro-Canada "in the national interest" was to return almost immediately.

FOURTEEN

Dancing the Bump

THE NEP'S government-backed, bank-funded buy-out of foreign oil may have damaged both relations with the U.S. and the Canadian dollar, but it had still not dislodged any of the largest foreign-controlled oil companies. Petrocan had bought BP's downstream, but BP had never been a big player on the Canadian scene. The majors — Imperial Oil, Gulf Canada, Shell Canada, and Texaco Canada — appeared more firmly entrenched than ever. They would have been difficult to acquire at the best of times. Now, with Petrocan apparently out of cash, they looked invulnerable.

When Gulf Canada finally came on the auction block, it was because of machinations unrelated to Canada's post-NEP takeover spree. An even more aggressive bout of acquisition had begun south of the border in the fall of 1983, as a brainstorm in the mind of a man named T. Boone Pickens.

Pickens, the swashbuckling Texan who ran Amarillo-based Mesa Petroleum, was an expert at "greenmail": buying shares in possible takeover targets and putting them in play, whereupon larger predators would come and gobble them up, leaving Pickens with hefty capital gains. He had played a role in Superior Oil being acquired by Mobil, in Cities Service falling into the arms of Occidental Petroleum, and in General American Oil being taken over by Phillips Petroleum. In each deal, Mesa had made a bundle.

But there was more to Pickens than greenmail. He was also a corporate crusader, sharply critical of Big Oil's diversification into unrelated businesses and its high-cost frontier exploration. Mobil had bought department stores, Exxon had moved into office equipment, Atlantic Richfield had gone into copper. But the strangest move of all had been made by Gulf Corporation: it had bought Ringling Bros. and Barnum & Bailey Circus.

Pickens's views on the wisdom of frontier exploration were powerfully supported by a well that was drilled off Alaska in the summer and fall of 1983. This well, Mukluk, proved to be the most expensive dry hole in history; it marked a turning point in attitudes towards frontier exploration. Pickens believed that rather than diversifying into businesses they knew nothing about, or drilling-billion dollar dry holes, companies with cash to burn should turn it over to shareholders.

In the fall of 1983, Pickens's incisive mind locked onto the problems and potentials of the Gulf Oil Corporation, the company that had acquired Ringling Bros. He soon decided that the clowns had taken over the circus.

Gulf was the smallest of the Seven Sisters. Its origins lay at Spindletop, in the great gusher of 1901. Spindletop soon dried up, but Gulf, under the control of the Mellons, the Pittsburgh-based industrialists, went on to make major discoveries all over the U.S. and then the world. Gulf opened the first U.S. drive-in gas station, in Pittsburgh in 1913, and made huge finds beneath the deserts of Kuwait and the swamps of Venezuela.

For Gulf and its Canadian subsidiary, the political and business turmoil created by the OPEC crises was greatly exacerbated by internal corporate problems. In 1973, in the course of Watergate, Gulf was revealed to have made major illegal contributions to Richard Nixon's re-election campaign. Between 1966 and 1972, Gulf was also found to have paid US$5 million to foreign politicians and parties, including South Korea's President Chung Hee Park. The Securities and Exchange Commission charged Gulf with falsifying financial records relating to slush funds. Gulf also became embroiled in an international uranium cartel.

These scandals had an important ramification for Gulf's 60-per-cent-owned Canadian subsidiary: they led to the replacement of Gulf's head, Bob Dorsey, by Gulf Canada's chief executive, Jerry McAfee. While Dorsey had been struggling in Pittsburgh, McAfee had taken Gulf Canada to the top of the multinational pack. The significance of McAfee's elevation was not lost on his colleagues at Gulf Canada's Toronto headquarters on Bay Street. When he left for Pittsburgh, they presented him with a T-shirt emblazoned with the words "Mr. Clean." But McAfee found Gulf's problems intractable. The company was faced with nationalization in Kuwait and Venezuela, plus a growing excess of refining and marketing capacity at home. McAfee handed Gulf's problems over to James E. Lee.

Jimmy Lee had a blind spot: he didn't understand Wall Street. In the summer of 1982, when Pickens had launched his first David-and-Goliath greenmail bid, tendering for the stock of Cities Service, Cities Service had sought a "white knight." The man who had galloped up was Jimmy Lee. But when Lee heard rumours that the U.S. Federal Trade Commission might intervene on anti-trust grounds, he rode off again. Gulf's withdrawal left a lot of unhappy Wall Street arbitrageurs, who had accumulated Cities Service stock in the hope of a bid-'em-up fight. Although Armand Hammer's Occidental Petroleum emerged as an alternative white knight, the arbs still lost around US$400 million. Jimmy Lee had cost them. If anybody took a run at Gulf, the arbs would participate with particular enthusiasm.

A run on Gulf became increasingly likely because of the company's depressed share price; its oil reserves were valued at US$4 a barrel when the average finding cost for new reserves was US$10. Why drill for oil when you could get it 60 per cent cheaper by buying Gulf? By the time Mukluk came up dry, Gulf was already in play.

On August 11, 1983, news of unusually heavy trading in Gulf stock came to the company's Pittsburgh headquarters. When Jimmy Lee and his executives heard that Pickens was buying, they were annoyed rather than scared. Gulf's 1982 revenues of US$30 billion were seventy times greater than those of Mesa. But Gulf executives had only to look at Pickens's record to realize that once he picked on a company, that company usually wound up being taken over. Although Pickens lost a proxy fight with Gulf, his actions, as he had hoped, stirred the interest in Gulf of much bigger corporate fish. Lee began to search for white knights, and found one in another of the Seven Sisters, Standard Oil of California. Socal eventually acquired Gulf for a mind-numbing US$13.2 billion, by far the world's largest takeover to date. The new company would be known as Chevron.

Wall Street's arbs made a fortune from the bidding war for Gulf, as did Pickens. He and his investment group hauled in a cool US$760 million. A dinner was thrown in Pickens's honour at Park Avenue's Regency Hotel. There, Ed Koch, the mayor of New York, presented Pickens with a crystal apple as a recognition of the huge volumes of money that Pickens's activities had generated for Wall Street, and hence the city. Pickens produced a live monkey. "I'd like you people," he said, "to meet Jimmy Lee."

• • •

Lee might claim he'd made a lot of money for Gulf shareholders, but that was little comfort to the Canadian subsidiary, which was now faced with an uncertain future. Either it would be absorbed into Chevron's Canadian subsidiary, Chevron Canada, or it would be sold. The former alternative held few attractions. Pittsburgh had always been a relatively passive major shareholder and had allowed Gulf Canada to go its own way; Chevron's head office in San Francisco, by contrast, was felt to have a much tighter grip on its Calgary-based Canadian operation. But then Chevron Canada had also been an enormous success, finding both West Pembina in Alberta and Hibernia off the East Coast.

Gulf Canada was Canada's second-largest oil company, but it was also one of its most troubled. Following McAfee's departure, it had been beset by problems of management succession and corporate direction. The man who had ultimately succeeded McAfee was John Stoik, a big, heavy-set, bespectacled engineer who had returned to Canada from running Gulf's operations in Korea. Stoik, who became chief executive in 1979, was a solid citizen and a charter member of the "Moose Jaw Mafia," the executive group that had trained at the company's big refinery in Moose Jaw, Saskatchewan. But Stoik was no McAfee. He lacked charisma and looked uneasy in public.

Under him, the corporate soul-searching deepened. The company was mired in bureaucracy and inertia. Management consultants were shown Gulf Canada's organization chart without being told the entity's name. Because of its myriad committees, the consultants decided it had to be either a hospital or a university.

To improve efficiency, Gulf was organized into upstream and downstream divisions, with a small corporate head office to give strategic direction. At least that was the theory. The resources arm was housed in a giant new glass-faced building on Calgary's Ninth Avenue. The squat building typified Gulf: massive but not outstanding. In front of the building sat a sculptured concrete structure that formed an outlet for the building's state-of-the-art energy conservation system. In the depths of Calgary's winter, the structure would wreath the entrance with white steam, making it look like the entrance to Hades. The mists were a fitting symbol of Gulf's clouded future.

Whereas Imperial took a strategic "rifle" approach, identifying and taking aim at specific targets, Gulf was seen as a "shotgun" company that tried for a little bit of everything. Gulf was a follower rather than a leader, and the company that it followed most often was Imperial. Imperial's supreme self-confidence galled Gulf's senior management. Gulf chairman J.C. Phillips once said in a company publication: "If Imperial jumped off a cliff, the others would follow. And when they hit the bottom and were hurting real bad they'd still say, 'It can't be all that bad because Imperial is down here with us.'"

Then, suddenly, Gulf's shotgun began hitting targets.

The first hit was at Hibernia, in partnership with Chevron, Mobil, and Petro-Canada. Gulf was also involved with Dome in a

Beaufort find that Dome claimed to be of major importance. Gulf was the only member of the Hibernia drilling consortium whose equity was publicly traded in Canada. In less than a month, its shares doubled to $100. By early 1980, they had reached an astonishing $190 before being split five-for-one.

In 1980, the value of trading in Gulf shares reached a record $5.4 billion. But just when it seemed that the oilman's greatest asset, luck, had pulled Gulf from its prolonged identity crisis, along came the National Energy Program.

For Stoik and his management and board, the prospect of "Canadianization" was not repugnant. After all, most of them were Canadians, and proud of it. More important, there was suddenly lots of money — in the form of the new discriminatory PIP grants — attached to being Canadian. But Gulf's Pittsburgh parent remained opposed to the notion of being blackmailed by the National Energy Program into selling out. As Alf Powis, chairman of Gulf Canada's executive committee, said: "Once the NEP came along, the Gulf Canada management was very keen to have the company Canadianized, particularly since we were so active in the frontiers... But at the end of the day, the only way they could Canadianize was to get Gulf Pittsburgh out of there, and Gulf Pittsburgh was reluctant to get out."

Inspired by its frontier success, Gulf Canada's management had decided to stop playing follow-the-leader. If they weren't Canadian enough to get their hands directly onto PIPs, they could at least take a bold initiative that would indirectly benefit from the grants.

Within six months of the NEP, Gulf Canada had committed itself to the largest single investment in its history, the $674-million Beaufort drilling fleet. But with the weakening of prices and the tighter monitoring of PIP grants by Ottawa, Gulf's drilling system began to look like yet another corporate error.

Gulf Canada was still a rare prize. Its 1983 earnings of $218 million on net revenues of $5.2 billion were well down from the 1980 peak of $380 million on sales of $3.8 billion, but it was still the country's fourth-largest petroleum reserve holder, behind Imperial, financially crippled Dome, and Shell Canada. These holdings made it an attractive company, but they also made it an expensive one. Gulf Canada was estimated to be worth around $5 billion, so it would take some $3 billion to buy out Gulf Corp.'s 60 per cent. Then Gulf Corp.'s 60 per cent became Chevron's 60 per cent.

When Chevron looked at its options for Gulf's Canadian subsidiary, it knew that its first stop had to be Ottawa. Chevron executives flew to the nation's capital, where they discovered that the Liberals had little desire to make an issue of the acquisition. There was an election coming. The government allowed Chevron to take title to Gulf Canada in return for promising to offer the company for sale to "Canadian-controlled entities." Chevron was quite keen to sell because it wanted to pay down its huge U.S. debt.

When the Tories came to power, the Chevron executives went back to Ottawa, but the Tories were still struggling with the reins of power, and Chevron's negotiators had problems getting answers. The Tories were facing several indirect takeovers in which the parents of Canadian companies had been acquired. In addition to Chevron-Gulf, there was also the acquisition of Superior Oil by Mobil, and of Getty Oil by Texaco. Both Superior and Getty had Canadian subsidiaries.

Although the Tories had declared themselves "open for business," and although the much-despised FIRA was now transformed into the more foreign-investor-friendly Investment Canada, the Tories were wary of letting all three companies pass to their new American owners. The attractions of "helping" one of the indirect takeover targets into Canadian hands were great. In February 1985, the Tories announced — as the Liberals had done — that they had allowed Gulf Canada to pass to Chevron on the condition that the American company put its block on the market "for sale to Canadian-controlled purchasers." A deadline of April 30, 1985, was announced, after which Chevron could dispose of Gulf Canada as it sought fit.

Pat Carney was an economic nationalist by inclination. Indeed, she was fond of telling people that the NEP's 50-per-cent Canadian ownership target for the oil industry had originally been a Tory policy. She believed that taking an active role in encouraging this largest of all Canadianizations would deflect any suggestion that the Tories, although they had dismantled the NEP, disagreed with its motherhood principles. Canadianization remained a flawed concept: Canadian did not necessarily mean competent; buying out foreigners meant sending money out of the country for assets that couldn't be moved anyway. But for economic nationalists, the only question was: Who could afford it?

Paul Reichmann, the strategic mastermind behind Olympia & York, a family-owned real estate company with a reputation for the magic touch, had been looking at Gulf for several years. The Reichmanns had made their reputation with two stunning deals. The first, described as the "deal of the century," was their acquisition of eight New York skyscrapers for US$320 million in 1976, amid widespread fears that the city might default. The city survived; the buildings' values multiplied and provided the collateral for further deals. Their second myth-making piece of business was the successful development of Battery Park, a landfill on the west side of lower Manhattan.

While Gulf's battle with Pickens had been in full swing in the final months of 1983, Paul Reichmann had been to Pittsburgh several times to discuss acquiring Gulf Canada, but Pittsburgh wanted too much. Following the takeover, Reichmann had spoken to Chevron, but Chevron too had wanted more than Reichmann was prepared to pay.

Gulf Canada was enthusiastic about a Reichmann takeover. Paul Reichmann had one big advantage over Chevron as far as Gulf was concerned: he wasn't in the oil business. He'd let them continue running the show — or at least that's what they thought.

Paul Reichmann's advisors told him he didn't want all of Gulf; he should ditch the downstream. When considering such a disposal, Paul Reichmann thought of an immediate candidate as a buyer: Petro-Canada. The other multinationals might be prepared to look at acquiring Gulf's downstream assets, but they were unlikely to pay as much as Petrocan. Moreover, the Tories did not want to be seen as promoting the multinationals' growth more than that of

Petrocan. Ideological opposition to Petrocan's growth was about to take second place to the political attractions of bringing Gulf Canada under Canadian ownership. Paul Reichmann was given the nod to approach the state oil company.

Bill Hopper had long lusted after Gulf Canada. He too had visited Pittsburgh, window-shopping for the acquisition that would make his the largest oil company in Canada, but he had never been able to muster political support from the Liberals. It seemed less than likely that he would receive it from the new government. But now Paul Reichmann appeared as a fairy godmother.

Hopper had previously told a reporter that Petrocan had a weakness: its slim downstream presence in the West. He said the surest way to increase the company's "critical mass" — a term much used in Ottawa both by Hopper and, in the early days, by Joel Bell — was through yet another acquisition. "If there were a refining and marketing operation available out West, we might look at it because adding to our current market share would allow us the efficiencies our competitors have," he told the *Financial Times of Canada*. Suddenly, in April 1985, Paul Reichmann appeared on Bill Hopper's doorstep offering him what he wanted, and then some.

Hopper told Reichmann it all depended on the government, but that he was primarily interested in Gulf Canada's refining and marketing operations west of Ontario. When Hopper reported to his political masters, he was told he should take more, not for commercial but for political reasons. The Tories wanted to force-feed him! There was a concern among the Tories that Petro-Canada would be perceived as the cat's paw used by the Reichmanns to pick up Gulf's choice upstream assets. Pat Carney wanted Petrocan to take part of Gulf's upstream assets too; that would "play better" in the public arena.

Soon serious negotiations began. Hopper and Petrocan senior vice-president David O'Brien camped out at Toronto's Royal York Hotel and began almost daily discussions with Paul Reichmann and other O&Y representatives. Reichmann was reluctant to sell any of Gulf's upstream, but Hopper didn't mind trying for some of Gulf's prime East Coast offshore acreage. Gulf's explorers, however, were strongly opposed to Petrocan walking off with their prize. Paul Reichmann told Hopper that the East Coast was not on the table. He would, however, let him take the Beaufort, where, although finds had been made, the prospects looked less certain.

Realizing that Carney wanted some upstream for cosmetic purposes, Paul Reichmann drove a hard bargain. Petrocan finally settled on a package consisting of all the downstream — although Hopper was unenthusiastic about Quebec and particularly unenthusiastic about Ontario, where overcapacity had led to fierce price wars — and pieces of the upstream. The cost to Petrocan would be a whopping $1.8 billion. The Tories were on the point of encouraging Petrocan's largest acquisition.

The Reichmanns, meanwhile, had made their $3-billion offer for Chevron's 60.2 per cent of Gulf Canada, but the offer was conditional on tax rulings. A key part of Paul Reichmann's complex strategy for acquiring Gulf was use of a tax loophole. Intriguingly, the manoeuvre had been used by Petro-Canada in its acquisition of Petrofina. It was nicknamed the "Little Egypt Bump," after a famous Chicago striptease artist of the 1890s.

The so-called "partnership step-up" rules had been put on the law books in 1971 as an innocuous measure relating to the liquidation of business partnerships. However, sharp legal brains had found that the law could be used to depreciate the same assets twice and thereby avoid lots of tax in takeovers. In cases where there was a large difference between the book value of a company's assets and their market value, the value of the bump became correspondingly large. Oil and gas assets were a prime example. If their value could be "bumped up," oil and gas assets depreciated once could be depreciated again, with a corresponding loss to the federal treasury.

There were three steps to the dance. First, Gulf had to roll its Canadian assets, tax-free, into a partnership. Second, a partner had to be found. This step was crucial because the amount paid by the new partner for his percentage of the partnership determined the value of the whole ball of wax. If the new partner paid $300 million for 6 per cent of the partnership, then the partnership's value for tax purposes was $5 billion. Finally, the partnership had to be wound up and its assets distributed between the partners. Gulf would have virtually the same assets — less whatever had been sold to the partner — but these would now be depreciable at their full market value as opposed to their much lower, depreciated value before they had been put into the partnership. This was clearly not the intent of the legislation, but it was the law.

The Department of Revenue regarded the move as little short of fiscal rape, and it had to give a ruling on the tax-free rollover. In the meantime, Paul Reichmann needed a partner. The state oil company was appropriate, because Bill Hopper had danced the bump before.

Petrocan's chairman, advised by the company's Toronto-based lawyers, Tory, Tory, Deslauriers & Binnington — where a number of former Department of Finance whiz-kids worked — had used the manoeuvre in the takeover of Petrofina in 1981. Even Petrocan had been surprised that they had managed to get away with it. They had, in the words of Hopper, sent the proposal over to Revenue Canada, then "held their breath." Although Auditor General Kenneth Dye had highlighted the loophole in his more general attack on the excessive costs of the Petrofina takeover, it had not been removed by the Liberals.

Pat Carney continued to think that Gulf Canada's Canadianization would be a particularly telling achievement if it could be pulled off through "free enterprise." Somehow, she saw no contradiction in the fact that enormous tax breaks and the participation of Petro-Canada were required. The curse of economic nationalism remained. While Maggie Thatcher in Britain simply dismantled the British National Oil Corporation in 1985 as having no more relevance or use, the government of Brian Mulroney continued to pursue wealth-destroying policies and the growth of state control. "Free" enterprise had acquired a whole new meaning: it meant enterprise where the private sector attempted to pay as little as possible by taking advantage of governments.

Industry Minister Sinclair Stevens liked the idea of Canadianization, but he didn't like the idea of Petrocan's planned involvement. Perrin Beatty, the young revenue minister, was as unenthusiastic about the Little Egypt Bump as his senior minister at Finance, Michael Wilson. They were both horrified at the thought of the Reichmann deal being used as a precedent and leading to a wholesale corporate raid on the Treasury. It was not clear where Prime Minister Brian Mulroney stood.

Chevron's negotiators were not party to these machinations. They knew that a tax ruling was involved, but they did not find out about Petrocan's role until late in the day. Their main concern was signing a deal and getting the money. But they knew that O&Y was having problems with the government because of Paul Reichmann's repeated requests for delays.

Paul Reichmann, meanwhile, was negotiating with other parties besides Revenue Canada and Petro-Canada. His style had always been secretive, but he also realized that the best price could always be obtained in negotiations when there were several bidders. O&Y, encouraged by Sinc Stevens, decided to look for another possible partner for the tax dance. The company chosen was Calgary-based Norcen Energy Resources.

Norcen was particularly interested in Gulf Canada's natural gas liquids subsidiary, Superior Propane, but Superior's value was only around $120 million. To be a "legitimate" partner, Norcen had to take at least 5 per cent of the planned $5-billion deal. So it also negotiated a selection of upstream assets to bring its total expenditure to $300 million, giving it a more legitimate 6 per cent of the partnership.

Lining up an alternative partner for the bump was a wise move, indeed almost prescient, because suddenly the heat over Petrocan's proposed involvement began to increase. Western members of the Tory caucus hit the roof when they discovered details of the acquisition. Pat Carney tried to explain that it was really all part of "rounding out" Petrocan's interests in order to make it a more attractive candidate for privatization, but the Western caucus members in particular weren't buying it.

This wave of political outrage hit the Prime Minister's Office just as the Cabinet passed the Order-in-Council approving Petrocan's expenditure of $1.8 billion to acquire all of Gulf

Canada's downstream and part of its upstream. At a critical lunch in the PMO, Sinc Stevens told the prime minister that Petrocan's involvement in the deal would do major damage. Astonishingly, only now, at the eleventh hour, did the political implications of the deal hit the prime minister. Mulroney gave the order to pull the plug. Instead of rescinding the Order-in-Council, Mulroney gave instructions for Hopper to call Paul Reichmann and tell him that whatever their previous understandings, Petrocan would not now participate. Hopper admitted that he made the call to Reichmann but refused to say who told him to do it.

"Look," he said during an interview, "what happened was this. We looked at the bundle and we said we'd rather not buy the upstream, and some of the downstream is just too much for us, so we said, let's carve it down. This happened all within a four- or five-day period that the thing went through Cabinet and Treasury Board. It got the Order-in-Council. Then we started to look at the whole thing and said, you know, we *could* do this — and of course I'm not sure that Paul *wanted* to sell the upstream — we said we could do this, but let's carve it back. We told Carney we don't like the deal the way it was."

Hopper admitted, however, that the primary motive for "rethinking" the deal was political rather than economic. He was plainly uneasy with the notion that the plug was pulled on the Reichmanns. "We had an understanding but it wasn't signed, sealed, and delivered, and we got ahead of ourselves and went back."

Paul Reichmann had in fact been growing increasingly worried about the direction of oil prices in the course of the summer, and thus about the value of Gulf. He had talked many times to Bill Hopper about the likely direction of crude prices. Hopper, trying at the time to buy upstream assets whose value was a function of the oil price outlook, had no compunction in painting a gloomy picture. But he had his own concerns. Said Hopper: "We were a little skittish and he was getting a little skittish."

There was enough reason for concern. Early in June, OPEC had a meeting at Taif in Saudi Arabia, where Sheik Yamani read his fellow oil ministers a letter from King Fahd, castigating them for widespread cheating on agreements to limit production. Saudi Arabia was the "swing producer" meant to control total OPEC output. When other members of OPEC sold more than their quotas at cut prices, Saudi Arabia sold correspondingly less. The Saudis had now had enough of this arrangement, and decided, in defence of their sales volumes, to introduce a new pricing system called "netback" pricing, under which the refiner was allowed a fixed profit off the top of the barrel and the Saudis got the rest. This gave the Saudis' customers an enormous incentive to push volumes. The consequences of boosting sales without regard for price would soon become apparent. If Paul Reichmann had known what they were, he might well have walked away from the deal for good.

Within a couple of weeks after the deal's apparent collapse, however, a new agreement emerged. Mulroney changed his mind again. The price Reichmann paid to Chevron fell almost $200 million. Petrocan's participation was carved back so that it now took none of the upstream and limited its downstream purchases to Gulf's refining and marketing assets in Ontario and the West, at a cost of about $1 billion. Hopper didn't want Ontario, and apparently bought it only because he wouldn't have been able to get the West without it. But he didn't pay a great deal of money for it. After further extensive negotiations, the downstream east of Ontario was sold to Ultramar.

For the Tories, any kudos they might have received from Canadianizing Gulf was destroyed by public perceptions of Mulroney's vacillations. Two other aspects of the deal also caused them trouble. With the oversupply of refinery capacity in Montreal, Gulf Canada had said it would close down its refinery in the city. The closing, since the Tories were obviously so deeply involved in Gulf Canada's sale, became a political hot potato. Then details of the Little Egypt Bump were leaked, causing a rumpus in the House of Commons and the press.

The principal purpose of the Little Egypt Bump had been for the Reichmanns to regain tax write-offs from Gulf's oil and gas assets. But one of the most contentious aspects of the deal was that the Reichmanns had also put Gulf's Edmonton refinery into the partnership. This enabled the Crown corporation to pay more for the asset, which helped the Reichmanns, but only at the expense of the Canadian taxpayer.

Further controversy erupted when Mickey Cohen announced he was joining Olympia & York, having been invited to do so by the Reichmanns the previous February. Cohen, a former Petrocan board member, had been deputy minister of finance while the negotiations were going on over the Little Egypt Bump, although he maintained he had taken no part in them.

Once again, Canadianization had proved to be motherhood with a sharp edge. Once again, the Tories had been burned. Once again, Petrocan had grown bigger. By the end of 1985, the corporation whose sails the federal Tories had promised to trim had increased the number of its employees from around 6,700 when the Tories came to power to 10,565.

Of the Gulf affair, Hopper said: "What happened is germane to the sort of political bullshit that goes on. But in the end we got what we wanted."

FIFTEEN

Unsuccessful Efforts

ILL HOPPER kept video monitors displaying international crude prices by the desks of both his Calgary
and Ottawa offices. He loved to play the international
oilman, lecturing visitors on market trends and swapping OPEC scuttlebutt, talking about "inventory
build," "differentials," and "seasonal swings." In late January
1986, Hopper stood in his Ottawa office, jabbing a pudgy finger
at the screen and expounding on the astonishing story that the
monitors were telling: "Boy," he said, "just look at those crude
prices. If I'd told you a week ago that Brent [North Sea crude]
would be quoted at $19.70 for February and $18.75 for April, you
wouldn't have believed it." Prices had slumped by more than a
third in two months and were heading much lower.

The slide had started in 1985 with the Saudis' switch to netback pricing. The Saudi move forced other OPEC producers to
make similar netback arrangements. Then OPEC turned on the
non-OPEC producers. Early in December 1985, the organization
made a dramatic announcement: it would no longer control output to protect prices. Now its objective was to "secure and defend
for OPEC a fair share in the world oil market consistent with the
necessary income for member countries' development." Although
the amount of oil pumped by OPEC increased by less than 10 per

cent, the impact on prices was dramatic, and far from beneficial to OPEC. West Texas intermediate crude sank from its November 1985 high of more than US$30 to a low of US$10 in the first quarter of 1986. OPEC might claim that it had forced the changes, but it was really bowing to necessity. The market had reasserted itself with a vengeance.

For Canadian producers, who had at last been granted access to international prices the previous summer, the collapse was both painful and ironic. Since the first OPEC crisis, Canadian prices had been held below world levels by the Liberals and, briefly, by the Clark Tories. Now the Mulroney government had given Canadian oilmen — including Bill Hopper — their wish, and the world price had promptly collapsed.

Because Hopper had received more than $4 billion of cost-free equity from Ottawa (that is, cost-free to Petrocan), plus well over another $1 billion in PIP grants, Petrocan's debt position was nowhere near as desperate as that of most of the industry. Nevertheless, the price decline threatened his plans for frontier oil and tarsands development. Moreover, it also threatened the prospects of privatization, for which Hopper was now more than eager. "I'm very much on side with the notion that now is the time, since this instrument has done its job, to sell it off," he declared.

Hopper wanted a share sale for two main reasons. First, Petrocan was desperate for cash, and the Tories had told him they weren't going to give it any more. Second, he wanted to be free of political control. The Tories, however, were beginning to have second thoughts. As an insider put it at the time: "The Tories are aware that Hopper is very keen for an equity sale because once it's done he's untouchable. The Conservatives have to decide whether they want him to be untouchable."

Mulroney and the Tories continued to struggle with their least favourite Crown. Petrocan's role in the Canadianization of Gulf had led to an uproar in Cabinet and caucus. Conservative MP Paul Gagnon had said: "It was simply asinine. The people of Canada voted for a change last year and all they're getting is a continuation of the status quo under the Liberals." Another Conservative

MP, Bobbie Sparrow, said: "We spent all of last fall talking about getting the government out of business and then we turn around and allow a Crown corporation to do something like this."

Also, despite earlier claims that it would "get to the bottom" of the Petrofina affair, the Tories had been persuaded by their mandarins that to give Cabinet documents to Auditor General Kenneth Dye would create a dangerous precedent; it could mean that *their* Cabinet documents might have to be made available. They found themselves in the uncomfortable position of appearing to hide details of Liberal fecklessness. They also realized, once they looked at the Petrocan books, that not only was there was little or no political advantage from privatizing Petrocan, there was a potential financial disadvantage — at least cosmetically, which is to say where it counted politically. Petrocan would need the proceeds of any share issue for itself; there would be nothing for the Treasury. Moreover, if Petrocan were sold for less than the value at which the government was carrying it on the books, the sale would actually increase the deficit.

The Tories tried to act tough. They chopped Petrocan's 1986 budget and demanded an $80-million dividend, but even that had to be cut to $50 million following the price collapse.

Public opinion was still a problem. The National Citizens' Coalition, a right-wing lobbying group, commissioned a Gallup poll that showed that 52 per cent of respondents did not agree with Petrocan's Gulf purchase; 33 per cent supported it. But another Gallup poll, which asked the question in a more neutral way, found those who supported and opposed the deal were exactly split: 41 per cent for and 41 per cent against. Bill Hopper claimed he had done his own polling, and that *his* polls found a majority in favour of the Gulf purchase.

Hopper had become close to Allan Gregg, the pollster who had warned Joe Clark's government back in 1979 that its Petrocan policy was heading for trouble. Just as Hopper had hired Frank Moores's consulting company, he had also hired Gregg's company, Decima, whose high-priced quarterly reports were required reading for followers of the political winds. The fact that Petrocan was paying fees to another powerful source of influence upon the government should have aroused disquiet. But then the Tories had — at Bill Hopper's insistence — told Petrocan to act like a commercial organization, and that's what a commercial organization would have done.

In any case, Hopper pretended he didn't care. "Adverse publicity doesn't seem to affect us," he said in his Ottawa office early in 1986. "The Decima guys said a majority of Canadians thought that buying Gulf was a good thing. Anyway, I don't give a shit. Every time we do something we get dumped on. I've got a hide as thick as a rhino."

Hopper needed his rhino hide. Attacks were coming from all sides. Husky and Shell had announced schemes to persuade Gulf credit-cardholders to switch to their cards rather than transferring to Petrocan. A Calgary-based group, Canadians For Less Government, started selling silver bullets with the name Petro-Canada engraved upon them, urging purchasers to send Ottawa a message: "Go ahead, waste my money, make my day."

The National Citizens' Coalition took out full-page ads suggesting the public should boycott Petro-Canada. The ads said Pat Carney had "betrayed and shocked free enterprisers across Canada" by permitting the Gulf downstream purchase. The coalition quoted Carney's words when she was in opposition: "Exploration, development and how capital should be re-invested should be controlled from the boardrooms of this country, not from government offices in Ottawa or Calgary... We believe in Canadianization that allows Canadian companies to flourish in an expanding oil and gas industry, not the approach of the Liberals." These words were compared with her statement in the wake of the Gulf deal: "Petro-Canada's purchase... should strengthen the Crown corporation's financial position for the future." The ad asked: "Will the real Pat Carney stand up?"

What Petrocan's critics had said from the start had turned out to be true. Petrocan had conspicuously failed to fulfill its original mandate of establishing security of supply; its frontier exploration had proved a bust; state-to-state oil deals had gone nowhere; the window on the industry, which was meant to help government make wiser policy, had led to the NEP. The company had grown in unintended directions that had nothing to do with energy policy and everything to do with political expediency and skillful manipulation by Bill Hopper.

Petrocan had grown at a rate nobody could have foreseen. It had grown not through creation of wealth but through the acquisition of foreign-controlled companies, using funds that had come mostly from the Canadian taxpayer and that subsequently flowed out of the country. Petrocan had become what its opponents had always predicted: a huge, unprofitable company that, having grown through access to the public teat, now wanted to separate itself from its parent, primarily because the teat had dried up.

Refining and marketing, activities of marginal significance in its original mandate, now dominated Petrocan's asset structure. Early in 1986, with the irony that marked all of Petrocan's dealings with the Tories, Pat Carney had to support Petrocan against opposition demands that it cut gasoline prices in response to the precipitous fall in the price of crude. The Tories' attempts to educate a braying opposition and a confused populace that Petrocan would never, and could never, be the source of a free fill-up were not proving popular.

Hopper made Petrocan's now massive presence in the downstream sound like serendipity. Referring to the Pacific purchase that had first brought gas stations into the organization, Hopper said during the January 1986 interview: "I'd go as far as to say that if Pacific had not had that little downstream interest we could be looking at a Petro-Canada without any downstream at all. I think it was the fact that we did pretty well with the Pacific stations in western Canada that gave us the confidence to know that we could do something with Petrofina's downstream." And then BP. And then Gulf.

Hopper's argument had always been that the downstream would provide funds for exploration in the frontiers. But the rationale had fallen on its face. By 1986, Petrocan had 21 per cent of the nation's refining capacity and 23 per cent of its gasoline and distillate market, but business was going to hell in a handbasket.

From its peak in 1979, Canadian demand for petroleum products had dropped 25 per cent by the end of 1985 and had continued dropping in 1986. In the same period, eleven refineries, representing 17 per cent of capacity, had closed, along with a quarter of all retail outlets. Even so, the average refinery utilization rate had still dropped, from 87 per cent to 80 per cent. A change in demand towards "lighter" refined products also meant major new investments. Increasingly stringent environmental regulations represented yet another financial drain.

The fight to retain sales volumes in a shrinking market had led to sustained price wars both at the wholesale level and at the gas pump. Low wholesale prices had allowed independent marketers, with no refining operations to support, to make significant inroads into the retail market.

According to Petrocan's 1986 annual report: "The average downstream rate of return from 1981 to mid-1986 was only 3.5 per cent, well below rates of return needed to raise new capital for continued reinvestment in this or any other industry." The *mea culpa* continued: "From the beginning of Petro-Canada's marketing activities, the expectation was that cash flow from product sales would help to finance the development of energy supplies for Canada's future... Yet in recent years the return on investment in the downstream has been so meagre that it has not even covered downstream reinvestment needs."

Not only did the downstream not provide money for the upstream, it represented a drain on overall resources. But at least Petrocan now had a strong corporate interest in disabusing the public of the notion that oil companies made too much money at the gas pump. The report continued: "Despite these weak financial results, many consumers continue to believe that product prices are unnecessarily high, and that they are kept high by some form of collusion among the major companies. The reality is that intense competition for the remaining market has forced prices down, to the benefit of the consumer. Exhaustive investigations, such as the five-year Restrictive Trade Practices Commission inquiry, have found no evidence of collusion or overcharging.

"Improved financial performance is clearly necessary. Adequate returns are needed to meet future investment requirements. They are needed to ensure the long-term survival of a downstream industry that is able to offer the range of services and quality of products that Canadians expect. They are also essential to provide ongoing employment and business opportunities, directly and indirectly, to hundreds of thousands of Canadians."

Petrocan, far from being a force for moderating prices, as its more naive supporters had hoped, was in fact the company that most desperately needed higher prices. It had paid premium prices to move into an industry in decline. This wasn't merely bad news for the taxpayer, it was bad news for the prospects of privatization.

• • •

As part of its lobbying effort towards privatization, Petrocan had "cooperated" with — in fact initiated — a report released in September 1984 by Toronto investment dealer Dominion Securities Pitfield. In an attempt to maintain that Petrocan's performance was comparable to that of the other big oil companies, the report noted, with somewhat twisted logic, that Petrocan's assets had cost a lot, but that if the other companies calculated their financial returns using current values instead of historical costs, then their performances would also look weak. In other words, if other oil companies had paid as much as Petrocan, they'd look bad too: if they'd acted stupidly, they'd be stupid too.

Hopper tried to explain the logic: "Let's put it this way. If Imperial is sitting there earning 12 per cent on the value of its book, that's not enough. It's like you bought a house for $100,000 ten years ago and rented it out for $500. If your rent hasn't gone up, and the house is worth $200,000, you're not getting a return on book value. A lot of things that are still valuable to Imperial were written off long ago and are no longer on the books. They're not making what the company's really worth."

The problem with Hopper's argument was that it didn't matter what the value of Imperial's "house" was, rents were determined by the market. To criticize Imperial's returns seemed almost suicidally hubristic, coming from a man who every year was destroying investment rather than enhancing it. Looked at another way, Imperial's low real returns confirmed that the government should never have become involved in the oil business, particularly in the downstream.

Interviewed for an article that appeared in the *Globe and Mail* in 1981, Andy Janisch, Petrocan's president at the time, had responded to criticisms that gas stations were just "showing the flag" by saying: "If we only want to show the flag, we can open a chain of candy stores." By 1986, Petrocan *was* selling candy through gas station convenience stores. In the same article, marketing vice-president Glenn Sundstrom had noted, "We don't have TV jingles and we don't give away prizes." By 1986, Petrocan had TV jingles and was giving away prizes, too. It had introduced its own brands of tires, batteries, and accessories; it ran car washes and gave quick lube jobs. It had dealer conventions as noisy and garish as any of the other majors. It had new wonder gasolines and motor oils.

Retailing took it deeper into the community, further into the Canadian psyche. Petrocan's "unique selling proposition" was its Canadianness, and it played the theme to the hilt. The problem was that it was inviting Canadians to share in a model of national failure. Acting under the banner of "corporate responsibility," it talked about encouraging activities that "touched the lives of Canadians." Dealers and agents were encouraged to promote programs such as women's car care clinics, children's bicycle safety presentations, and junior soccer teams. Retail gasoline promotions were linked to support for "worthwhile Canadian initiatives," such as restoration of the *Bluenose II,* supporting Canadian Olympic athletes, and helping fund Ronald McDonald House. The company entered chuckwagons in the races at the Calgary Stampede. They were roundly booed.

But what did entering chuckwagon races have to do with preventing Canadians from freezing in the dark? Hopper claimed it was all part of generating cash for frontier exploration and development. But the downstream wasn't generating free cash; the frontiers were dead; the oil crisis seemed over. The rationale had disappeared but Petrocan lived on, a Crown corporate zombie moving under its own momentum, begging to be put out of its misery and made "normal" by being privatized.

Petrocan was trying to make itself indistinguishable from the other major oil companies, but unlike the others it was losing money hand over fist. Corporate executives undoubtedly got off on handing out cheques for educational or charitable purposes, but it was ultimately taxpayers' money, part of the whole perverse laundering operation through which taxes were transformed into the dross of Petrocan's self-promoted public purpose.

Just as patriotism has been called the last refuge of the scoundrel, now "social conscience" and "good corporate citizenship" seemed the last refuge of the unprofitable. And, although it was almost impossible to conclude so from its accounts, Petrocan *was* very unprofitable.

In one way, the plunge in oil prices in early 1986 was a good thing for Hopper. One reason why he could be relatively sanguine despite the price drop was that the decline offered to reduce the financial burden on his downstream operations. Lower oil prices meant less capital had to be tied up in inventory — the oil and refined products making their way through the refining and marketing system. Still, the prospect of absorbing yet another organization, the fifth in less than ten years, created severe internal problems.

Petrocan had not wanted Gulf's Ontario assets but had had to take them in order to get the West. Now Petrocan controlled one in three of Ontario's gas stations and faced enormous cutbacks and layoffs. An additional problem was that Gulf's downstream operations had been divided into east and west not at the Ontario-Quebec border but at the Ontario-Manitoba border, so Petrocan had acquired two separate organizations.

In taking over Gulf, Petrocan was for the first time acquiring the downstream operations of a *major* major. Effectively, it became a reverse takeover: Gulf wound up taking control of the hotch-potch of regional marketers Petrocan had acquired in Pacific, Petrofina, and BP. Hopper gave the Gulf people their head. This inevitably caused frictions with those already running the refining and marketing show. The downstream head office, which had been a moveable feast — in Montreal after Petrofina, in Toronto after BP — now moved to Calgary. Bill West, meanwhile, the former Imperial executive who was running the downstream, resigned.

The company had faced severe staff cutbacks in 1983. Now, a chill moved round the company's coast-to-coast operations. This time, they knew, there would be cutting to the bone. There was an executive meeting in Calgary. Hopper's opening words were: "The first guy who suggests I get rid of my plane gets fired." It was meant to be a joke. Many of those present didn't think it was too funny.

Not only was Petrocan facing a petroleum price collapse and the absorption of yet another downstream organization in a lousy market, rationalization was also necessary because the whole company was running fat, despite Hopper's frequent protestations of how commercial and "lean" it was.

· · ·

In the summer of 1984, Petrocan had introduced an "inter-action centre" computer terminal at a service station on Highway 400 near King City, Ontario. The location already carried two video display terminals. One transmitted information about offshore drilling, complimentary car care clinics for women, and a "skid school" in Oakville, Ontario; the other provided information about local travel, recreation, and road conditions. The "inter-action centre" would answer questions such as "Why does the price of gas go up and down?" and "Just how profitable is Petro-Canada?"

Now *there* was a question.

Earlier that year, when Bill Hopper had appeared before a parliamentary committee, Michael Wilson, then opposition finance critic, had launched a devastating attack on Petro-Canada's financial reporting. Although Petrocan's results appeared poor, said Wilson, they were in fact much worse. The company was in the black, he claimed, only because of "misleading" reporting practices. The company had already had skirmishes with the Canadian Institute of Chartered Accountants over recommended changes in accounting that would make its figures look even worse. Petrocan had argued with the CICA over accounting for the NEP's taxes and grants, and over deferred taxes. Meanwhile, it used inappropriate, even bizarre, financial ratios as indicators of its relative "success," such as "capital additions per employee": that is, it congratulated itself on its ability to spend money.

One of Wilson's principal complaints was Petrocan's treatment of the US$1.25 billion of preferred shares sold to finance the Pacific purchase. The dividends on these preferreds were not shown as a deduction from earnings. Instead, they were buried in the notes. Wilson said he had found no other company that had reported its earnings "in this devious way."

But the treatment of preferred dividends was only the most obviously cosmetic feature of Petro-Canada's accounts, and of the way that results were massaged for public consumption. From the start, it had been the organization's political survival rather than fiscal reality that had dictated how it presented its figures. Billions of dollars of losses had been concealed through perfectly legal but misleading treatment of the company's huge frontier expenditures, while Bill Hopper had also preached the self-serving and ultimately delusive line that earnings didn't matter; it was cash flow that counted. For support — typically seeking to shift responsibility — Hopper noted that Petrocan board member Harrison McCain had told him: "At the end of the day, what counts is cash in your pocket. Forget all those accountants."

Hopper claimed he had had trouble getting this argument over to politicians. Pat Carney's eyes, he claimed, "glazed over." But it was also a tough point to get over because it was bogus. In fact, the higher the costs of assets, the greater the write-offs against them. The larger the write-offs, the bigger the cash flow. The size of Petrocan's cash flow was therefore, to a degree, a measure of its fiscal fecklessness.

Assets in accounting are strange creatures in any case, and in oil accounting, they sometimes border on the mythical. Media reports often spoke of Petrocan after the Gulf acquisition as a "$9-billion company," or as a company with $9 billion in assets. A naive individual might be forgiven for thinking that that was the value of the company. If he was a little more sophisticated, he might realize that the company's debt would have to be subtracted from those assets to determine the company's net worth. But neither approach even began to address the smoke and mirrors of Petrocan's balance sheet, or Hopper's insistence on what really counted.

The first full year under the Mulroney Tories, 1985, demonstrated how much fiction there is in accounting. In March, the company announced record profits of $252 million for 1984, still reporting the figure *before* the preferred dividends, the practice that Michael Wilson had called "devious." With one eye on privatization, Hopper declared at a press conference that the company's financial position made it "very attractive to the share-buying public." David O'Brien, who would spearhead efforts to have the company privatized, declared: "If the government looks around at Crown corporations and decides on a program of privatization we would be one of the most attractive." Later in 1985, Petrocan announced a whopping $486-million write-off on its frontier exploration lands. When the full-year figures were announced, Petrocan's write-off for 1985 mounted to $865 million, wiping out not only 1984's "record profits" but all the supposed profits it had made since its creation. "The write-offs were mostly associated with the public policy emphasis," Hopper confided to a newspaper reporter. Nothing to do with me.

Despite the huge 1985 write-offs, the biggest potential skeleton in Petrocan's financial closet was not addressed until 1989. That skeleton was how the company accounted for its frontier exploration. Petrocan did not write off the cost of unsuccessful wells against current profits. Instead, it "capitalized" those costs and wrote them off over a longer period. This meant that if the company spent $100 million drilling an East Coast dry hole, it would not write $100 million off as an expense; it would declare itself to have acquired a $100-million asset, which it then amortized over time. The $865-million write-off was only a partial acknowledgment of a growing problem.

The rationale for this "full cost" form of accounting was that exploration expenditures, whether successful or unsuccessful, should be treated in one lump. This was realistic if one was exploring in conventional areas, where the odds of success were relatively high, and well costs were relatively low. But Petrocan was exploring in areas where well costs were enormous and the chances of success were slim.

A strong case can be made that Petrocan should never have been permitted to account in this way, since all the companies exploring the frontiers — the majors — used the more conservative principle of "successful efforts" accounting, writing off dry hole costs as they were incurred. Nevertheless, Petrocan declared in its 1983 report that it believed "that its practice is both conservative and appropriate." In fact, the practice was never conservative, and it was appropriate only in cosmetic political terms.

Most charitably, Petro-Canada's adoption of the full cost approach rather than the successful efforts method had been predicated on Ottawa's naiveté: the belief that it would immediately find oil in the frontiers. Less charitably, it was a means of concealing the enormous costs of Petrocan's frontier mandate, quite apart from the $1.8 billion of PIP grants the company ultimately received. If Petrocan had accounted on the successful efforts basis from the beginning, it would have shown large losses every year and provided the Tories with a powerful weapon for attacking it. Full cost accounting enabled reality to be swept under the carpet.

By the late 1980s, the bulge under the carpet was becoming embarrassing. Moreover, it had to be dealt with before the company could be privatized. In 1989, the company at last changed from full cost to successful efforts accounting. This was the major factor contributing to almost $2 billion more in write-offs. To cope with the problem, the government cancelled $1.434 billion of its shares. Declared Hopper, with a masterpiece of understatement: "Petro-Canada did not do well financially in 1989." This manoeuvre went almost unnoticed in Parliament and the media. Neither was it prominently or clearly laid out in the annual report.

The company had now written off close to $3 billion, but that didn't mean it had taken care of another fundamental problem related more to corporate culture than to accounting: it had a fat lifestyle that started at the very top, with Hopper's two corporate jets, lavish offices, and executive chefs. Hopper refused to get rid of his personal jet in 1986, but he managed to chop 23 per cent of the company's staff.

The 1986 cuts provided only a temporary improvement in results. After record earnings of $172 million in 1987, results slumped again in 1988. And despite yet another round of statements by Hopper about the company tightening up, its expenses were in fact increasing. In the 1987 report, Hopper had spoken of "the cumulative impact of dozens of efficiency-seeking initiatives." But marketing, general, and administrative expenses were up 4 per cent over 1986 to $819 million, while those for producing and refining were up a whopping 26 per cent at $727 million. The following year, marketing, general, and administrative expenses rose another 9 per cent to $891 million, those for producing and refining by 7 per cent to $777 million. This didn't seem like a company committed to cutting costs.

In Petrocan's annual report for 1984, the year the Mulroney Tories had come to power, Hopper had spoken of Petrocan's "excellent performance." He claimed: "Over its nine-year history, Petro-Canada has moved quickly, adjusting its operating direction to suit changing business conditions." He said, "Canadians now own and control an integrated oil company that is as large and as competent as the Canadian arms of the multi-national majors." He spoke of "streamlining," "running a tight ship," and "focusing on early returns." He concluded: "Our financial situation is good, we are lean and efficient and well-positioned for growth." The following year, the company announced a net loss of $769,335,000.

In 1986, Hopper acknowledged that, because of plummeting

oil prices, the industry was in a state of crisis. Nevertheless, he claimed: "Petro-Canada's performance in this exceptionally difficult year signals the successful transition from a policy-guided to a commercially-driven company. While in the past Petro-Canada was directed to invest aggressively in Canada's frontier areas, its activities and expenditures are now geared to enhancing the Corporation's already substantial financial health and operating capability." He wrote of the company's "strong commercial performance." In the 1987 report, Hopper boasted that "Petro-Canada entered 1987 as a lean and tightly focused organization."

But by 1988 the fiction was becoming harder to maintain. Hopper returned to his old standby of blaming the "expensive mandate" and external circumstances, which had hit all oil companies. "These factors," Hopper declared, "have left Petro-Canada with a short- to medium-term performance gap that management has deemed unacceptable." But who, if not management, and if not Bill Hopper in particular, was responsible for the "performance gap"? Hopper declared that yet another "major overhaul" was under way, which would "radically" alter the company's cost structure, asset balance, operating practices, and organization.

The following year, yet more radical changes were announced. The 1989 report, which described a new corporate "vision," declared: "Recognizing that a 'business as usual' operating mode could not lead to progress toward the vision, management initiated a number of important change programs in 1989." "Business as usual"? But what about all the leanness and meanness that Hopper had been talking about for the past five years?

Now that the company was on the point of privatization, its report and accounts were more incomprehensible than ever. The five-year financial summary presented in the 1989 report was a masterpiece of financial complexity, which made the huge write-offs as hard to track down as possible. All previous years' earnings had been hauled downwards. The 1988 annual report had shown shareholder's equity of $3.915 billion. In 1989, the 1988 figure had been reduced to $2.727 billion. In 1990, the 1988 figure was declared to be $2.402 billion. Lies, damned lies, and statistics: this was generally accepted accounting principles with a vengeance. But nobody in Ottawa was going to blow the whistle.

The Tories continued to take up the pretzel position, jerking into spasms of convoluted confusion every time the word Petrocan was mentioned. Not only did the trauma of 1979 remain in the collective memory, but the party had also compromised itself in the Gulf deal. Its privatization program had gone aground. Meanwhile, defence of the state oil company was still motherhood as far as the political opposition was concerned.

Michael Wilson's seemingly bland remark in a speech in Calgary in March 1987 that Petrocan no longer had a public policy role, and that the government was planning to move ahead on privatization, led to a storm of opposition protest, as well as confusion within Tory ranks. Liberal leader John Turner still spoke of Petrocan's role as promoting frontier exploration and keeping gasoline prices down, even though the corporation had failed expensively in the former and had explained time after time why it could not deliver the latter.

Nevertheless, the Tories were still so scared of Petrocan that Turner's remarks were followed by a cacophony of crossed signals. Brian Mulroney said in the House of Commons that Petrocan was not up for sale, but could be later. At an announcement of further Petrocan drilling off Newfoundland, John Crosbie declared: "Contrary to recent statements in the press, Petro-Canada has been and will continue to be a strong positive force in the development of oil and gas activities in Newfoundland and Labrador." Barbara McDougall, then privatization minister, declared that a Petrocan sell-off was being pursued "very actively." Energy Minister Marcel Masse further muddied the waters by introducing a non-issue: he declared boldly that Petrocan could not be sold to one of the foreign-owned majors. "This is clearly what we will not do," the francophone minister told reporters, "if ever we do something."

Bill Hopper continued to pressure the government, telling them that if they weren't going to give him any more money, then he had to go to the public. He couldn't possibly borrow the money, he said; that would be fiscally irresponsible.

Hopper also seized upon a powerful new bargaining lever: Hibernia.

SIXTEEN

On the Rocks

WHEN GERRY Henderson retired as head of Chevron Canada in 1986, he was presented with a long scroll, which was ceremoniously unrolled on the floor of the Petroleum Club. On it were the names of 486 dry holes he had drilled for Chevron, including a consecutive string of 57. This was the record of one of the most successful and respected oil finders in Canadian history. Under Henderson's leadership, Chevron had drilled both West Pembina, the most significant Alberta oil discovery of the 1970s, and Hibernia, Canada's largest offshore find.

But when governments looked at the oil industry, they saw only successes. They didn't see Gerry Henderson's 486 dusters. It was this skewed view that led to the "delusion of facility," the belief that the oil business was easy and that Petrocan, armed with a "need to know," could simply drill a few wells and find all the oil the majors had somehow been "hiding."

Henderson, a tall, distinguished geologist with a long string of qualifications and a wry sense of humour, got on well with Bill Hopper. Most people did. But he also once said to Hopper: "If I ever hear you take credit for Hibernia, I'm going to have to cry bullshit!"

Despite Henderson's friendly warning, Hopper had always sought at least part of the credit for the big East Coast discoveries.

East Coast exploration had emerged as a key rationale for Petrocan's existence. Hopper had used the high costs of frontier drilling as justification for "buying cash flow" through a string of expensive acquisitions. The acquisitions had not turned out well, so if his exploration efforts were a failure too, then Hopper had a lot of explaining to do.

Since he was spending so much taxpayers' money, Hopper was a welcome visitor in Halifax and St. John's, where he tended to meet with premiers rather than provincial energy ministers. But success in the oil business, unlike politics, is predicated on more than merely spending money.

In his message in the 1981 annual report, in which he spoke of East Coast success and declared that the Hibernia find on Newfoundland's Grand Banks and the Venture discovery on the Scotian Shelf were commercial, Hopper said: "We believe that this occurred much sooner than if Petro-Canada were not active in the frontiers for the last five years." In 1985, the report declared more boldly that, in the offshore, "the Corporation's efforts to accelerate exploration led to discoveries such as Terra Nova, Hibernia and Venture." This was not true; Mobil's tough farm-out arrangements had forced Petrocan to drill the deep Venture find against the company's will; Hibernia would have been drilled whether Petrocan had been there or not; one of its partners had had to nudge it to drill the Terra Nova discovery, 35 kilometres southeast of Hibernia, in 1984, even though Petrocan was the operator.

There had been powerful hostility, particularly from Mobil, to Petrocan's backing into the Hibernia exploration play under preferential federal land provisions. But antagonism had subsided and Petrocan had come to be seen as a "good partner." Following initial euphoria in 1979, plans for the field's development had become bogged down in the dispute between Ottawa and Newfoundland, and then in haggling between both governments and the consortium.

In February 1985, Mulroney's Tories had finally reached agreement with Brian Peckford over offshore jurisdiction. But other federal Tory policies were problematic. It was announced that PIP grants, which had driven East Coast exploration, were to be ended by 1987. Then in early 1986, the world price collapsed. Newfoundland's dreams of wealth, it seemed, were once again about to disappear into the fog. In April 1986, when the Canada/ Newfoundland Offshore Resources Board approved, "with a number of terms and conditions," a Hibernia Development Plan, the process seemed like hair continuing to grow on a freshly dead corpse.

Given the long lead times and the price uncertainty, the project was at best marginally economic. The partners needed concessions, but federal and provincial negotiators clung to the "economic rent" mentality of the 1970s, in which the oil companies' take had to be whittled to the bone lest they got away with any windfall profits.

Ottawa's preferred form of support for the project was loan guarantees, because they didn't add to federal spending and the deficit unless things turned sour. Then, of course, they would be left holding the baby. In politics everything is cosmetics; the important thing was that there was no baby to hold *yet*. But loan guarantees weren't enough.

For two years after the jurisdictional dispute ended, the sides haggled but remained far apart on what was necessary to make the project go. Lubrication was provided to the negotiating process when the widely respected Arne Nielsen returned to head Mobil Canada following Mobil's acquisition of Superior, whose Canadian subsidiary he was heading. Mobil in New York still had misgivings about the project. Chevron and Gulf were more enthusiastic. Petrocan was prepared to go with the flow. It was in a difficult position: it was a state oil company negotiating, on the same side as private-sector partners, against the state that controlled it.

In the summer of 1987, with no movement from Ottawa, Mobil told Nielsen, who was now chairman of the consortium's negotiating committee, to pull the plug. The partners agreed. At a meeting in Montreal over the August civic holiday, Nielsen told Energy Minister Marcel Masse that the consortium had decided there was no point in negotiating further. They were going nowhere.

Masse's face reddened. This was a terrible shock. He asked for a recess. Fifteen minutes later he returned to the negotiating table, stared straight at Arne Nielsen, and declared: "Mr. Nielsen, what you propose is not acceptable to the Canadian government. We want Hibernia to go, it *must* go." Masse said the consortium should go away and tell them *whatever it needed* to go ahead. Ottawa was taking a strangely tough stance: it would stuff money into the consortium's mouth until the consortium cried uncle. It was Nielsen's turn to be taken aback. He called for a recess. The feds seemed to be making an offer the consortium couldn't refuse. The two sides separated.

When the consortium returned, it presented its bottom line: on the $5.2-billion project, a grant of $1 billion plus loan guarantees equal to 40 per cent of the balance, around $1.7 billion. The deal looked rich for the oil companies, who knew it would be interpreted as a "giveaway." Nielsen didn't believe the government would go for it. Then he got a call. The government would give the consortium everything it had asked for.

Once again, fiscal responsibility had been cast aside in pursuit of political advantage. When Masse had said "the project must go," he hadn't been talking about energy security or the benefit of Canada; he'd been talking about electoral politics, and in particular about federal giveaways to the province of Newfoundland. The federal Tories were flagging in the polls. An election was due the following year. As a Tory insider said: "We had to demonstrate that there was a plan, there was action, there was activity, there were regional considerations, there was industrial development."

Despite Ottawa's accession to the consortium's financial demands — indeed, because of it — there was a great deal of negotiating left to do on the form of the project: in particular, how many local jobs would be provided for Newfoundland. There were also technical issues, such as what would happen in the event of cost overruns. Nevertheless, such discussions were limited by the timing of the next federal election in the fall of 1988.

The partners had decided to use a fixed concrete-based production platform, which Mobil had experience with in the North

Sea. The biggest safety problem on the Grand Banks came from icebergs. A fixed "gravity-based" system, whose perimeter was armed with jagged concrete teeth, was designed to take icebergs on, although nobody was particularly keen to test the theory's effectiveness. But such a structure was also attractive for political reasons, because it offered more local employment. "Do not forget," Bill Hopper later told the Senate Standing Committee on Energy and Natural Resources, "the gravity-based system is a big chunk of cement you put on the floor. It employs a lot more people and it uses a lot more cement from the island than [the floating production system planned for] Terra Nova would."

Building the gravity-based structure in Newfoundland was also going to add significantly to the consortium's costs. Another partner said: "If we built it somewhere else, such as Norway, it would not only be cheaper, but we wouldn't have to build a construction site that's going to cost us $600 million to $700 million. We got that grant *not* to build outside Newfoundland. It's a subsidy to do things that are uneconomic and to do them in Newfoundland."

The Tories claimed that Hibernia would, via the magic of "technology transfer," provide skills and jobs for the future of Newfoundland; they said that helping Hibernia would encourage further exploration and development; they declared Hibernia would be the bell cow for a herd of similar East Coast developments. All these claims were debatable.

Politicians have always liked big expensive schemes that can be announced with much fanfare — preferably, as in the case of Hibernia, several times. But it is now almost universally acknowledged that the mega-approach is inappropriate as a development tool.

The Third World debt crisis resulted from the failure of flashy megaprojects, whose primary asset was their appeal to the egos of bankers and governments rather than their ability to meet the needs of the people of developing countries. Newfoundland was not the Third World, but the megaproject approach had the same political and psychological appeal, and the same economic shortcomings. Since there was little or no local knowledge of such oil developments, insistence on using locals would both increase costs and lengthen construction time.

Government apologists pointed out that there would be 1,000 permanent jobs in Newfoundland once Hibernia came into production, but they would have existed *wherever* the production facility was built. In the meantime, Canadian taxpayers were shelling out $100,000 per man-year for each temporary job building the production facilities.

Like most pieces of supposedly well-intentioned government intervention, the Hibernia development was likely to have the reverse of its intended effects. If governments had allowed oil companies to develop according to their own plans, and build their production systems where they wanted, rather than forcing them to build locally, then further development would be more likely. "Natural" rig and supply jobs would then come to the province in greater numbers. But the free market approach didn't satisfy the desire to make the Big Announcement, or address the obsession with comforting — if ultimately meaningless — concepts such as "encouraging" technology transfer.

Canadian governments appeared to take a mystic view of technology transfer: you stood beside somebody with skill, and some of it somehow rubbed off. But the process did not work like that. The contractors involved with the building of the gravity-based structure and part of the sophisticated superstructure, the "topsides," in Newfoundland might set up Newfoundland offices and take Newfoundland partners; but what would remain once the project was finished was debatable. The government had said it would provide no subsidies for future projects, but without subsidies, on the basis of existing price projections, no further work would be justified.

The development's funding and form were not the only points of controversy. Hibernia's crude could not be refined at East Coast refineries. It would have to be exported. The word that oil was "just a commodity" still hadn't reached many economic nationalists, who spoke of Canadian petroleum as if it was the nation's lifeblood.

In July 1988, the Hibernia consortium and the two levels of government met for one final, gruelling week of negotiations in Toronto. The terms were settled on a Saturday morning, so that Brian Mulroney and Brian Peckford could make a joint announcement the following Monday in St. John's. That day, details of the "statement of principles" were announced. Apart from the $2.7-billion grant and guarantee package, the most significant concession was that neither government would take any royalty or profit interest until the consortium had recovered its investment plus a 15-per-cent rate of return. The agreement indicated a significant change in attitudes from the early 1980s, when federal and provincial governments had been so busy fighting over the spoils that they had forgotten that the oil companies had to produce oil before they could tax it. Now the pendulum seemed to have swung all the way to hand-out city.

Governments always overplayed their hands in energy: the Liberals had been greedy and arrogant when they thought there were huge windfall energy profits to grab; the Tories had been reckless and craven when falling prices threatened to leave the energy cupboard bare. Hibernia was not unique. The Tories had already pumped subsidies into other uneconomic energy schemes, such as a heavy oil upgrader in Saskatchewan and a gas pipeline to Vancouver Island. But Hibernia was the biggest and most uneconomic.

Typically, Bill Hopper embarrassed the government by dumping on the economics of the Hibernia project and the length of the negotiations. Hopper didn't want to get stuck in that loop to develop Terra Nova. Instead of an uneconomic concrete platform, he wanted an offshore-built floating system. He told the Senate energy committee: "The rate of return on Terra Nova should be at an acceptable level to us and to our partners, without any government loans and grants. As operator of that project, I would rather not ask the government for anything. First of all, I do not think they can afford it. Secondly, the agony of trying to negotiate Hibernia with government over the years has been so difficult that I think we had best do without it."

Once again, Hopper was taking unconcealed delight in skewering his political masters. In fact, Hopper provided the ultimate argument against Hibernia when he said, "I do not think they can afford it." Even if the federal government had been in sound financial shape, Hibernia would still have represented a very risky project, involving the likely destruction of taxpayers' wealth. But the federal government was not in sound financial shape.

Hibernia was a classic example of the failure of the political system to control expenditure and act in the country's best long-term interests. It was a prime example of that perversion of capitalism that might be called "deficitism," in which uneconomic projects are funded with money that will have to be extorted from future taxpayers. It represented a system of dishonest bookkeeping, in which the present was credited and the debit was shoved into some vague future, to be paid by immigrants, or our children, or whoever. But the price would have to be paid.

The huge subsidies promised for Hibernia indicated that Canada's marginally economic petroleum resources had turned out to be not a blessing but a curse. Like the false lights shone by less scrupulous Newfoundlanders in earlier days to lure ships to destruction so that they might be "salvaged," Canada's frontier reserves had been an *ignis fatuus* that had led governments onto the deficit rocks. Hibernia represented the subsidized purchase of temporary political advantage at a potentially disastrous cost to the entire system. In the long run, just as encouraging the Gulf Canada acquisition in the name of Canadianization had brought the Tories no credit, so subsidizing Hibernia would prove to be yet another disastrous intervention.

The Mulroney government had claimed when it came to power that it would put an end to boondoggles. Instead, it had erected a destructive system of competitive regionalism, a system in which commitment was judged primarily in terms of expenditure. As a cynical Tory insider put it: "Spending anywhere in Canada is regarded as okay in Ottawa, but you have to give everybody else an IOU. If you want to do it in one part of the country, you have to do it in another too. They don't squawk about

Hibernia in Newfoundland because they get most of the benefits. Quebec gets benefits too. They don't squawk in Ontario because there are also spinoffs, plus it would be unseemly to attack 'poor little Newfoundland.' They don't squawk in the West because they are not opposed to government-funded economic development. Nobody speaks for the taxpayer."

Because of Mobil's desire to change the rig configuration, negotiations carried on for more than a year after the signature of the statement of principles in July 1988. The process was lengthened because a new federal energy minister, Jake Epp, had to be brought up to speed, and a new provincial premier, Clyde Wells, had to be brought on side. Epp didn't know much about energy; Wells had been a severe critic of the project. The political good news was that it gave the politicians a chance to announce the project yet again. Typically, in the run-up to the re-announcement, the important consideration was not the huge subsidy involved, but whether Mulroney wanted to be seen on the same platform as Wells, with whom he had fallen out over constitutional reform. Following yet another signing on September 14, 1990, there was a big party at the house of Craig Dobbin, a St. John's magnate who'd made his money in the helicopter business. This really was it. Wealth at last.

Almost immediately, the bulldozers and graders went to work to carve out a branch road from the Trans-Canada Highway, 100 kilometres west of St. John's, to the construction site at Great Mosquito Cove, an inlet of Bull Arm, which thrusts deep inland from Trinity Bay. It would be the biggest construction site in North America. Ironically, it sat close to Come By Chance. Even more ironically, and no thanks to Petrocan, Come By Chance had now come back into commission. The state company had wanted to bulldoze the facility, but at the last moment, Brian Peckford had found an American buyer. Petrocan had in the end allowed the sale only on condition that the American buyer did not put gasoline into the Canadian market; it didn't want any more competition. At the end of October, Epp told the Senate energy committee that — apart from any technological problems — it was

Petrocan's condition of sale that would prevent Hibernia crude being refined at Come By Chance. Irony upon irony.

The month after Epp's Senate committee appearance, in November 1990, the salon of the St. John's Convention Centre was packed with businessmen who had come to listen to Derek Owen, the British-born general manager of the Hibernia Management and Development Co. Ltd. They wanted to hear what they could do for Hibernia and what Hibernia could do for them. They all wanted a piece of the Bull Arm action. They listened intently to Owen as he delivered a conceptual blueprint of the branching hierarchies of engineering and purchasing that would oversee procurement and cost and quality controls. They heard Owen emphasize how important it was to "do it right the first time."

But some still harboured skepticism about Hibernia, still wondered if the project was for real. Like a variation on the story of the boy who cried wolf, politicians and speculators had been crying Hibernia since the field had been discovered. The businessmen's skepticism was well based. Even as the project was under way, it was still threatening to fall apart. Petrocan was deeply concerned about the $1-billion commitment it had made, but another of the partners was even more concerned: the company that the Tories had taken such great pains to Canadianize five years before, Gulf Canada.

. . .

Since Gulf Canada had been acquired by the Reichmanns, it had been forced through a complex choreography in the name of creating shareholder "value." Its Beaufort drilling fleet had proved a white elephant, and despite a significant find at Amauligak, Gulf, like the other Beaufort explorers, had eventually pulled out. Then (again, with a certain irony given the thrust of Canadianization) Gulf brought in an American, C.E. (Chuck) Shultz, from Tenneco to take over as chief executive. Shultz told shareholders at the 1989 annual meeting that he had joined Gulf because he saw a well-managed company with an outstanding inventory of business opportunities. In fact, he had been brought in by the Reichmanns to kick butt.

Gulf had liked the Reichmanns because they weren't in oil. Gulf executives had been persuaded they would be allowed to "go their own way." That hadn't turned out to be the case. The Reichmanns weren't in oil, but they were in money, and Gulf had found itself jumping through hoop after financial hoop. In 1985, Gulf had been "persuaded" to buy paper giant Abitibi-Price from the Reichmanns in order to provide the funds for its own takeover. In 1986, the Reichmanns had used it to acquire Hiram Walker Resources. In 1987, they had "deconglomerated" it, splitting off Abitibi and the rump of Hiram Walker, and Gulf had found that it was an oil company once more.

Concerned at criticism that he had "used" Gulf, Paul Reichmann declared that the company would be revitalized. He had himself appointed head of a committee of Gulf directors set up "to guide the new initiatives for frontier and international exploration and development." He also took a contrarian stance in favour of Beaufort development, although this was partly making a virtue of necessity, since Gulf still had its $674-million Arctic drilling fleet. Despite a sale and leaseback arrangement that enabled the company to take the fleet's debt off its balance sheet, Gulf still had to make the lease payments.

Investors, obsessed by the Reichmann "mystique," apparently believed that Paul Reichmann, a man with no knowledge of geology, would somehow help Gulf's drilling prospects. The mystique was a key selling point for the record $519-million Gulf Canada equity issue in June 1987. But Paul Reichmann was no oilman. Indeed, he could hardly have bought Gulf at a worse time. His skill was demonstrated in squeezing as much value as he had done from the situation. But that had hardly helped Gulf's financial prospects.

In 1990, Shultz was faced with another round of complex financial manoeuvres that were all part of the Reichmanns' Olympian financial game. Gulf purchased Imperial's stake in Reichmann-controlled Interhome, which in turn controlled

Interprovincial Pipeline and Home Oil. This was the first step in a plan under which Interhome was to be split and Gulf was to be merged with Home. But the prospective Gulf-Home merger — which had created further employment uncertainties at both Gulf and Home — fell apart when the Interhome board decided the Reichmanns wanted Home too cheaply.

Surrounded by these shifting corporate sands, Shultz had nevertheless moved quickly to sharpen up the company. He had moved Gulf's exploration thrust away from the frontiers towards western Canada and overseas, where there would be more immediate pay-offs. Ironically, Gulf saw better prospects even in the Soviet Union — where it had entered into a joint venture — than in Canada. Then, critically, Shultz decided that Gulf couldn't carry its whole commitment to Hibernia. As the situation deteriorated throughout 1991, Shultz began to realize that Gulf might not be able to carry *any* of its commitment to Hibernia. Gulf held negotiations with more than seventy companies but could find no buyers for all or part of its stake.

In the fall of 1991, Shultz went to see federal Energy Minister Jake Epp. "Look, Jake," he said, "we cannot carry Hibernia. I will not sacrifice the company for Hibernia." The federal government wasn't interested in bailing Gulf out, so Gulf then talked to its partners about mothballing the project. That proposal, too, was rejected, although the most enthusiastic of the other partners was Hopper, who also saw Hibernia as an enormous drain. He had already announced that half of Petrocan's interest was also up for sale.

On February 4, 1992, Gulf dropped its bombshell: it was pulling out of Hibernia. "Gulf has a number of very attractive investment opportunities under development," said Shultz. "Proceeding with our full interest in Hibernia commits too large a portion of Gulf's resources to a single project."

Epp and other federal Tory ministers turned angrily on Gulf. Referring to the huge tax break the Reichmanns had received in 1985, Epp declared: "I was very disappointed because Gulf has gotten some very good deals from the Canadian taxpayer apart from Hibernia." John Crosbie subsequently declared that Gulf's walking away from Hibernia at the same time as it was investing in the Soviet Union amounted to "bad faith." In fact, it was simple common sense. Epp and Crosbie were suggesting that one bad deal deserved another: that because taxpayers had involuntarily kicked in money so the Reichmanns could purchase Gulf, and then involuntarily kicked in money so the uneconomic Hibernia project could be announced, so Gulf now should abandon economics — nay, had a moral obligation to abandon economics — and join in the wealth destruction game.

Hibernia came to symbolize the federal government's political bankruptcy; it had no political strategy for winning votes other than misspending borrowed money. The Tories had dismantled the NEP and returned to a system of market pricing, but they proved incapable of allowing the market to work.

Bill Hopper chose this particularly delicate time to stick his foot in his mouth. Emerging from a speech in Washington a month after Gulf's withdrawal, Hopper met two Canadian reporters. During the speech he had jokingly asked: "Does anybody wanna buy a project?" The Canadian reporters asked him about Hibernia. He said: "Within sixty days, if we don't find somebody to step into Gulf's shoes, we'll move toward mothballing the project."

When Ottawa and Newfoundland politicians were told of Hopper's remarks, their reactions ranged from confused to ballistic. "Maybe he's trying to put some pressure on the federal government," opined Premier Wells. In fact, Epp had said just a few days before that the partners had closer to a year to find a partner. Hopper contradicted Epp, and said that the sixty-day deadline was an internal matter. "I'm not optimistic about somebody stepping into Gulf's shoes, although it's altogether possible," said Hopper. "Maybe the government will come up with some new incentives."

Epp was outraged, but there was little that he could do to Hopper. In fact, there was little that any minister had ever been able to do to Hopper. And now Hopper was completely invulnerable because he had at last received his fondest wish: in July 1991 Petrocan had been privatized. Ironically, Hibernia had been a key factor in finally forcing the government to allow the Crown corporation to sell shares.

The Tories had said when they returned to power in 1984 that they would give no more funds to Petrocan. They had been as good as their word. But then, in order to win votes for the 1988 election, they had committed themselves to Hibernia, of which Petrocan was a major partner. Where, Bill Hopper asked them, was he expected to get the money to fund his share?

While the two Brians, Mulroney and Peckford, had smilingly been holding up the 1988 Hibernia agreement for the cameras at a St. John's press conference, Bill Hopper had taken the opportunity to pull out the begging bowl. He said he hoped Petrocan's participation in the project would add urgency to his pleas for privatization: "We don't have the money."

With consummate irony, and in an almost total reversal of his stand of a decade earlier, by the fall of 1989, Hopper was threatening to dismantle the company *himself* unless the Tories allowed him to make a share issue. He claimed he would have to sell off Petrocan's frontier assets: the very rationale for its existence.

But of course Hopper wanted a public share issue for more than simply money. Once he had private shareholders, he would be free of government interference.

SEVENTEEN

Jobs for the Boys

ETROCAN HAD become a full member of the association of South American state oil companies, called ARPEL, in 1976. The link was justified, Hopper claimed, because Canada sought state-to-state oil deals with Venezuela, and also planned exploration in places like Colombia and Ecuador. But there were important psychological undertones to the association. Canadian nationalists, like those of Latin America, inevitably sought to denigrate the damned Yanquis and seek the path of "authenticity," usually through government intervention. In ARPEL, Petrocan was among friends.

Where the Latin Americans had gone wrong was in allowing both corruption and irrationality to run away with them. In 1981, for example, Pemex, the huge and corrupt Mexican state oil company, was forced to raise prices against the market in the name of "Mexican pride." It lost $1 billion in a month.

Latin American corruption had historical, institutional roots. In the Spanish colonial empire, judges and policemen were poorly paid; they were expected to supplement their incomes by graft. This attitude pervaded the political system and all state institutions. Jorge Diaz Serrano, head of Pemex in the late 1970s and early 1980s, had given contracts to his own drilling company, taken kickbacks, and embezzled millions in tanker contracts. He was not unusual; he just had the misfortune to get caught in a high-profile political clean-up. Hopper would never have done anything so crass. He wasn't on the take in any crude, hand-in-the-till sense, but his corporate perks and his huge discretionary budgets gave him the ability to bestow financial favours.

Petro-Canada's membership in ARPEL was symbolic. Hopper got on well with South Americans because he understood them. Indeed, he had an essentially Latin, come-up-to-the-*palacio*-and-see-me-Chico style. Hopper created a web of obligations. He did people favours. He gave old cronies jobs. He got the politicians and journalists on his jet. He announced petroleum discoveries when the party wanted him to. He put the projects in the ridings.

In the period leading up to Petrocan's privatization, Hopper had almost every consultant influential with the Tory government on his payroll: former Mulroney chief of staff Bill Fox; big Mulroney buddy Frank Moores; former Clark inner Cabinet member Bill Neville; key Tory advisor Nancy Jamieson; Jamieson's husband, another top consultant, Bruce Anderson; Harry Near, former executive assistant to Ray Hnatyshyn and Pat Carney; ace pollster Allan Gregg. From all of these he bought newsletters or quarterly reports or polls or communications advice. At their height, Petrocan's consultancy fees totalled more than $10 million a year.

Of course, it was noted, these consultants weren't lobbyists. Indeed, Crown corporations were not permitted to have lobbyists. Petrocan made all of its consultants sign a document that they would do no lobbying on Petrocan's behalf. A more cynical document could not be imagined. The Tory insiders believed themselves to be honourable people, but Bill Hopper knew that once you pay somebody, you've got them in your pocket; they have a vested interest in your future. Hopper realized this and used it to Petrocan's advantage.

The Canadian media had higher standards than their Mexican colleagues of the 1980s or 1990s, but Hopper courted journalists and writers too. Reporters were fed stories and found jobs. Two prominent local writers who had been harsh critics of the company — Earle Gray, former editor of *Oilweek,* and Tom Kennedy, a colourful and often controversial energy writer for the *Globe and Mail* and the *Calgary Sun* — wound up writing Petrocan-funded books.

Petrocan also subsidized a book written by the former head of Westcoast Transmission, Ed Phillips. Writing about Petrocan's seizing control of Westcoast, a Pacific subsidiary, Phillips declared that Westcoast management was naturally concerned about the prospect of being a "crown-corporate satellite." But Phillips then gushed: "The distinguishing difference in Petro-Canada was its second chairman, Bill Hopper, who was anything but the quintessential head of a crown corporation. Although he was a public servant at the time of his appointment, Bill's academic preparation and working experience had been in the private sector of the petroleum business... At Westcoast, Bill Hopper gave management unrestrained room to move. In fact, he pressed the concept of expansion... With Bill as chairman, they never lacked for ideas, which meant the management could concentrate on execution of all the plans... In my opinion, there is not another oilman in Canada more suited to the unique requirements of Petro-Canada than Bill Hopper."

Phillips was right, but he didn't expand on what the "unique requirements" were.

As well as the huge consulting fees, Hopper controlled a multi-million-dollar budget for "corporate image advertising." This could be doled out willy-nilly to the pet causes of senior corporate executives who might consider themselves rabid free-enterprisers. All they had to do was get through to Bill, and the cheque was in the mail. They would gratefully accept money for their favourite educational or cultural causes, without reflecting that the cash had ultimately been laundered from the federal treasury. When it was pointed out to one executive who had accepted such largesse that it ultimately came from the taxpayers, he looked shocked, thought for a second, then responded: "I'd rather he gave it to me than to the Olympic Torch."

Corporate image advertising was also a wonderful slush fund

for buying off the cultural community. Petrocan pumped more than $2.5 million into a 1989 television series called *Democracy.* Petrocan had asked the highly respected journalist and broadcaster Patrick Watson to draw up a list of ideas for family television programs to sponsor. Watson offered Hopper sitcoms, movies, even a revival of the Ed Sullivan format. Without great hope, he threw in his democracy idea, a pet project he'd been trying to persuade the CBC to make. According to Watson, Hopper said, "Wait! Wait! Wait! How much would that cost?" Watson told him five or six million. Hopper said: "Hell, I could get that without even going to my board. I want to do that! That's class!"

Wrote *Maclean's*: "At a time when support for Canada's documentary tradition is flagging at both the CBC and the National Film Board, private investment offers a novel source of financing."

Private investment?

Maclean's continued: "The company took a low-key approach in sponsoring *Democracy.* Cutting the usual number of commercials in half, it is filling the spots with personal anecdotes about Canada from such prominent individuals as the CBC's Peter Gzowski and novelist W.O. Mitchell. Like Petro-Canada's successful sponsorship of last year's Olympic torch relay for the Calgary Winter Games, its commercial backing for *Democracy* enhances the Crown-owned company's patriotic image." Thus muddying the Maple Leaf logo and the financial disaster behind it with national institutions like *Morningside* and *Who Has Seen the Wind,* and further confusing a nation prone to identity crisis.

Then there were jobs for the boys. Hopper had put political advisors, like Marc Lalonde's executive assistant, Mike Phelps, on the payroll. Phelps wound up as president and CEO of Westcoast, the same subsidiary where Hopper pulled in a healthy salary for being chairman.

Like any self-respecting corporate giant, Petrocan had its jets and limos, in which Hopper could give lifts to politicians, bureaucrats, and private-sector oil executives. "A corporate jet can be a good communications tool," said a former Petrocan director, "if you use it to keep in touch with parts of a widespread empire."

But that wasn't all Hopper used it for. He used it for flying home to Ottawa on weekends and zipping across the Atlantic to meetings with Sheik Yamani in London; he used it for zooming down to petroleum congresses in Buenos Aires.

Petrocan certainly had international operations, but these had become yet another example of the inevitable perversion of corporate power when it is unfettered by the responsibility of a bottom line. The most egregious instance of Petrocan's distortion of good intentions was the Petro-Canada International Assistance Corporation.

PCIAC was yet another expensive and misguided child of the National Energy Program. A Canadian organization, brimming with the proceeds from windfall taxes on $90 oil, would be set up to realize the Third World's oil potential. Its raison d'être, like so much else in the NEP, was the multinationals' greed and selfishness. Declared the NEP: "A new firm, Petro-Canada International, will be created to explore solely in developing areas, where multinational oil companies are often reluctant to invest.

"This company will harness the skills of many private sector firms in Canada for the benefit of developing countries." It would seek to do business with state oil companies like those of Mexico and Venezuela. An immediate $50 million was granted as "seed money" for "equipment acquisition and start-up costs." It wasn't clear what equipment would be needed, apart from a pen. But then these were heady times. What was $50 million? The budget for the first five years was soon set at a more weighty $250 million.

In line with the NEP's all-embracing pretensions, PCIAC would go beyond merely dealing with the Third World's problems. It would be "part of an international effort to solve the world's oil problem. Moreover, Canada has the skills to help solve it and, in doing so, can open up industrial and trade opportunities to strengthen our own economic growth." Once again, Ottawa regarded giving taxpayers' money to specially selected private companies as synonymous with national growth, rather than destructive of it.

"We are not looking for oil for ourselves," stressed Peter Towe, the first and only chairman of PCIAC, as if keen to assert that it had no useful commercial purpose. Towe, the urbane former Canadian ambassador to the U.S., had known Hopper when he was Canada's ambassador and permanent representative to the OECD in Paris; Hopper at the time was Canada's chief representative to the International Energy Agency. PCIAC would be the source of much exotic travel for both of them.

Towe, in a speech shortly before he took up his appointment, peddled the Big Bad Oil justification for his new job. "Most major oil companies," he told a Washington conference, "are interested in fields that can produce even a minimal excess capacity for export. But what of the small, sparsely populated countries where … an oil puddle or gas bubble may mean the difference between energy dependency and self-sufficiency?" Federal officials declared that PCIAC would "take up the slack in areas the multinationals have abandoned."

Upon Towe's appointment, "a senior official in charge of building the new company" was quoted as saying: "Somebody might argue that it would have been better to appoint an oilman. But an oilman doesn't know the intricacies of foreign aid and the North-South dialogue as Towe does." Not just any bozo could be given a chequebook. There were sensitivities to doling out free money.

According to the original plan, Petrocan would provide technical assistance to PCIAC, help it find places to drill, and tell it which Canadian service companies to use. Petrocan's lack of overseas operating experience was not seen as problematic. However, according to a senior Ottawa energy official: "It was the height of pomposity to think Petrocan could find oil and gas in the Third World. The majors had been doing geology all over the globe for fifty years. They had an enormous amount of fundamental geological science. If anyone really believed that Petrocan could come from Calgary to Africa and find oil, they must have been crazy." But then the framers of the NEP *were* a little crazy, with all that oil-wealth-in-the-sky. Surely they should spread the wealth around a little?

Benefitting the Third World proved to be more difficult than buying the support of the Calgary service industry, which was hired to do all the geophysical work and drilling in the far-away places with the strange-sounding names. Also, PCIAC proved a useful way to help pay for the horrendous costs of East Coast offshore exploration. According to one former PCIAC employee: "International exploration was a great place to utilize East Coast offshore equipment during the off season. The rigs were very expensive. It was great to be able to get another company to take that equipment off you." Thus drillships wound up fleeing the advancing ice floes of the Labrador winter to drill off the coast of Ghana.

PCIAC bought lots of friends in Alberta. It even, at Petrocan's suggestion, obligingly drilled wells in places where Calgary-based service companies happened to have rigs, such as Madagascar. PCIAC turned into a sick version of the classic joke about the oilman who went to the dentist and was told he had nothing wrong with his teeth. "What the hell," the oilman replied. "Drill anyway."

Since Third World countries made no distinction between PCIAC and Petrocan proper, PCIAC's free money was a useful way for the state oil company to get its foot in the exploration door. PCIAC was also seen, at least initially, as a good staff training ground for Petrocan. Eventually, when the oil markets fell apart, PCIAC became a place to stash displaced Petrocan employees at the expense of Ottawa's aid budget.

The one group that didn't get too much from PCIAC was the people of the Third World. As a senior Ottawa energy mandarin says: "They drilled an expensive well off Tanzania that represented a big chunk of our aid to Tanzania. It was a dry hole. What good did that do the people of Tanzania? They could have used the money to build a hospital."

Sometimes the Third World managed to outsmart the do-gooders. The company became involved in drilling in the South China Sea with BP. Both companies thought they were going to teach the Chinese how to do things. At least $25 million later

Petrocan realized that the Chinese knew *exactly* what they were doing. They had given the foreigners their lousiest prospects to drill.

As PCIAC evolved, it had less to do with finding Third World oil and became more of an instrument for the aggrandizement of Bill Hopper and Peter Towe. Those who had tried to put PCIAC into smaller projects that might actually help the Third World were told not to rock the boat. A former PCIAC executive says: "Hopper and Towe used to love to fly off in the corporate jet to big signing ceremonies. The principle for operation became not the chance of finding oil but which countries were your friends. Also, turning up with a $10-million aid cheque in Bangkok makes you a pretty big wheel. That turned Towe's crank." And Hopper's.

And there was lots of potential adventure in not finding oil. One of Petrocan's drillships became involved in an offshore border dispute between Senegal, for whom it was providing assistance, and Guinea-Bissau. The rig was boarded by troops from Guinea-Bissau, bristling with Soviet-made armaments, and then buzzed by Senegalese MiGs. The drill site had been chosen by Senegal. Why Senegalese MiGs should have been buzzing a drillship that was meant to be helping them was never explained.

Sometimes it was tough to give money away. PCIAC had a lot of trouble persuading Nepal to take its assigned loot because the king's antechamber was filled with competing aid bureaucrats waving chequebooks. But then there were the fulfilling moments, the moments that made it all worthwhile. As a gushing reporter put it after the inauguration of a PCIAC drilling venture in Ghana: "Ghanaian officials describe Canada as 'a special friend,' and one that appears to understand the kind of transformation going on in the country. Coming from a government which, since it came to power in a coup two years ago, has continued to be suspicious of the West's motives in Africa, the compliment is extraordinary."

The "kind of transformation" going on in Ghana consisted of executions of former heads of state by firing squad, public floggings and canings, and an official declaration of national bankruptcy. But Canada could bask in the "extraordinary compliment" of being a "special friend." All we had to do was open the chequebook.

When the Tories came to power in 1984, they threatened to disband the PCIAC boondoggle, but the oil patch rushed to its defence. So the bands that accompanied the cheque-signing ceremonies played on: in Kingston, Jamaica, in 1985 when Towe signed over $5.3 million to refurbish a refinery; in Accra, Ghana, in October 1986, when another $8.5 million was committed to exploration; in Madagascar and Vietnam, in Bolivia and Morocco, in Botswana and Peru.

Five years after the Tories had come to power, PCIAC was still there, still spending $60 million a year, although the agency had by then become involved in a turf fight with the huge bureaucracy of the Canadian International Development Agency. Said Towe: "Large agencies such as CIDA are less able to move with the speed desirable particularly in the oil and gas sector. We need to use rigs that are available on a seasonal or cyclical basis in Canada, and to take advantage of seasonal and cyclical slack in Canada."

Astonishingly, Towe was giving the game away: one of PCIAC's main functions was to use Canadian drilling equipment as it became available "off season." It was a makework project for Calgary service companies. By the end of 1989, it had spent close to $400 million in more than thirty countries, with conspicuously little success in finding oil.

Shortly after PCIAC was announced, Hopper had said in a speech in Montreal, "Petro-Canada International can set an important precedent as a new form of international aid geared more closely to developing countries' needs." Ten years later, it had gone the way of all bureaucracy, becoming an organization that was there primarily to serve itself and its private-sector friends. Those worthwhile visions of "puddles of oil and bubbles of gas" that were too small for Big Bad Oil had turned into the reality of chauffeur-driven limousines, private jet flights, suites in Bangkok, and signing ceremonies with khaki-clad despots. Another dream shattered, another stepping-stone to the entrenchment of Bill Hopper. One final step was now needed: privatization.

EIGHTEEN

Quick Flip

WHEN FINANCE Minister Michael Wilson announced in his budget of February 20, 1990, that the Tories would be privatizing Petro-Canada, even Petrocan's own executives were taken by surprise. They had been pushing the issue for more than five years. There had been so many false dawns.

Following the announcement at an Ottawa press conference, Bill Hopper was all smiles as he sat beside Energy Minister Jake Epp and Privatization Minister John McDermid. "I've waited a long time for this," he said. "It's been a real shot in the arm for our people in Calgary, Toronto, and elsewhere." Significantly, Hopper took the opportunity to say a few words in praise of Hibernia. But Hopper seemed to find it hard to be nice to a government without making up for it elsewhere, so when asked about one of the Alberta government's pet megaprojects, the proposed OSLO tarsands plant, he called it "a dog," thus precipitating rage in Edmonton, a review of all Petrocan's Alberta tarsands and heavy oil commitments, and a quite uncharacteristic apology from Hopper.

McDermid, at the Ottawa press conference, continued to demonstrate ideological fuzzy-headedness. He acknowledged that Petrocan needed huge amounts of capital, but said the government was strapped for cash. The only alternative was to turn to public markets. But this made it sound as if the only reason Petrocan was being privatized was that the government was short of money; under other circumstances, he was suggesting, Ottawa might kick in more funds. Once again, any argument on principle was avoided.

The Tories — typically lacking conviction — continued to pursue economic nationalism even in privatization. They placed restrictions on Petrocan's proposed public ownership, and thus on its financial discipline. Individual ownership would be limited to 10 per cent, and foreign ownership to 25 per cent, of the publicly held shares. But if nobody could own more than 10 per cent of the shares, the company was invulnerable to takeover. Bill Hopper had told the Senate energy committee the previous fall that without the threat of a takeover, management could become complacent. "I don't think that's wise," he said. "Eventually, if you do that, you basically do tend to give the company to the management."

His tongue must have been planted firmly in his cheek.

The Tories were in a difficult position. They had to be careful about criticizing Petrocan and its performance. On the one hand, they wanted to raise as much money as possible from a sale so that Petrocan could afford its share of Hibernia; on the other, since they had used Petrocan themselves for Gulf's Canadianization, they couldn't afford to shine too harsh a light into the financial morass they had helped create.

Petrocan's below-par economic performance was comprehensively analyzed in a report prepared in June 1990 for the Senate energy committee. The report noted that, over the ten-year period from 1980 to 1989, Petrocan's return on shareholder's equity was 1.43 per cent, compared with 10.8 per cent for Imperial and 9.46 per cent for Shell. In fact, subsequent write-offs would mean its performance was even worse.

The report also stressed that Petrocan's performance had not improved since it started operating under its supposedly "commercial" mandate in 1984. "The under-performance in terms of the financial tests has become more marked in the recent periods...

Five complete years have passed since the mandate was changed to a commercial one without a clear trend to relative improvement."

This was a damning indictment of Petrocan management, but Hopper continued to treat Petrocan's performance as somehow separate from his own, or else as permanently affected by the original mandate. These Teflon characteristics raised wry chuckles among some of his executive rivals. One senior Calgary executive remarked: "I like Bill Hopper, but how can he get away with this? You'd swear if you didn't know the history that this was a new chief executive who'd just taken over, and he's going to make a real difference." But Bill Hopper thrived because almost nobody "knew the history."

The Tories were still terrified of being seen as selling off national patrimony and abandoning security. They became even more terrified in August 1990, when Saddam Hussein invaded Kuwait. Just as scary images of Sheik Yamani had been the backdrop for Petrocan's creation, and even scarier images of the Ayatollah Khomeini had undermined the Clark Tories' threats of dismemberment, so now the most frightening image of all, that of a megalomaniac with his hands on the world's oil valves, inevitably raised concerns about security. But political uncertainty no longer produced the kneejerk support for state intervention it once had.

Nevertheless, the privatization debate did become marginally entangled with the ongoing impasse over constitutional reform and the future of the country. A rudderless nation was looking for a flame to share. Petrocan's privatization, it was suggested, might further damage Canada's fragile nationhood. The *Globe and Mail's* respected columnist Jeffrey Simpson wrote: "There is, across Canada, a sense of the country slipping away. Too many Canadians believe they have lost the capacity to do great things together through their governments. To be selling Petro-Canada, which has been and might still be a collective agent for doing great things together, merely contributes to that sense of things slipping away."

But if Petrocan stood for any form of collective action, it stood for the unprofitable pursuit of misguided goals. That may well have been some sort of definition of the Canadian way in the past, but it had been a destructive way.

Parliamentary debate on Bill C-84, the Petrocan privatization bill introduced on October 1, 1990, was marked by a parade of all the old delusions about the usefulness of government instruments in general and Petrocan in particular. So, too, were presentations before the legislative committee on Bill C-84. The NDP in particular had a great many difficulties with the notion either of wealth creation or of wealth destruction. They seemed to believe that if $6 billion plus of debt and equity had been sunk into Petrocan, then that $6 billion still had to be hanging around somewhere, most likely in a Swiss bank account. They couldn't comprehend that most of the funds had been destroyed in poorly conceived exploration and investment.

The Tories, meanwhile, rather than laying out why Petrocan hadn't worked and couldn't work, found it necessary instead to quote approval of their own actions from unlikely sources. The most improbable was former Liberal energy and finance minister Marc Lalonde, interviewed on CBC's *Morningside* shortly after the introduction of C-84.

The arch-Trudeaucrat who had introduced the disastrous NEP exploded many of the myths about Petrocan that had germinated amid the rich fertilizer of economic nationalists' wishful thinking. Lalonde noted that Petrocan was never meant to protect Canadians against the market; that nobody had ever guaranteed that Petrocan would mean cheaper oil; that the "window on the industry" was redundant. He concluded: "If the government of Canada can get a good price for us as taxpayers by privatizing Petro-Canada, if we can keep it as Canadian, under Canadian ownership, I don't see that it is essential to the national interest that Petro-Canada should be forever government-owned." John McDermid and Jake Epp lost no opportunity to throw Lalonde's words across the Chamber.

Final passage of Bill C-84 went almost unremarked. Politically, it was something of a relief for the Tories. Still, the last thing the Tories wanted was for the sale of Petrocan shares to become, as it were, a non-issue.

· · ·

The path-breaking privatizations undertaken by Margaret Thatcher's government in Britain were usually pitched at attractive prices as a way of promoting "people's capitalism." Canada's Tories also wanted to sell shares as widely as possible, so they encouraged a heavy push at the retail end of the brokerage industry. All the registered representatives got on the phones to their clients. "Buy Petrocan," they said. "It's a sure thing. And if you want a few extra shares, I may be able to swing something for you."

According to a Toronto broker, the Tories were trying very hard to sell the stock to "Mom and Pop in Wawa, Ontario." The problem, said the analyst, was that not only were Petrocan's earnings of lower quality than those of either Imperial or Shell, but, because of its heavy emphasis on the downstream, they were also more volatile. "Because of its volatility," said the analyst, "this is not a stock that Mom and Pop should be putting into their retirement fund." The analyst was proved abundantly correct.

Size was a potential problem. This would be one of the largest issues in Canadian history. The last comparable issue was Gulf Canada's during a bull market in the summer of 1987. That issue had to be sold in Europe, the U.S., and the Far East as well as Canada. Repeating the performance with Petrocan would be more difficult because of restrictions on overall foreign ownership, although international brokers and merchant banks were beating down Petrocan's doors for a piece of the action and a share of the underwriting fees. Virtually every broker in Canada would have to be involved in selling the issue, raising a major problem for potential shareholders: where to get objective, independent advice on Petrocan's value?

Reports prepared before the issue by two prominent oil analysts, Robert Robinson of Scotia McLeod and Eleanor Barker of Sanwa McCarthy Securities, were both broadly bullish. Robinson predicted a dramatic financial improvement at Petrocan, largely due to the funds from the proposed $500-million-plus issue itself.

Both analysts expected sharply higher earnings and cash flows on the back of a better outlook for the downstream; also predicted were higher oil and gas sales in the intermediate and long term, when Hibernia would kick in and overseas holdings might begin to bear fruit. Nevertheless, both also acknowledged that higher cash flows were going to be matched by higher investment demands, in particular the $1 billion Petrocan had to invest for its share of Hibernia.

Perhaps surprisingly, given the conclusions of the 1990 Senate committee report, both analysts mentioned managerial strength as a positive factor, citing in particular the refining and marketing management acquired with Gulf Canada's downstream in 1985. Barker, a former Gulf and Petrocan employee, wrote: "Four of the nine senior officers are essentially the strong Gulf downstream management. Prior to the takeover of Gulf by Petro-Canada in 1985, this group had just turned its business around and led the top performing downstream operation in Canada." Wrote Robinson: "The existing management is very competent and the company has come a long way through a series of restructurings and downsizings of the organization."

Nevertheless, to suggest that Petrocan could move from being a chronic underperformer to outgrow Imperial and Shell was to promise the biggest comeback since Lazarus walked out of the tomb. Robinson believed Petrocan's annual growth rate between 1990 and 1995 would be 21.3 per cent, compared with 16.4 per cent for Shell and 19.7 per cent for Imperial. His report also indicated, however, that if oil prices stayed flat and refining margins failed to recover as projected, the company would soon find itself strapped for cash.

Neither Robinson nor Barker was permitted to comment after the prospectus had appeared, since both their companies were involved in the underwriting. But other analysts were privately less sanguine about the company's prospects, in particular the chances of shedding the extravagant lifestyle acquired during the years when profits didn't matter. According to one Calgary analyst, "Until it generates consistent earnings, I'll stay away. I believe that from the bottom to the top, it's fat. It will be very difficult to change that. It's a psychological thing."

Crude prices quickly fell following Saddam Hussein's defeat. Because of the delay in passing through crude costs, Petrocan found itself, in the first quarter of 1991, selling gasoline made from some of the most expensive crude of the decade. Retail prices were depressed by both recession and cheap gasoline imports from the U.S. Since Petrocan was more geared than either Imperial or Shell to the downstream, it would be particularly hard hit. The day the preliminary prospectus was issued, May 9, Petrocan announced a $52-million loss for the first three months of 1991, in contrast to a profit of $40 million for the first quarter of the previous year. This did not seem a propitious time to go to the market.

In June, Hopper led a road show across the nation and through Europe. It treated potential salespeople and investors to a flashy, split-screen presentation backed with rock music. In London, he hosted elaborate receptions and meals at the Savoy. But many observers came away unimpressed, noting that the company talked too much about the past and not enough about the future. In fact, Hopper didn't put up a good performance on the road because he just *hated* having to kowtow to brokers. He had always been a buyer. Now suddenly he had to play the role of salesman. He hadn't minded selling big acquisitions to Ottawa; that was easy. But selling to all these lowly analysts and brokers — who were asking some difficult questions — proved to be no pleasure at all. When one investment broker told him that the price they were talking about was too high, that it was the institutions who would determine the price in the "aftermarket," Bill Hopper gave a typical response: "It's political. It's out of my hands."

Despite a comprehensive campaign to sell the press on the notion that the shares would be bargain-priced at $15, when details of the issue finally emerged on June 18, the price was lower and the volume of shares to be sold higher — 39.5 million at $13 a share — than the government had wanted. Even though the institutional investors were lukewarm to the issue, the government's underwriting juggernaut, led by RBC Dominion Securities, had managed to sign up retail buyers for more than half the shares, even though they didn't know the price. The European tranche had also attracted strong interest.

The $523-million issue valued the government stake in Petrocan at $2.25 billion, little more than half book value. At least, with the offering under way, the Tories could claim some kind of victory in their struggle with Petrocan. But there were further slings and arrows to be suffered.

Following the share sale, the government was forced to take a write-down on its investment in Petrocan. As had been feared, the privatization increased the deficit. The Tories attempted fiscal sleight of hand: instead of taking the $1.25-billion hit in 1991, they tried to hide it by shoving the losses into the past, and increasing the deficits for the years prior to 1984, when the investments in Petrocan had been made, mostly under the Trudeau Liberals. In February 1992, Auditor General Denis Desautels sharply criticized this accounting method as improper. He said the action violated the government's own established accounting practices. "If you record things retroactively," he told the House of Commons finance committee, "it essentially causes transactions to disappear." And of course when such actions disappear, "they escape public scrutiny."

But that, of course, was exactly what the Tories had in mind.

Nineteen ninety-one turned out to be even worse for the industry than had been projected. After the Petrocan share issue, one piece of bad news followed another. The company reported a whopping $149-million loss for the first six months. In September, it drew criticism when it reported that it was looking to sell half its stake in Hibernia. In October, it sold 5 per cent of its Syncrude stake to Mitsubishi Oil for $132.5 million, taking yet another $138-million write-off in the process.

In his report before the share issue, Scotia McLeod's Robinson had estimated that Petrocan's 1991 earnings would be $54.1 million. Sanwa McCarthy's Barker had estimated $100 million. In the event, Petrocan's net loss for 1991, after write-offs, was $598 million. The shares fell virtually from their opening trade. Within a year, they were trading at close to $8, presenting investors with a loss of more than a third from a stock that many brokers had recommended as a "quick flip."

With Petrocan's share sale, Hopper was now subject to the discipline of the financial market, but if he failed to meet it, he was going to be a hard man to shift, especially given the government's ownership restrictions. Certainly the government didn't seem prepared to challenge him. John McDermid, who regarded himself as an enemy of financial waste and bureaucratic incompetence, spoke with remarkable sympathy of the man who had presided over such an enormous loss of public money. "I guess it's kind of like being the prime minister," said McDermid. "If you're CEO and chairman of the board, you get blamed for everything."

In fact, Hopper had survived sixteen years at the helm without taking a single direct hit. But if Hopper wasn't subject to ultimate market discipline in the form of a takeover, he was still subject to the wrath of shareholders, particularly when those shareholders were also employees.

NINETEEN

Question Time

THE SILENCE that greeted Bill Hopper when he walked into Calgary's Jack Singer Concert Hall for Petro-Canada's first annual meeting on Tuesday, May 5, 1992, was palpably hostile. Of the 1,500 shareholders present, 80 per cent were Petrocan employees. The previous Friday, the company had announced that 660 jobs would be axed from its refining and marketing arm, the human costs of a huge downstream rationalization involving the closing of more than 1,000 gas stations, which had been announced the previous January.

Bill Hopper had wanted privatization in order to be free of political interference. He was finding it wasn't as much fun as he'd thought. He was experiencing the downside of personal responsibility. The symbol of his stewardship was the Petrocan share price, which had gone straight down virtually since the day shares started trading. One hundred thousand people had bought shares. They were now disappointed and angry. The most disappointed and angry were those on Petrocan's payroll. Many had borrowed to buy equity as an act of faith. They had also been persuaded that the company was being sold "cheap." Finally, they had been lured in by what looked like a deal too good to refuse: interest-free, or nearly interest-free, loans.

Executives had borrowed $8 million to buy shares. Other employees had borrowed $11 million. Hopper had borrowed $720,200, president James Stanford $681,200. But the board had given Hopper, Stanford, and the other executives a sweeter deal than the average worker: executive loans were repayable over ten years; other employees had to pay up within twelve months. The twelve months were almost up. An employee who had bought 5,000 shares was sitting on a loss of more than $20,000.

These losses, combined with the layoffs, had caused more than a further deterioration in already low employee morale; they had caused employees at last to turn on Bill Hopper. Discontent had erupted in the form of an anonymous letter that had been faxed and photocopied round the company the week before the meeting. It began:

Dear Fellow Employees:

In the next few weeks we will hear the announcement of yet another massive layoff. The company is going to cut as many as 1000 to 2000 jobs because they say that Petro-Canada is in such financial trouble that it just can't survive with these many employees. The real story is that Bill Hopper has to face the music at the Annual Meeting, and somehow make excuses for his terrible mismanagement of the company all these years.

The company has said that we don't have enough money to fund any new projects, and many of the current projects we have sweated blood over all these years are now going to die too.

What the company doesn't tell us, as shareholders is what Bill Hopper costs us: Did you know...

The letter went on to a list of allegations about Hopper's extravagant lifestyle, including his jets, limos, and chefs. It claimed that Hopper couldn't stand anyone who disagreed with him. It concluded:

Hopper wastes many, many millions of dollars each year, and doesn't contribute anything to the company except to make us a laughing stock in the business community. Maybe we're trying to save money in the wrong ways. If you agree with this letter please make copies of it and circulate it within the company. The Annual Meeting is May 5 in Calgary. Let's go to it and boo Hopper off the stage so the company can get a decent leader.

At the directors' dinner the evening before the AGM, in the 51st-floor dining room of the Petro-Canada Tower, one of the directors had said: "Our problem is Bill Hopper." Hopper acknowledged that he'd been getting a lot of bad press. In fact, the board had received another letter earlier in the year. It came from Bill Wheeler, head of a Vancouver-based investment institution. Wheeler's letter, too, had concentrated on the widespread allegations about Hopper's fat lifestyle. It alleged that, during the road show for the share issue, a fleet of limousines had been kept waiting outside meetings for hours on end. The letter also accused Hopper of not selling Petrocan's stake in Westcoast because he wanted to retire to Vancouver. That allegation seemed wide of the mark. Petrocan's stake in Westcoast had been questioned since it had been acquired as part of the Pacific takeover. But Hopper, described by colleagues as a "collector," hated to part with any of his empire. Hopper brushed off Wheeler's letter as the grumbling of a "kooky institution."

Both the anonymous employee letter and Wheeler's had contained some inaccuracies, but they had also hit some important targets. Hopper had been telling the board that he'd been trying to sell the second jet, but in fact he had only been trying to sell half the jet — that is, sell it and lease part of its airtime back, so the company could carry on using it. The private chefs, too, had been a cause of concern at the board. Before the annual meeting, Hopper was told they had to go. The employee letter had mentioned the PR department that "has to clean up after all the stupid things he says"; this was also particularly relevant, given Hopper's remarks about the sixty-day clock running on Hibernia, remarks that had angered federal Energy Minister Epp and surprised Petrocan's partners. Actually, hardly anybody at the company, including the PR department, had known that Hopper was making a speech in Washington, even less that he was going to start shooting off his mouth about Hibernia to reporters.

A jibe about Hopper loving "to travel around the world like

some big shot from Exxon" was also on the money. But Hopper's wings were already being clipped. Petro-Canada International Assistance Corporation had finally been closed down in 1990, and Petrocan was moving out of international operations. As it happened, however, international operations would provide a wonderful opportunity for Hopper to divert the spotlight from himself at the annual meeting.

The poison-pen letters encountered a keen response. Petrocan employees had never been able to understand why they weren't performing as well as other big oil companies. After all, as Hopper liked to point out, 99 per cent of them came from the industry. The majority were experienced, skillful, and dedicated. In the past, they had become angry when the company was attacked. They had taken it personally.

Back in 1984, the *Calgary Sun,* which had always been staunchly, even rabidly, anti-Petrocan, had declared that "no proud Canadian" would work for the state oil company. The *Sun's* editor had been inundated with angry phone calls from Petrocan employees, one of whom had even challenged him to a fistfight. Spontaneously, a group of Petrocan employees had taken up a collection to pay for a half-page ad in the *Sun's* rival, the *Calgary Herald*: "A Calgary tabloid recently questioned the patriotism of Petro-Canada employees," the ad read. "We object. We are loyal Canadians and proud of our achievements. Best wishes to all Canadians on Canada Day 1984." Petrocan employees devoted a great deal of time to community activities. Their dedication had helped make the Olympic Torch Relay such a hitchless success; they had even made the largest-ever corporate contribution to the Calgary United Way. But now morale was at an all-time low. Petrocan's employees began to believe that they weren't the problem; the problem was upstairs.

Understandably, Hopper approached the AGM with trepidation. As the unnatural silence in the hall continued, Hopper introduced himself and his executives: president Jim Stanford, chief financial officer Wesley Twiss, and corporate secretary Bob McCaskill. This wasn't the feisty Bill Hopper who had spoken to the analysts' conference the previous fall, damning fools and critics left, right, and centre. This was repentant, low-key, serious Bill, his voice a contrite monotone.

As he went through the formalities of the meeting, Hopper almost seemed to be trying to put the audience to sleep. Eleven directors — those already sitting on the board — were nominated and seconded and, in the absence of other nominations, elected "by acclamation," a strange term under the circumstances. Hopper then introduced the board, who sat in a group, wearing white carnations. Each director stood. There was no applause. Auditors were nominated.

Hopper's tone moved up a notch on the contrition scale. He mentioned the privatization, which had been "gratifying" at the time, but had taken place during "the worst year I can remember since I started in this industry thirty-seven years ago." Hopper reaffirmed the company's net loss of $598 million. Things would remain difficult, he said, but the downstream looked promising. Now that major restructuring was under way, there would be "substantial improvement" in profitability. He reiterated the job losses announced the previous Friday. He announced that the company would be focusing on western Canadian light oil, natural gas, natural gas liquids, and oil developments on the Grand Banks.

Then came the shocker. Hopper announced that the number of salaried employees in the resources division would be reduced by 40 per cent. A gasp ran round the the hall. Hopper also announced that corporate support staff would be cut. Petrocan's payroll would be slashed from 6,200 to fewer than 5,000 by the end of 1993. At the end of 1985 it had been over 10,000.

Following the announcement of accounting changes and continued support for Hibernia, Hopper acknowledged the poor performance of the company's stock, and said that 1992 would be another difficult year. The company would maintain a "conservative financial posture."

Then there was a long silence, a deliberate silence, almost a controlling silence. "Before I call on Jim Stanford," Hopper continued, "I would like to touch on one other issue. Recent months have been difficult for our employees as well as our shareholders. Many employees have carried exceptionally heavy workloads in a frustrating business environment with much uncertainty about their ongoing employment. These circumstances may have fostered the anonymous communications which have been receiving some media attention. As chief executive, I take full responsibility for Petro-Canada and I expect to be the recipient of any criticisms as to the manner in which the corporation is managed. Some criticisms concern arrangements for our senior people and mine in particular. They have involved unfounded allegations which are irksome, particularly when they involve family members."

Another anonymous letter had questioned why Hopper's wife, Pat, had never moved to Calgary, and accused her of using the jet for shopping trips to Vancouver.

Hopper continued: "Corporate aircraft carry a certain image which is unrelated to business efficiency or cost effectiveness. We operate two executive aircraft. Efforts to sell the one which we own were initiated last fall and we hope to complete the sale within the next two months. Last August, we froze salaries of senior management and decided against any bonuses for 1991. In the past year, seven officer positions were eliminated."

But Hopper went on: "I am not going to address specific matters such as company cars, club memberships, or my own living arrangements. Your board of directors is well aware of all these matters. The board determines the policy with respect to them, and the board will continue to set policies."

In fact, the story about Hopper's wife using the jet was unfounded. The notable thing about Bill Hopper's wife, as far as most executives were concerned, was that they'd never *seen* her. Unlike other executives, he rarely if ever brought his wife to company functions. The real scandal in the jets lay in Hopper's use of them to curry favour with politicians. He'd lent the jets to ministers or given rides to politicians many times over the years. But the accusation about Hopper's wife enabled Hopper to display a little self-righteous indignation. On the other hand, for Hopper to talk about freezing executive salaries the previous August was a little self-serving, since Hopper had received a large increase after the share issue. Still, there were no boos.

Hopper handed over to Jim Stanford. There was coughing in the audience, but still no applause. Stanford went to a podium at the side of the stage and proceeded to review results and describe management's actions and plans for the future. Pictures of horse-head pumps and gas flares and bar charts were beamed onto the triple screen at the front of the auditorium. Stanford — according to the anonymous letter, one of Hopper's "yes men" — at least delivered his speech in a more upbeat style.

On the other side of the stage from Stanford, a young woman signed his remarks to a block of seats reserved for the deaf. Only one person sat there. It was the relief signer. The two women swapped positions several times during the meeting, translating Hopper's and Stanford's remarks into the language of the hearing-impaired. But only, apparently, for each other.

Stanford concluded. There was still no applause. But now an expectant murmur ran down the aisles: it was question time.

Shareholders' meetings seldom produce relevant questions. They usually provide the opportunity for either the certifiably wacky or the terminally disgruntled to have their fifteen seconds in the limelight. This is not unwelcome to managements, who frequently appear to cultivate the kooks. By most AGM standards, the first questioner was on the mark. He drew an eruption of applause when he suggested that, instead of a freeze, management might consider a "10- or 15-per-cent salary cut." The questioner was obviously well known to the corporation. Hopper said he would have brought the questioner's file with him, but he couldn't carry it. Despite themselves, the audience laughed. He told the shareholder: "You've become something of a legend around the corporation." Schmoozerama. He suggested he go speak to other executives after the meeting. The man sat down, flushed with recognition.

Then up to a microphone came a man named Bill Davis, who held the proxy for the United Church of Canada. Bill Davis want-ed to ask about Petrocan's activities in Myanmar, formerly Burma, a country now under military rule, where there had been many instances of human rights abuses.

In 1988, the military dictatorship in Myanmar had imposed a bloody crackdown on students, killing more than 3,000. But then it had promised "free and fair" elections and the opening of the country to foreign investment. When the opposition leader won those elections, she was placed under house arrest. Petrocan had rushed in where the multinationals had feared to tread. In 1989, the company had paid a $6-million "signing bonus" to Myanmar's dictatorship in return for exploration rights.

As shareholders had filed into the Jack Singer Hall that morning, they had passed a small group of very respectable-looking middle-aged protesters carrying placards, one of which featured an incongruous skull-and-crossbones. The protesters were demanding Petrocan's withdrawal from Myanmar.

Bill Davis's arrival at the microphone was no surprise to Bill Hopper; in fact, he welcomed it. Petrocan executives, including Hopper, had met Davis the previous week to hear about his concerns. Nobody on stage minded when Davis spent several minutes talking about Myanmar, because the more time he spent on Myanmar, the less time could be spent questioning Hopper's stewardship.

Hopper was happy to discourse on Petrocan's presence in that distant country. If they weren't there, he pointed out, some other company would be. As it was, there were already a couple of state companies operating in the area. Petrocan was only a small player, and employed local people. But Hopper said he was "deeply troubled" by events in the military dictatorship. Following a long, rambling reply, he declared: "We'd like to spend more time with you." Perhaps Bill could work out a strategy, an "action plan." Schmooze a little.

The clock ticked on.

Next up was a big man named Jack Downey, who also had Myanmar on his mind. Downey, a former soldier with a worldwide network of human rights interests, gave a graphic description of dealing with gunshot wounds and victims of gang rape. But

Downey supported Petrocan's presence in Myanmar, because it gave him a channel for applying pressure, for harassing management. Applause. Go get 'em, Jack. Downey, an admitted faxaholic, wanted a hand-out to support his good work in Burma. Hopper would have no trouble with Jack; he was an expert at giving hand-outs. "Are you going to be in Calgary tomorrow morning?" asked Hopper. "Yes, sir," said Big Jack Downey. "Then come and see me in my office." "What time, sir?" asked Big Jack. "What time do you want?" asked Hopper. Reluctant giggles broke out again in the crowd. "Seven o'clock," said Jack Downey. There was laughter and applause. Big Jack was going to make little Bill get up early.

The next questioner threatened to get relevant: How could the company not have known it was going to take huge write-downs in the months after the share issue? The questioner wanted more shares to be doled out gratis to make up for the decline in the shareholders' value. His proposal was out of the question. It was applauded. Hopper said it would be considered. More time passed.

There were questions about a gas station in Kleinburg, Ontario, the closing of the company's Port Moody refinery in B.C., and other issues, but the angry shareholder-employees with the questions written out with shaky hands on now sweaty pieces of paper never got up.

One shareholder received applause when he suggested that if Hopper came back with similar results next year, he might look to his "golden parachute." But nobody questioned exactly *why* Hopper had a golden parachute. In most cases, a golden parachute — in Hopper's case, three years' salary in the case of dismissal without cause — is installed so that executives have security in the case of a hostile takeover. But Petrocan was invulnerable to takeover. The government's restriction on shareholdings had taken care of that. Hopper's had been installed to protect him from *government*. He'd even joked to the board that he wouldn't mind if they fired him, because then he could walk off with a couple of million.

Other shareholders wanted to know how many vice-presidents the company had; some asked questions about directors' fees that were answered in the proxy statement. One shareholder wanted to question Hopper's claims of having been in the industry for thirty-seven years. Myanmar was raised again. But Hopper was like a matador, the crowd like a weak bull. The shareholder-employees cheered on the weak charges, but Hopper kept waving his cape and stepping out of the way.

After the meeting, directors were buttonholed by shareholders and employees. Many were angry with Hopper. The directors found themselves defending him; after all, look at the state of the industry.

Hopper, meanwhile, sitting between Jim Stanford and Wesley Twiss, was answering questions at a press conference. Most questions dealt with the specifics of downsizing. When asked again about perks, Hopper referred to "unfounded allegations" in "brown envelopes." But he said he wasn't going to get into details "because one detail leads to another, and soon you're going to want to know my waist size." Nobody asked Hopper's waist size.

When it was all over, the directors returned to the Petro-Canada Tower for a post-meeting meeting. Previously, they would have enjoyed a lavish lunch. This time, they were given sandwiches.

Hopper had survived the meeting virtually unscathed. The challenges thrown at him had been slim. The board had been re-elected. Hopper now had virtually total control because he was chairman of the board committee that nominated the eight out of eleven directors who were not government appointees. The government had agreed not to interfere or vote its shares beyond nominating its three directors.

As he treated all sources of supposed authority over him, Hopper treated the board with a combination of charm to their faces and contempt behind their backs. Giving evidence before the Senate energy committee, Hopper had said: "We probably have too many lawyers on the board... When the Liberals were around, we had a bunch of lawyers too. Politicians appoint lawyers, I guess. I think lawyers only have time to be bagmen, so I mean, everybody else works for a living."

But suddenly Hopper seemed to need all the friends he could

get, even the Tory bagmen. The groundswell of ill feeling inspired by layoffs and slumping share prices had reached Hopper. He was sensitive to criticism, but he showed little sign of moving. Some had reckoned that, with his remarks about Hibernia two months before, Hopper had actually been trying to get himself fired; but his ego was much too large to take such a blow. He had persuaded most board members that if Petrocan had any problems, they were related to the heavy costs of the original exploration mandate, established in a period before any of them had been around.

While Petrocan had been losing huge amounts of taxpayers' money, there had been hardly any criticism of Hopper. But what privatization had done was to introduce at least some private individuals — that is, shareholders — to the direct consequences of the government's original investment in Petrocan and its management by Bill Hopper. Petrocan shareholders were mad because they felt they'd been sold a pig in a poke. Petrocan workers were unhappy because they were losing their jobs. Both groups were casting around for someone to blame. The obvious choice was Bill Hopper. His corporate jets and limos and executive chefs made him an easy target. But although Hopper was sensitive to the criticism, he had no plans to change his lifestyle.

His next big date was at the June 1992 conference on the global environment in Rio, which would be chaired by his old boss, Maurice Strong. The conference didn't have a whole lot to do with tidying up Petrocan's desperate condition, but then everyone who was anyone was going. Hopper would be taking the corporate jet.

TWENTY

The Bottom Line

WHEN LIBERAL Energy Minister Donald
Macdonald made his presentation to Cabinet
in 1973 on Petrocan, he talked about creating
"reliable import supply links" and enhancing
the "rate and pattern of the development of
Canadian energy resources." He spoke of filling in "undesirable
gaps" and taking "direct steps to improve the security of the supply." He emphasized providing a "more significant Canadian presence in a foreign-dominated industry." He talked about "coordi-
nation" and "stimulation" and using "instruments."

Macdonald didn't say anything about a coast-to-coast network
of tunnel car washes and convenience stores with gas stations
attached. He didn't project that Petrocan would enter chuckwagon
races at the Calgary Stampede, run an art gallery, and sponsor an
Olympic Torch Relay. He didn't point out that Petrocan would
spend millions annually to support charities and arts organizations, from the Vancouver International Comedy Festival to the
Sudbury Symphony. He didn't talk about the chief executive's
limos and jet and perks. He didn't mention those things because
he did not foresee them. Was Donald Macdonald naive?

Over the years, there emerged a huge gap between the good
intentions under which Petrocan was created and the corporate
carnival that Petrocan became. What went wrong? Did the world

change? Was the mandate flawed? Did politicians interfere too much? Did management escape control? Was going astray inevitable?

The answer is all of the above.

It wasn't so much that the oil world changed as that few people understood the economics of oil. During the first and second OPEC crises, the delusion grew that petroleum was somehow beyond economics, that the laws of supply and demand did not apply. Everybody had always known that gluts tended to drive the price to the floor, but what nobody really understood was what higher prices would do to supply and demand. Both sides of the equation seemed "inelastic," in the terminology of the dismal science. A petroleum-hooked world seemed to have no immediate alternatives to refined products, particularly when it came to the automobile; nobody was sure how much more oil would be brought on stream by higher prices.

In fact, the petroleum market behaved just as the most fundamental of economic theories said it would: higher prices led to conservation, technological improvements, and the development of alternatives. The world became much more petroleum-efficient, although it took time. On the supply side, higher prices made it economic to drill prospects such as the North Sea, as well as boosting exploration in more conventional areas. Oil finding techniques continued to become more sophisticated.

The vast majority of government programs merely attempted to make the market work but more so, and thus too much. Ottawa subsidized people to over-insulate their houses, and companies to over-explore in regions that were not economic. In this it was not alone.

But misunderstanding of oil markets was due not merely to ignorance but to ideology as well. Many Ottawa analysts didn't like markets, because for markets to work, some people had to get richer and some poorer. More important, corporations had to get richer. The super-bureaucrats were obsessed with distribution of wealth and market "fine-tuning," which they had been taught were the proper concern of economics.

The emergence of OPEC provided the immediate rationale for government intervention. Bureaucrats detected a supposed need for "countervailing" power. In addition, in Canada as in OPEC countries, anti-American economic nationalism supported the interventionist approach. Petrocan was thus born both of the widespread Keynesian-Galbraithian dream of benevolent intervention that ruled much postwar thinking, and of Walter Gordon's economic nationalism and xenophobia. But its godparents were those who, while embracing Keynes, Galbraith, and Gordon, were also attracted by the prospect of powerful jobs as the guiding hands of the guardian state.

These self-styled "policy entrepreneurs" were quite inappropriately described as "public servants." From the start, Petrocan was an organization peopled by very human actors with very human desires for personal wealth and self-aggrandizement. Its political masters and bureaucratic monitors were people too, with their own selfish interests. Although this simple reality did not explain everything about the company's birth and evolution, it was a critical element in explaining how the vision went awry.

It did not seem unreasonable for citizens to ask: "How can we trust foreigners to provide jobs and technical skills for Canadians?" The blunt answer was that we couldn't. But neither could we trust Canadian businesses. The group we could trust least of all was the government, whose claims to job "preservation" or "creation" were based on beggaring the future for the sake of the present, destroying two jobs tomorrow so that one job — usually temporary — could be created today.

Petrocan was part and symptom of a larger trend. Since the days of Pierre Trudeau, program has been piled upon program at an accelerating rate, and with little noticeable difference between parties; the government machine has grown beyond control. But it would be a mistake to imagine that better monitoring or supervision would bring government to heel, because the monitors are themselves ultimately the problem. Like doctors whose only known remedy is the application of leeches, their response to the increasing sickness of the economic patient was simply to pile on the suckers. Even the Mulroney Tories, apparent champions of privatization, engaged in it with much less conviction than Tories elsewhere. Like most Canadians, their ultimate problem with Petrocan may have been one of cognitive dissonance. Privatization seemed to go against the whole Canadian history and ethos of supposedly benign government intervention.

In fact, government intervention has almost invariably been disastrous. There are myriad examples at both the provincial and federal levels: the Glace Bay heavy water plant, Bricklin, Canadair, de Havilland, Churchill Forest Industries, Consolidated Computer, Sysco, Devco, Candu, Quintette, the Alberta telecommunications fiasco, Ontario's investment in Suncor, Mirabel airport, the $12-billion-plus cost overrun at Ontario Hydro's Darlington nuclear power station, Hibernia, the Lloydminster heavy oil upgrader, the Vancouver Island gas pipeline, and on and on. The truly astonishing aspect of this catalogue of disaster is that few seem willing to draw the ultimate conclusion: government does not, *can* not help the economy in the long term. It can only slow it down by misspending taxpayers' money, which means less tax revenue for social programs.

Numerous academic studies have been made of direct government intervention in the economy. While recording the stream of failures, even the most critical stop short of recommending that government should not attempt to run companies. But unless companies are subject to the discipline of the "bottom line," they inevitably — like Petrocan — fall prey to the whims of management, monitors, or politicians. Even when Crown corporations do their accounting according to private-sector rules, it is possible to conceal the real financial picture for a long period, as Petrocan demonstrated.

So Petrocan began life with a mandate fatally flawed by misunderstandings about markets and business in general, and oil markets and the oil business in particular. Successive governments perverted the mandate by insisting on using Petrocan for political objectives that had little or nothing to do with energy: using Petrofina to "show the flag" in Quebec, allowing the acquisition of part of Gulf in the name of "Canadianization." But the ultimate size and scope of Petrocan's failure — and its huge cost to the Canadian taxpayer — had a lot to do with Bill Hopper's skill in manipulating the system. A less skillful operator than Hopper wouldn't have been able to play the political game. A less likeable character would have been easier to can.

Just before the privatization, an experienced analyst said: "Hopper is a guy who, if you give him a mission, he accomplishes the mission. That was his mandate. You give him a new mandate and he's doing pretty well. You can't shoot the messenger. His mission was to build the company to compete with Imperial and Shell." But the experienced analyst had it wrong. Petrocan's original mandate was *not* to compete with Imperial and Shell. That was where Bill Hopper led it.

In his 1982 interview with *Executive* magazine, Bill Hopper said: "There's one thing you ought to understand about public sector corporations, particularly in the oil business, because I know them worldwide. You can plot their mandate, you can describe their functions in economic terms and so on. But a great deal depends on the personal drive and ambitions of the people who run them... I'd like to be able to leave this world thinking I accomplished something, that I built that thing."

Ten years later, Hopper was trying to distance his "personal drive and ambitions" from the fiasco. To an astonishing degree, he had succeeded. The reason was that he had used the same techniques to cover his tracks as he had used to influence Petrocan's growth: a potent combination of charm, charisma, and deviousness.

There was no doubt that Hopper, through his position, received substantial salary and perks; there was nothing unusual in that. The problem was more complex. Hopper wasn't interested purely in money. He wanted to be the *legitimate* recipient of a high salary and utilizer of a corporate jet. That's why he needed to build a big company.

Hopper thought he could create a viable and competitive entity by acquiring other companies. In doing so, like his masters, he mistook form for substance; he underestimated the importance of corporate culture and corporate legitimacy. Interventionist governments do not understand the fundamental nature of corporate enterprise. Governments create simulacra, corporate voodoo dolls. They acquire assets, invest money, build plants, employ workers, but what is ultimately missing is the motive power of enterprise, the drive to create wealth by taking risks, to pull out more than you put in.

Although a government can seize or buy the corporate fruits of individuals' labours, it cannot seize talented and experienced entrepreneurial minds. It cannot seize the *process* of wealth creation, only its results. Some managers will stay on, but many of the best will leave as they discover that, in a state organization, ingratiating oneself with political powers is more important than objective performance. At that game, Hopper was a master.

The bureaucrats who were meant to monitor Petrocan either were true believers, were not as smart as Hopper, or could be schmoozed. The board was never an effective control mechanism, except perhaps for a brief period in the first three or four years. By the time of its first annual meeting, Petrocan had had more than forty directors over its seventeen years. Scarcely any had oil experience. But most important, there had been enormous turnover, primarily because the Tories had pitched virtually the whole board in 1984. Admittedly, the majority of those thrown out were Liberal patronage appointees; but installing a completely new board, which would experience significant further changes, deprived the company of continuity.

In any case, Hopper played the directors like a violin. As a former EMR insider, now a consultant, says: "The company ended up being way different from what was originally intended. Energy ministers came and went. Bureaucrats played musical chairs, and all the while Bill Hopper was at the wheel, so he was the only one people could ask about where the ship was going. They'd all forgotten the original mandate, so they went along with what Hopper told them. It was his destination that the ship headed for."

The only really strong executive to have emerged under

Hopper's stewardship was David O'Brien, who was clever enough to know how to work Hopper and his ego. Says a fellow executive: "He worked twice as hard as Hopper, and he worked *on* Hopper." But O'Brien departed in 1988, partly because he was tired of living in Hopper's shadow, partly because he believed Hopper was still thinking expansively when he should have been pulling in his horns, partly because job opportunities were opening up.

Hopper didn't know how to pull in his horns. He was turned on by the rush of buying. "I'm a builder," he'd tell his Ottawa bureaucratic colleagues. But by 1992 the days of buying and building were over. By the time of the annual meeting, Hopper was becoming more and more reclusive. Colleagues reckoned he'd become bored with Petrocan. For many of the employees in the Jack Singer Hall, it was the first time they'd ever seen him in the flesh. Increasingly, he took off in the jet for international oil meetings without telling anybody. And yet, astonishingly, because of his control of the board, he looked irremoveable, despite Petrocan's horrendous costs.

It can fairly be claimed that Canada is at least $10 billion deeper in debt because of Petrocan, a debt for which there is no corresponding asset. The money has gone. Those responsible for creating Petrocan might say, "Well, so what? We made mistakes. Let's not harp on it." But although the original investment has been largely destroyed, the debt lives with us. We are like bad gamblers in debt to loan sharks, our obligations growing geometrically. The annual interest cost of the Petrocan-associated debt is about $1 billion, and all the income tax from 100,000 average Canadian families will have to go to pay that annual charge.

Government has become like a coin-clipper, those villains of old who used to shave just a little off each gold or silver coin, then melt down the results. In fact, our coins are now half-moons. Governments take almost half the average family's earnings in taxes, but we have little idea which shaving goes where, and the government doesn't plan to start helping us, and of course many get more than they put in.

Large numbers numb minds, but it's important to remember

that the dollars that go into $10 billion are the same as the dollars that go into $1,580 —the average loss suffered by Petrocan's shareholders after a year — or the tax that comes out of your paycheque or is added to your restaurant bill. They represent wealth, that is, the fruits of people's effort, of sweaty or wrinkled brows. They are the same dollars that buy Hamburger Helper and Cadillacs, the same dollars that pay for day care centres and medical bills and welfare cheques. When government levies taxes for social policy, it may fairly claim that there will be fewer Cadillacs so there will be more welfare cheques. But when it creates something like Petrocan, it ensures that there will be *both* fewer Cadillacs and less money for welfare.

Is this view too crudely bottom-line? Did Petrocan provide non-financial or non-economic benefits to the nation to offset its huge costs? After all, a key plank of its original mandate was to help "security of supply." Did it contribute anything there? No. Hibernia would have been found anyway. The finds Petrocan made in the West were probably less than those that would have been made by Arcan, Pacific, and Petrofina if they had not been taken over. Oil and gas discovery, according to the "multiple hypothesis" taught to all geology students, including young Bill Hopper, is likely to be more successful the greater the number of players. By taking players out, Petrocan reduced the number of views available, and probably the amount of oil found.

Did Petrocan carry out useful research that might not have been done by the companies it took over? Nope. State-to-state oil deals? *Nada.* Overseas exploration? A bust. What about Canadianization? Petrocan was certainly responsible for a major chunk of the increase in Canadian ownership, from 26.1 per cent of the industry revenues in 1980 to its height of 48.2 per cent in 1985. But the fact that Petrocan's market value in mid-1992 was little more than the price it paid *either* for Pacific in 1978 or for Petrofina in 1981 shows that these acquisitions were poor value, or that their assets were dissipated, or both.

Petrocan's privatization, meanwhile, is hardly the end of the affair. The government still owns 80 per cent of Petrocan. The

Mulroney Tories had wanted to sell additional shares to bring public holdings to more than 50 per cent before the next election. But given the disaster of the initial privatization, and the further deterioration in the oil business, by the summer of 1992, that appeared a pipe dream.

In a rational world in which the government's top priority is returning value to the taxpayers, or at least minimizing taxpayers' losses, the government would scrap all ownership restrictions on Petrocan and sell its remaining holdings — at the appropriate time — to whoever could offer the most money. Or Petrocan could be bought lock, stock, and barrel by a buyer of any nationality, thus enabling 100,000 shareholders — and Canadian taxpayers — to recoup at least part of their capital losses. Even if that unlikely event should come to pass, the hidden burden of Petrocan within the national debt will probably be with us forever. At least the same cannot be said for Bill Hopper, who will have to retire eventually.

For the moment, however, Bill Hopper continues to win friends and influence people. Big Jack Downey, the ex-soldier who had been invited at the annual meeting to meet with Bill Hopper to discuss Burma/Myanmar, turned up in the enormous sky lobby of the Petrocan tower the following morning at the appointed time. He was impressed that an assistant was there to carry his briefcase. Jack spent an hour and a half with Bill, and came away more of a convert than he realized.

"They even let me smoke up there," said Jack, "because I'm addicted. We discussed the situation in Burma and other places, and it is my opinion and the opinion of a lot of people that it's absolutely essential that Petrocan stay there. They made a mistake going in, but you have to live with mistakes — $26 million plus a $6-million signing bonus. They are treating their people well, as well as they can. And Canada cannot afford to lose another $26 million, because it'll be bought out by the Venezuelans or somebody else so fast it'll make your head spin."

Jack Downey wouldn't say what, if anything, Bill Hopper had given him. "Now look here," he says conspiratorially, "this is a sensitive issue. People will get killed. The dictator will find out in a minute, and then that's it for Petro-Canada. Everything has to be done quietly."

Would Jack describe himself as a fan of Bill?

"No, I'm not a fan of Bill Hopper, but he's a sensitive man. He's a good leader. He's prepared to make hard decisions."

But hadn't they lost a lot of money over the years?

"You're goddamn right they have. Any time the government's involved in anything you've got to snivel to the senators and all the rest of these bastards.

"But you can't hang that on Bill Hopper."

Damn right.

Sources

I have followed Petrocan since I started to cover the energy beat for the Financial Post in 1977, the year in which I first met and interviewed Bill Hopper. I left the Post in 1979 to complete a book on the Canadian oil industry, The Blue-Eyed Sheiks. In that book, I identified Petrocan as one of a trio of companies that seemed to be the wave of the future, since they all held favoured status with government. The other two were Dome and Alberta Gas Trunk Line (later Nova).

My second and third books, *The Sorcerer's Apprentices* and *Other People's Money,* dealt with the disasters of the Trudeau government's National Energy Program and Dome Petroleum respectively. Petrocan appeared in both as a prominent corporate character. In 1984, I wrote a commissioned history for Bow Valley Industries, *From Rigs to Riches*, which gave me a further opportunity to study the disaster wrought by the NEP, particularly as it affected East Coast exploration. In 1986, I finished a book on the Reichmanns, *The Masterbuilders,* in which Petrocan again appeared, this time as a partner in the Reichmann's takeover of Gulf Canada.

I have written a number of articles about Petrocan over the years, the chief of which were "The Power of Petrocan" and "The Empire Builder," which appeared in *Saturday Night* in October

1981 and June 1986 respectively; and "Hopper's Folly," which appeared in the *Globe and Mail Report on Business Magazine* in August 1991. Two other articles I wrote for *Saturday Night*, "The Battle of the Sectors" and "Strong Politics," in March and August 1983, were important in crystallizing my views about economic nationalism and "policy entrepreneurs," in particular Maurice Strong.

Over the years, I have interviewed most of the main actors who appear in this book. Between 1977 and 1986, I interviewed Bill Hopper a number of times. He has refused to see me since my second *Saturday Night* article. I carried out a large number of additional interviews in 1991 and 1992 for this project. Because of this project's controversial nature, the majority of people who spoke to me did so on condition of non-attribution.

I first thought of writing a book about Petrocan ten years ago. I'm glad that I didn't. Petrocan's privatization in July 1991 provided the perfect opportunity for an assessment of the state oil company's sixteen-year history, a history wrapped in delusion and obfuscation.

"A New Western Power." *Maclean's.* November 25, 1985.

Anderson, Ian. "The Godfather." *Canadian Business.* June 1983.

Bagnall, James. "Ottawa Denies Petro-Canada Share Issue for Near Future." *Financial Post.* May 30, 1989.

Barber, John. "A Wolf in Sheik's Clothing." *Today.* August 22, 1981.

Barker, Eleanor J. "Petro-Canada Update 1991." *Sanwa McCarthy Securities Limited.* April 1991.

Base, Ron. "The Elegant Fiction of John Ralston Saul." *Quest.* April 1978.

Best, Dunnery. "Petrocan Cuts, Shapes and Glues to Get It All Together." *Financial Post.* October 15, 1983.

Bliss, Michael. *Northern Enterprise: Five Centuries of Canadian Business.* Toronto: McClelland and Stewart, 1987.

Boinod, Pierre. "111 St. Clair." *Imperial Oil Review.* June 1957.

Bott, Robert. "Carney's Gamble." *Saturday Night.* June 1985.

—. *Mileposts: The Story of the World's Longest Petroleum Pipeline.* Calgary: Interprovincial Pipe Line Company, 1989.

—. "The Perils of Petro-Canada." *Canadian Business.* June 1979.

Camp, Dalton. *Points of Departure.* Toronto: Deneau and Greenberg, 1979.

Campbell, Colin, and George J. Szablowski. *The Super-Bureaucrats: Structure and Behaviour in Central Agencies.* Toronto: Gage, 1979.

Canada. Department of Energy, Mines and Resources. "Privatization of Petro-Canada." Confidential discussion paper and secret report to Cabinet, August 21, 1979; written by David Scrim.

Canada. House of Commons. Standing Committee on National Resources and Public Works. *Minutes.* Issue No. 5 (May 31, 1984). (For Michael Wilson's attack on Petrocan's accounting methods.)

Canada. Senate. Standing Committee on Energy and Natural Resources. *Petro-Canada. Report...* Ottawa: The Committee, 1990.

Canada. Task Force on Petro-Canada. *Report...* Ottawa: The Task Force, 1979.

"Canadian Takeover is Urged of Big Foreign-Controlled Firms." *Toronto Star.* February 17, 1977.

Carlisle, Tamsin. "Ottawa Slowly Strangling Alberta Energy Aid Agency." *Financial Post.* September 11, 1989.

Carlisle, Tamsin, and Peter Morton. "Gulf Quits Giant Hibernia Play." *Financial Post.* February 5, 1992.

Chandler, Alfred D., Jr. *Scale and Scope.* Cambridge, Mass.: Belknap Press of Harvard University Press, 1990.

Chenoweth, Chris, and James Dawe. "PetroCan Brief Predicts Higher Oil Price by 1990." *Toronto Star.* December 3, 1983.

Considine, Bob. *Larger Than Life: A Biography of the Remarkable Dr. Armand Hammer.* London: W.H.Allen, 1975.

Cox, Kevin. "Firm Tries Hard to Gain Acceptance in Calgary." *Globe and Mail.* September 21, 1985.

—. "Petro-Canada Sets a Record with Profit of $252 Million." *Globe and Mail.* March 16, 1985.

—. "Petro-Canada to Test Drill Terra Nova Find." *Globe and Mail.* March 10, 1987.

Cox, Kevin, and Richard Cleroux. "Petrocan Quitting Petroleum Club." *Globe and Mail.* November 19, 1985.

Cox, Kevin, and Drew Fagan, Alan Freeman, Cathryn Motherwell, Margaret Philp. "Gulf Canada to Quit Hibernia Oil Field Project." *Globe and Mail.* February 5, 1992.

Dabbs, Frank. "Hopper Takes Another Kick at the OSLO 'Dog' Project." *Financial Post.* February 27, 1990.

—. "Jordan's Progress Earns Praise for Canada." *Financial Post.* October 17, 1989.

—. "Petro-Canada's Energy Source." *Montreal Gazette.* January 26, 1979.

Davis, L.J. "The Biggest Knockover: T. Boone Pickens and the End of Gulf Oil." *Harper's.* January 1985.

DeMont, John, and David Hatter. "PetroCan Buy Stirs Tory Revolt." *Financial Post.* August 24, 1985.

Dewar, Elaine. "O Petro-Canada! We See Thee Rise." *City Woman.* Summer 1981.

Doig, Ian. "PetroCan's Black Trail of Troubles." *Financial Times of Canada.* May 20-26, 1991.

"Dome Canada, Petrocan Given Lion's Share of Frontier Grants." *Globe and Mail.* June 22, 1984.

Donville, Christopher. "Debt Too Heavy, Petrocan Warns." *Globe and Mail.* November 17, 1989.

—. "Kicking the Tires of Our Oil Company." *Globe and Mail,* May 18, 1991.

Doucet, Lyse. "Canada Key Player in Ghana's 'Revolution.'" *Financial Post.* March 17, 1984.

Downey, Donn. "Devoted Career to Promoting Cause of Economic Nationalism." [Walter Gordon obituary]. *Globe and Mail.* March 24, 1987.

—. "Petrocan's Gas Station Buy Unpopular, Gallup Poll Finds." *Globe and Mail.* October 23, 1985.

Doyon, Richard. "PetroCan's 'Hip Pocket' Global Arm Eager to Go." *Financial Post.* November 21, 1981.

Duncan, Stephen. "Ideology: The Name of Our New Energy Game." *Financial Post.* February 14, 1981.

—. "Imagine PetroCan Stations Coast to Coast." *Financial Post.* April 26, 1980.

Dunwoody, Derm. "The Big Move." *Imperial Oil Review.* August 1957.

Fagan, Drew. "Epp in No Rush to Sell Petrocan." *Globe and Mail.* December 19, 1989.

—. "Hibernia Delays Possible: Epp." *Globe and Mail.* February 8, 1992.

—. "Hibernia Project at Risk As Ottawa Bars Extra Cash." *Globe and Mail.* February 6, 1992.

—. "Ottawa Set to Open Oil Patch to Further Foreign Investment." *Globe and Mail.* March 21, 1992.

—. "Petrocan Asset Sale Under Fire." *Globe and Mail.* September 14, 1991.

Fagan, Drew, Cathryn Motherwell, and Kevin Cox. "Stark Realities Envelop Hibernia Dream." *Globe and Mail.* April 11, 1992.

Fife, Robert. "Petrocan Names Moores' Firm as Consultants." *Globe and Mail.* December 27, 1985.

Fife, Sandy. "An Upheaval at Petrocan." *Maclean's.* December 10, 1984.

Foster, Peter. "The Big Chill." *Canadian Business.* April 1984.

—. *The Blue-Eyed Sheiks: The Canadian Oil Establishment.* Toronto: Collins, 1979.

—. "Boon or Boondoggle?" *Canadian Business.* February 1991.

—. "The Destruction of Wealth." *Saturday Night.* January 1987.

—. "The Empire Builder." *Saturday Night.* June 1986.

—. "Energy Nationalism Leaves Sad Legacy." *Financial Post.* October 19, 1987.

—. *From Rigs to Riches: The Story of Bow Valley Industries Ltd.* Calgary: Bow Valley Industries, 1984.

—. "Hopper's Folly." *Globe and Mail Report on Business Magazine.* August 1991.

—. "Many Uncertainties Ahead, but PetroCan Carving Own Niche in Oil Industry." *Financial Post.* April 22, 1978.

—. *The Masterbuilders: How the Reichmanns Reached for an Empire.* Toronto: Key Porter, 1986.

—. "NEP 'Bunker' Mentality Still Alive and Well." *Financial Post.* September 14, 1987.

—. *Other People's Money: The Banks, the Government and Dome.* Toronto: Collins, 1983.

—. "PetroCan: 'A Number of Disquieting Questions Remain.'" *Financial Post.* February 14, 1981.

—. "PetroCan Chief Holds All the Aces." *Financial Post.* March 16, 1987.

—. "PetroCan Seems Bent on Being Mirror Image of Imperial Oil." *Financial Post.* November 13, 1982.

—. "PetroCan Stakes Out the Long Term." *Financial Post.* February 12, 1977.

—. "Pie in the Sky." *Canadian Business.* February 1992.

—. "The Power of Petrocan." *Saturday Night.* October 1981.

—. *The Sorcerer's Apprentices: Canada's Super-Bureaucrats and the Energy Mess.* Toronto: Collins, 1982.

Fotheringham, Allan. "The 52-Storey Federal Insult." *Maclean's.* November 14, 1983.

Francis, Diane. "CBC to Air 'Less-Flattering' Film About Petrocan chief." *Toronto Star.* March 27, 1984.

—. "Idle PetroCan Oil Rig Costs $272,000 a Day." *Toronto Star*. March 6, 1984.

—. "Only Traces of Oil in Controversial Newfoundland Well." *Toronto Star*. November 24, 1984.

—. "PetroCan Chief Speaks Out on 'Painful' Layoffs, Closings." *Toronto Star*. January 25, 1986.

—. "PetroCan Staff Send Tabloid Proud Message." *Toronto Star*. July 6, 1984.

—. "Petro-Canada Adjudged Healthy in Brokerage Analysts' Report." *Toronto Star*. November 1, 1984.

—. "Petro-Canada: Profits Are In, Perks Are Out." *Toronto Star*. May 26, 1983.

Frankel, Paul. *Mattei: Oil and Power Politics*. New York and Washington: Praeger, 1966.

Fraser, Graham. "Ottawa Decides at Very Last Minute to Sell Petrocan." *Globe and Mail*. February 21, 1990.

Freeman, Alan. "Federal Deficit Understated by $2-Billion, Desautels Says." *Globe and Mail*. February 5, 1992.

French, Richard D. *How Ottawa Decides: Planning and Industrial Policy-Making 1968-1980*. Ottawa: Canadian Institute for Economic Policy, 1980.

Galbraith, John Kenneth. "Walter Lockhart Gordon Remembered." *Financial Post*. March 30, 1987.

Gates, Bruce. "Torch Has Lots of Canada in It." *Financial Post*. November 9, 1987.

—. "Torch-Relay Trek Burns Brightly for PetroCanada." *Financial Post*. November 9, 1987.

Gessell, Paul. "The Tories' Rising Star." *Maclean's*. November 11, 1985.

Gibbens, Robert. "Oil Companies Defend Role of Petro-Canada." *Financial Times of London*. June 12, 1979.

Gillespie, Alastair. "How PetroCan Can Ensure Our Future Energy Supply." *Financial Post*. November 25, 1978.

Gorham, Beth. "Hibernia Deadline Passes Quietly." *Calgary Herald*. May 2, 1992.

Gray, Charlotte. "Giving Peace a Chance in the Oil Patch." *Globe and Mail Report on Business Magazine*. March 1986.

Gray, Earle. *The Great Canadian Oil Patch*. Toronto: Maclean-Hunter, 1970.

—. *Super Pipe*. Toronto: Griffin House, 1978.

—. *Wildcatters: The Story of Pacific Petroleums and Westcoast Transmission*. Toronto: McClelland and Stewart, 1982.

Growe, Sarah Jane. "Carney Is First in Man's World." *Toronto Star*. November 16, 1984.

Gwyn, Richard. *The Northern Magus*. Toronto: Paperjacks, 1981.

Hammer, Armand, with Neil Lyndon. *Hammer*. New York: Putnam's, 1987.

Hatter, David. "Corporate Jetsetters Eye Latimer's Fall." *Financial Post*, June 29, 1985.

Hay, John. "Spreading the Know-how Around." *Maclean's.* January 11, 1982.

Hayek, Friedrich A. *The Road to Serfdom.* Chicago: University of Chicago Press, 1944.

Heilbroner, Robert L. *The Worldly Philosophers: The Lives, Times and Ideas of the Great Economic Thinkers.* New York: Touchstone/Simon & Schuster, 1972.

Heise, Horst. "PetroCan's Advance Guard Sets Up Camp." *Financial Post.* January 10, 1976.

Henderson, Helen. "Petro-Canada Chief Earned Respect from Tough, Free-Enterprise Oilmen." *Toronto Star.* July 29, 1976.

Howard, Ross. "Liberals Would Challenge Move to Sell Petro-Canada, Turner Says." *Globe and Mail.* March 9, 1987.

Hull, Ken, and John Ridsdel. "From Atlantic to Pacific, Petro-Canada Presence Felt." *Calgary Herald.* April 20, 1979.

——. "Oil Shortage, Public Distrust Midwives to Petro-Canada." *Calgary Herald.* April 19, 1979.

——. "Petrocan Walks Middle Ground Through Critics." *Calgary Herald.* April 21, 1979.

Hunter, Nicholas. "Foreign Aid Agency Faces Political Battle at Home." *Globe and Mail.* January 30, 1984.

——. "Question of Financing Key to Future of Petro-Canada." *Globe and Mail.* November 27, 1984.

——. "West Quits Petrocan Job over Move." *Globe and Mail.* November 23, 1985.

Hustak, Alan. *Peter Lougheed.* Toronto: McClelland and Stewart, 1979.

"It's Ours! But Fewer Want to Keep It, Poll Finds." *Toronto Star.* April 18, 1983.

Jamieson, Robert. "Introducing: PetroCan's President." *Financial Post.* July 24, 1976.

Johnson, Paul. *Modern Times: The World from the Twenties to the Eighties.* New York: Harper and Row, 1983.

Johnston, Donald. *Up the Hill.* Montreal: Optimum, 1986.

Jutras, Catherine. "Cancorp: A Very Canadian Company." *Canadian Business.* June 1980.

Kennedy, Tom. *Quest: Canada's Search for Arctic Oil.* Edmonton: Reidmore, 1988.

——. "Strong Claims Petrocan's Entry May Prove Blessing in Disguise for Petroleum Industry." *Globe and Mail.* January 21, 1976.

Lancashire, David. "When Will the Privileges Pay Off?" *Globe and Mail.* February 28, 1981.

Laxer, James, and Anne Martin, eds. *The Big Tough Expensive Job.* Toronto: Press Porcepic, 1976.

"Learning to Love Petro-Canada." *Maclean's.* April 4, 1988.

Linton, George. "Petrofina Jumps $10.37 on Bid Rumor." *Globe and Mail.* December 12, 1980.

Little, Bruce. "Petrofina Canada Takeover Probe Set." *Globe and Mail.* November 1, 1984.

Macfarlane, David. "Escape Artist: In His Novels and His Life, John Ralston Saul Plays Romanticism to the Hilt." *Toronto*. November 1988.

"Making 'Democracy.'" *Maclean's*. January 16, 1989.

Martin, Tony. "Sponsors Count on Games to Polish Corporate Image." *Financial Post*. November 9, 1987.

Mayers, Adam. "Boosting Olympics Gave Petro-Canada a Lift, Too." *Toronto Star*. January 9, 1989.

——. "Petro-Canada Wins Respect as Major Player in Oil Scene." *Toronto Star*. April 9, 1988.

McCall-Newman, Christina. *Grits: An Intimate Portrait of the Liberal Party*. Toronto: Macmillan of Canada, 1982.

McCallum, Anthony. "Petro-Canada's Chairman Hopper is Report on Business Man of Year." *Globe and Mail*. January 1, 1981.

McCallum, Anthony, and Robert Gibbens. "Petrocan Confirms Bid for Petrofina." *Globe and Mail*. February 3, 1981.

McDonald, Terry. "Petrocan Bets on the Frontier. And Unloved Bob Meneley Is on the Hot Seat." *Financial Times of Canada*. April 6, 1981.

McIntosh, Gord. "Petrocan Not for Sale: Mazankowski." *Globe and Mail*. February 26, 1988.

McMurdy, Deirdre. "A Matter of Privacy: Petro-Canada Says That It Is Ready to Stand on Its Own Against Any Oil Company." *Maclean's*. March 4, 1991.

——. "A Radical New Beginning for Petro-Canada." *Globe and Mail*. May 17, 1990.

Moon, Peter. "Petrocan Helps Pay Lalonde's Assistant." *Globe and Mail*. October 2, 1981.

Morton, Peter. "Hibernia Will Launch Industrial Age for Newfoundland, Minister Says." *Financial Post*. September 13, 1990.

——. "Petro-Can May Not Be a Quick-Buck 'Flip.'" *Globe and Mail*. June 24, 1991.

——. "Petro-Canada Stock to be Sold in Chunks." *Financial Post*. February 22, 1990.

——. "Plan for Rig-building Centre." *Financial Post*. March 12, 1990.

"Most Believe in Energy Role of Crown Firms, Poll Indicates." *Toronto Star*. December 5, 1985.

Motherwell, Cathryn. "Petrocan Thrashing in 'Blood Bath' Waters." *Globe and Mail*. August 2, 1991.

——. "Reshaping Costs Put Petrocan Deep in the Red." *Globe and Mail*. February 21, 1992.

"Nationalize Oil, Gordon Suggests." *Montreal Gazette*. February 18, 1977.

Nelson, Barry. "A Drama in the Oilfields." *Maclean's*. April 22, 1985.

——. "Petro-Canada Spending Millions to Rent Empty Space in Calgary." *Globe and Mail*. November 19, 1982.

"Newfoundland Refinery Takeover Ruled Low Priority by Petrocan." *Globe and Mail*. March 3, 1976.

Newman, Peter C. *The Canadian Establishment*. Toronto: McClelland and Stewart, 1975.

—. "Still Preaching in the Wilderness." *Maclean's*. May 21, 1983.

Noble, Kimberley. "Petrocan Slogan Changes Image." *Globe and Mail*. July 11, 1984.

O'Connell, Joe. "Move to Sell PetroCan Is Huge Error, Turner Says." *Toronto Star*. March 8, 1987.

"The Oil Problems That Plague John Shaheen." *Business Week*. March 1, 1976.

Our Industry: Petroleum. London: British Petroleum, 1977.

Oxtoby, David. "Petrocan Sell-off Firmly on Track." *Financial Times of Canada*. March 16, 1987.

Perry, Robert L. "The CDIC: Jobs for the Boys or Jobs for the Country?" *Financial Post 500*. June 1983.

"PetroCan Called Big Loser in Calgary's Office Glut." *Toronto Star*. May 8, 1986.

"Petrocan to Focus on Consolidation." *Globe and Mail*. November 18, 1983.

"Petrocan Found to be Charging High Prices." *Globe and Mail*. May 7, 1986.

"Petrocan Is Obstacle to Domestic Refining: Epp." *Financial Post*. October 29, 1990.

"PetroCan Joins Group Critical of Energy Plan." *Toronto Star*. February 11, 1984.

"Petrocan Not for Sale but May Be Later, PM Says." *Globe and Mail*. March 10, 1987.

"Petrocan Threatens Mothballing of Hibernia." *Globe and Mail*. March 4, 1992.

"Petrocan Turns Down Dome Drilling Venture." *Globe and Mail*. May 5, 1976.

"Petrocan Writes Off $486 Million." *Globe and Mail*. August 21, 1985.

"Petro-Canada Gets New Auditors." *Montreal Gazette*. August 14, 1985.

Phillips, Frances. "PetroCan Veteran Speaks for the Oil Industry." *Financial Post*. April 1, 1988.

"Plotting Petro Can's Path After Takeover." *Financial Post*. December 9, 1978.

"Poverty Plea on Hibernia." *Financial Post*. July 19, 1988.

Quirin, G. David. "Public Ownership in the Petroleum Industry — Some Economic Considerations." Paper presented to a conference on "Government Involvement in the Energy Industry," University of Calgary, October 27-28, 1976.

Reguly, Eric. "Petrocan Geared Up for New, Private Role. Direction is Changed 'Totally.'" *Financial Times of Canada*. November 26, 1984.

—. "PetroCan Loses Precious Ground at the Pumps." *Financial Post*. January 12, 1987.

Riding, Alan. *Distant Neighbours: A Portrait of the Mexicans.* New York: Vintage, 1989.

Robinson, Robert H. "Petro-Canada. A Competitive and Comparative Analysis with Shell Canada and Imperial Oil." ScotiaMcLeod, Equity Research. May 7, 1991.

Ross, Alexander. "Joel Bell." *Energy.* November/December 1981.

Rowan, Geoffrey. "CN Productivity Right off the Tracks." *Globe and Mail.* October 9, 1991.

Sallot, Jeff. "Tories Reappoint Hopper as Petro-Canada Head." *Globe and Mail.* December 15, 1984.

Sampson, Anthony. *The Seven Sisters: The Great Oil Companies and The World They Shaped.* New York: Viking, 1975.

Sawatsky, John. *The Insiders: Power, Money, and Secrets in Ottawa.* Toronto: M&S Paperback, 1989.

—. *Mulroney: The Politics of Ambition.* Toronto: Macfarlane Walter & Ross, 1991.

Sellar, Don. "Paper's Attack Riles Petro-Can Workers." *Southam News. June* 29, 1984.

Sheppard, Robert. "Former Lougheed Press Aide Hired by Petrocan as PR Head." *Globe and Mail.* January 4, 1984.

Simpson, Jeffrey. *Discipline of Power.* The Conservative Interlude and the Liberal Restoration. Toronto: Personal Library, 1980.

—. "Why the Federal Tories Should Think Twice Before Selling Petro-Canada." *Globe and Mail.* October 30, 1990.

Slocum, Dennis. "1987 Could Be Year of Decision on the Privatization of Petrocan." *Globe and Mail.* January 19, 1987.

—. "Shares in Petrocan May Be Offered, Subject to Carney's Plans, Oil Prices." *Globe and Mail.* April 22, 1986.

Smith, Dan. "Petro-Canada Gets New Custom-Built Multi-million-dollar Home in Calgary." *Toronto Star.* March 21, 1982.

Smith, Philip. *The Treasure Seekers.* Toronto: Macmillan, 1978.

Solomon, Hyman. "PetroCan Share Sale Faces Hurdles." *Financial Post.* September 7, 1985.

Squires, Alex. "Petro-Canada: An Examination of Its Position in the Canadian Oil Industry." Dominion Securities Pitfield. September 29, 1984.

Steward, Gillian. "Who Should Buy Our Oil." *Energy.* November, 1982.

Stoik, J.L. "Finding Oil Requires the 'Multiple Hypothesis.'" *Financial Post.* June 14, 1975.

Tarbell, Ida. *The History of the Standard Oil Company.* David M. Chalmers, ed. Norton Library, 1969. The book originally appeared as a series of articles in *McClure's* from 1902 to 1904, and was published in two volumes by Macmillan in 1904.

Taylor, Paul. "Petrocan Mulls over Alternatives As It Waits for Election Outcome." *Globe and Mail.* August 20, 1984.

Thampi, Radha. "Petrocan Opens Office of the Future." *Toronto Star.* November 21, 1983.

"Time Ripe to Offer Shares, Petro-Can Official Feels." *Toronto Star.* June 25, 1987.

Toulin, Alan. "Masse Rules Out PetroCan Sale to Big Oil Firms." *Toronto Star.* March 10, 1987.

Tupper, Allan, and G. Bruce Doern, eds. *Public Corporations and Public Policy in Canada.* Montreal: Institute for Research on Public Policy, 1981.

Waddell, Christopher. "Crash-landing Crown Corporations." *Globe and Mail Report on Business Magazine.* April 1986.

Walker, Dean. "Blunt and Surprising Opinions." [Hopper interview]. *Executive.* December, 1982.

Walker, James. "Latest Petrocan Buy Sets Stage for Tougher Gasoline Battle." *Financial Times of Canada.* November 8, 1982.

—. "Petrocan Reorganizes After Buying Spree." *Financial Times of Canada.* April 25, 1983.

"Walter Gordon Dies, Economic Nationalist Called 'Gentle Patriot.'" *Toronto Star.* March 24, 1987.

"What PetroCan May Stand to Gain from Arcan." *Financial Post.* March 13, 1976.

Yaffe, Barbara. "U.S. Firm to Resuscitate Come-by-Chance Refinery." *Globe and Mail.* October 28, 1986.

Yaffe, Barbara, and Bruce Little. "Ottawa, Mobil Study $1 Billion Guarantee." *Globe and Mail.* July 16, 1986.

Yergin, Daniel. *The Prize: The Epic Quest for Oil, Money and Power.* New York: Touchstone/Simon & Schuster, 1991, 1992.

Index

This book is typeset in Adobe Garamond. Designed by Robert Slimbach, the typeface is based on the original sixteenth-century design of Claude Garamont, and is one of the finest modern revivals of the letter form.

Design by Ken Rodmell

Typeset by Heidy Lawrance Associates

Epilogue: End of the Line

NOTHING SO CHALLENGES a board of directors as the prospect of firing its chief executive, particularly when he is also the board's chairman. This most wrenching and revolutionary act of corporate governance is surrounded by inevitable feelings of guilt and ingratitude, some of which have been quite deliberately induced. Chairmen/CEOs inevitably develop close relationships with their boards; they frequently cement the bonds with perks and personal favours. These favours have a clear defensive purpose that might be summed up by a Biblical paraphrase: let him who has not ridden on the corporate jet cast the first stone.

Throughout his tenure as both chairman and CEO of Petro-Canada, Bill Hopper held his board in a velvet grip. As chairman, he controlled the flow of information on which his performance as CEO was to be judged. But why would directors rock the boat anyway? Petrocan had always been different from public companies, where boards are historically charged with representing the interests of shareholders who have little or no access to management. In Petrocan's case, the sole shareholder from 1976 until 1991 had been the federal government. Few Petrocan directors had ever been foolish enough to think that they were representing the people of Canada. Moreover, successive ministers had had no problems in gaining access to Hopper. Or his jet. However, Petrocan's 1991 privatization had brought a change of emphasis in Petrocan's governance, which ultimately led to Hopper's undoing.

Ostensibly, the privatization left Hopper in a stronger position than ever. The board still consisted of Hopper's and the government's appointees. The number of "official" government nominees was limited, and the government had promised not to vote its shares or interfere with management. Hopper was also chairman of the board's nominating committee, which decided who would be invited onto the board. But the board also now answered to a significant minority of private shareholders whose primary concern was commercial performance and its impact on the share price. Also, both the management and employees — many of whom were also shareholders — had shown themselves increasingly discontented with Hopper, and they made sure that the board knew about it.

Towards the end of 1992, Jim Stanford, Petrocan's president and chief operating officer, decided that he just couldn't take operating under Hopper any more. He wanted early retirement. To obtain his retirement benefits, he needed the permission of the board. Stanford had once worked for Petrocan director Ed Barroll at Mobil Canada, so when he made his decision, he approached Barroll. (Norm McIntyre, president of the resources division, was the third member of Petrocan's ex-Mobil executive "mafia.")

Barroll felt Stanford's departure would be a blow to Petrocan and decided to share his concerns with other directors. He asked Stanford to speak to, among others, Tom Kierans, who had come onto the Petrocan board at the time of the initial share offering. Kierans is president and CEO of the C.D. Howe Institute, the high-profile, Toronto-based public policy analysis organization. Ironically, it was Hopper who had invited Kierans onto the Petrocan board. After interviewing Stanford at length, Kierans, who had himself grown increasingly concerned about Hopper's performance, became convinced, as did Barroll, that Petrocan should keep Stanford and ditch Hopper.

In the wake of Petrocan's turbulent 1992 annual meeting, where Hopper had had to face angry employee-shareholders who were watching the share price flag and their jobs disappear, Petrocan's supremo had become a little more circumspect about his flamboyant lifestyle. But Hopper had still not thrown himself into the arduous but necessary task of corporate downsizing. He found chopping corporate employees easier than letting go of corporate assets, but the Hibernia project still threatened to bleed the company dry. It would cost Petrocan $170 million in 1993 alone.

By the fall of 1992, sixteen years of empire building at Petrocan had produced the oil patch's answer to Mr. Micawber, a corporation desperately hoping that something would turn up. What turned up was RBC Dominion Securities, the giant Bay Street investment house. RBC Dominion offered to raise almost $250 million for Petrocan via a "bought deal," in which an investment dealer, or group of dealers, slaps a cheque on the CEO's desk for a block of shares the dealers then have to sell. RBC Dominion would give Petrocan $240 million and sell 30.35 million Petrocan shares for $8.25 each.

The deal turned out to be a disaster of epic proportions for almost everybody except Petrocan. There were few buyers. Institutional investors continued to hold misgivings about the company. Smaller investors weren't going to be burned twice. RBC Dominion's consortium was left holding 20 million Petrocan shares. Junior consortium members were annoyed with RBC Dominion — subsequently described as "greedy and arrogant" — for leading them into such a débâcle, having assured them that the stock would sell. The deal held no joy for taxpayers either. Since the proceeds of the sale went to Petrocan, the government's equity holding was further diluted, to 70 per cent, without any return. And yet there was still no general cry of complaint from the toiling masses, who continued to hand over, on average, 44 cents of every dollar they earned to the government. Politicians, meanwhile, looked the other way. Nevertheless, the constituency of those who wanted Hopper's head was growing. Ultimately, the only group that could wield the axe was Petrocan's board.

Following the private meetings with Stanford, Kierans and other directors — in particular Barroll and Bill Siebens, the hard-nosed Calgary oil millionaire who had been on the board since 1986 and who had always been a strong private critic of Hopper — began to dig further into Hopper's management performance and rumours of his extravagance. An example of Hopper's continuing to serve his own interests came to light when the Petrocan board learned that early in 1992, Hopper's employment and severance package with Westcoast Energy Inc. had been rewritten. Petrocan's 37-per-cent ownership of the Vancouver-based pipeline and energy company, of which Hopper was also chairman, had long enabled Hopper to draw two salaries. The Westcoast stake had been sold in September 1992, but not before Hopper's pension package had been significantly sweetened. Hopper and Westcoast's president and CEO, Michael Phelps, went back a long way. They were both veterans of the energy wars who knew how to work the Ottawa system. While Phelps was executive assistant to the then minister of Energy, Mines and Resources, Marc Lalonde, back in 1980, Petrocan had paid him an additional salary. His rise within Petrocan-controlled Westcoast had been remarkably rapid considering his lack of executive experience. He and Hopper were described by another former Ottawa insider as "two peas in a pod."

Under a new agreement with Westcoast, Hopper's salary was boosted to $220,000 from $150,000. He was also given a special bonus, reputedly $250,000, plus an interest-free loan. Moreover, his pension arrangements were changed so that, if he resigned as chairman at or after the age of sixty, he would receive 70 per cent of a figure that included not only the average of his best years' earnings but also a proportion of his highest and most recent bonuses. The new provisions thus significantly boosted his pension, with his sixtieth birthday little more than a year away.

After Petrocan sold its Westcoast stake for $342 million, taking yet another $54-million charge against earnings, Hopper resigned as Westcoast chairman, although he remained on the board. His pension arrangements had apparently been preserved. Westcoast refused to clarify the issue. Phelps took the attitude that it was nobody's business but the company's. However, Petrocan's board was disturbed by Hopper's arrangements with Westcoast. Stanford had been in a unique position to know about Hopper's package because he was on the compensation committee of Westcoast's board. However, the package wasn't the main reason that the directors with whom Stanford had met — and ultimately the rest of the board — became convinced that Hopper had to be removed.

Hopper was increasingly perceived as a negative force within Petrocan. He was not only resisting change, he was continuing to pursue his old divide-and-conquer management strategy, flattering people to their faces and then denigrating them behind their backs. This inevitably had a further detrimental effect on corporate morale. The showdown came at the end of January 1993. A regular board meeting had been scheduled for Friday, January 29. At the beginning of that week, Kierans arrived in Calgary to plot strategy with Barroll and Siebens. Another director, Gail Cook-Bennett, was part of the group and kept in touch by phone. The four had decided that it would be Hopper or them.

The rebel group realized they were dealing with a master strategist. They had to put together a strong case to present to the remainder of the board. The group planned to do this at a special "information meeting" that they called for Thursday, January 28, the day before the regular board meeting. The meeting would be followed by a special board meeting at Petrocan at which a vote would be taken on Hopper. The information meeting would be held at the venerable Palliser Hotel, where so many meetings that had shaped the Calgary oil patch had been held over the years.

Kierans, well versed in the ways of politics, realized that they had to close down one possible escape route for Hopper: Ottawa. He made a handful of phone calls. He wasn't seeking approval for the rebel group's action; he was letting Ottawa know what was happening and why. For their part, the Tories were more than happy to stick with their "philosophical" position of no interference. They had been burned too many times by Petrocan. They were also still smarting from the uproar over their January 1993 bail-out of Hibernia, in which the federal government had had to kick in close to another $360 million of taxpayers' money to prevent the project from cratering.

On Tuesday, January 26, Hopper had separate meetings with

Barroll and with Kierans and Siebens at which they told him they were going to challenge his stewardship. The directors came away with the impression that he wasn't taking their challenge too seriously. On Wednesday night, when Cook-Bennett arrived in Calgary, the rebel group of four were joined by Claude Fontaine, a highly regarded Montreal lawyer who had been on the board since 1987. One of the key issues in Hopper's removal was his employment contract, which few, if any, of the board had ever seen. The rebels were shocked when they saw the contract's provisions. Written in 1982 before the Tories had returned to power, the contract gave Hopper virtual *carte blanche*, with a gold-plated severance package. Firing Hopper would carry a heavy price.

The purpose of the Palliser information meeting, which began after lunch on Thursday, was to lay out the rebel group's case against Hopper, which was based on a number of instances of "inappropriate behaviour." Of the directors who had not been part of the original dissenting group — Reuben Cohen, Bill Elliott, former Tory MP Bill Jarvis, and Guylaine Saucier — some were miffed that they had not been informed earlier. Moncton lawyer and businessman Cohen didn't like the way it was being done; it lacked decorum. He thought it would be better if Hopper were allowed to retire gracefully at the annual meeting. However, the rebel group believed that if Hopper were given that much time, he would mount a counter-attack that would leave him in control. The arguments went back and forth throughout the afternoon.

At 6 P.M., the group moved to the Petrocan headquarters for the special board meeting at which Hopper's fate would be determined. Hopper attended briefly and then departed. Kierans was elected chairman. The meeting was adjourned several times in order to continue the discussions of the information meeting. Eventually, at about 9 P.M., the special meeting was called to order and a vote was taken. Neither Hopper nor Stanford was present. Eight of the remaining nine directors voted for Hopper's removal. Cohen abstained.

Once the vote was taken, Kierans, Barroll, and Fontaine went to inform Hopper in his fifty-second-floor aerie, the office with the million-dollar view of the Rockies. If Hopper was shocked, he did not show it. There was a discussion about severance, then Hopper returned to his Calgary apartment. Bob Foulkes, vice-president of public affairs, was summoned into the boardroom and told to issue a press release. The news must have been traumatic for Foulkes, one of Petrocan's first employees, who had spent the best part of his career as a kind of Sancho Panza to Hopper's grand ambitions. Once, he had been a true believer. Latterly, his experiences at Petrocan, not to mention the chunk of Petrocan shares he had bought with borrowed money, had rendered him a good deal more cynical about his job. At times he was still Hopper's greatest fan; at others, he referred to himself as Hopper's "shit-eating lap-dog."

That Thursday night, Foulkes had to write one of the toughest press releases of his life. It would lead with Stanford's appointment as president and CEO. Further down, it announced that Hopper had been "relieved of his duties." No reason was given for Hopper's dismissal. When the news hit the press, there was inevitable speculation that Bay Street had had its knives out for Hopper after the costly bought deal. But the proximate cause of his ouster lay in the growing discontent of management and, in particular, Stanford. Stanford was considered a moral man, but although insiders reckon that he was moved by a combination of distaste for Hopper's abusive lifestyle and concern for the welfare of the corporation, the fact remained that the coup left him on top. Stanford had lived fourteen years in Hopper's shadow. One of his mottos had always been "No surprises," but he had been instrumental in delivering the biggest surprise of all to Hopper. At his first press conference as CEO a week later, Stanford noted that his personality differed from that of his predecessor: "I think that I probably have a reputation as being a little more austere than the characteristics that were attributed to Mr. Hopper."

In the 1992 annual report, Stanford's message declared: "Sincere thanks are due to Bill Hopper, who stepped down in January, 1993, after 14 years as chairman and chief executive officer. He will be remembered for his key role in the development of Petro-Canada. We will build on his contribution as we press forward to increase profits and value for our shareholders." Elsewhere, Bill McKnight, the new energy minister, was quoted as saying: "Mr. Hopper served well and long, but the company now has a new focus."

Petrocan's 1993 annual meeting, its second as a public company, was very different from its first. There were no fireworks. Barroll, who had been appointed non-executive chairman, sat in the chair. Stanford announced a first-quarter 1993 profit of $40 million, or 16 cents a share, versus $32 million the previous year. The best news was that, although the shares were well below their 1991 issue price, they were at least off their bottom, trading at about $9.37 in a much more buoyant oil and gas market. Ironically, the RBC Dominion group that had participated in the disastrous bought deal the previous November had unloaded its huge position in February at $7.25, taking an estimated $25-million bath. By mid-year, Petrocan shares would be trading at more than $12.

At the annual meeting, Barroll refused to elaborate on Hopper's departure or the terms of his severance package. In so doing, he was obeying the unwritten rules of corporate etiquette, under which directors treat the boardroom as priests treat the confessional. As long as the job gets done — or so goes the theory — then neither shareholders nor the general public should concern themselves with the whys and wherefores. Forget the personalities, concentrate on the system. Too many details of executive shortcomings might feed the cause of those who would still attempt, unwisely, to regulate. But Petrocan was different. The Canadian people, as well as private shareholders, deserved to know more about just why Hopper had been ditched. Taxpayers had poured billions of dollars into Petrocan. And they had lost most of it.

On January 29, the day after he was fired, Hopper boarded a scheduled Air Canada flight for Ottawa. Ironically, he met David Scrim, one of the men who had accompanied him on the flight to Calgary seventeen years before to set up Petrocan. As a bureaucrat, Scrim had played a critical part in sabotaging the Tories' attempt to dismantle the state oil company during their brief reign in 1979. Now he was an energy consultant. Like almost every Ottawa consultant, he had at one time been on Petrocan's payroll. Scrim still had affection for Hopper. The two men sat together and reminisced. Hopper didn't seem despondent.

Hopper was intercepted at Ottawa airport by a reporter from the *Globe and Mail.* "It didn't come out of the blue," he said. "Was there a difference of philosophy? Yeah. Can I be more specific? No. I feel terrific. I'm sixty years old, I've been in this for a long time. For seventeen years I've commuted, much to the dismay of Calgarians. . . . I'm not unhappy about all this."

Why was he not unhappy? Well, there were those two pension packages, one from Petrocan and one from Westcoast, and his Petrocan severance arrangement. Insiders estimated that, together, they represented a lump sum of close to $3 million and a combined pension of more than $500,000 annually. The two companies would make sure that Hopper continued to be well served.